ASSAULT
ON THE
LEFT

ASSAULT
ON THE
LEFT

The FBI and the Sixties
Antiwar Movement

JAMES KIRKPATRICK DAVIS

PRAEGER

Westport, Connecticut
London

Library of Congress Cataloging-in-Publication Data

Davis, James Kirkpatrick.
    Assault on the Left : the FBI and the sixties antiwar movement /
James Kirkpatrick Davis.
        p.   cm.
    Includes bibliographical references and index.
    ISBN 0–275–95455–2 (alk. paper)
    1. Vietnamese Conflict, 1961–1975—Protest movement—United
States.   2. United States. Federal Bureau of Investigation.
3. United States—Politics and government,—1963–1969.   I. Title.
DS559.62.U6D38   1997
959.704'3373—dc20   96–44675

British Library Cataloguing in Publication Data is available.

Library of Congress Catalog Card Number: 96–44675
ISBN: 0–275–95455–2

First published in 1997

Praeger Publishers, 88 Post Road West, Westport, CT 06881
An imprint of Greenwood Publishing Group, Inc.

Printed in the United States of America

(∞)™

The paper used in this book complies with the
Permanent Paper Standard issued by the National
Information Standards Organization (Z39.48–1984).

10 9 8 7 6 5 4 3 2 1

For
Winifred Lee Kirkpatrick Davis
John Plantz Davis II
and
Whitney Anne Kirkpatrick Davis Kretsinger

Contents

Acknowledgments   ix

1. The 279th Meeting of the National Security Council   1

2. The New Left and the Emergence of Anti-Vietnam War
    Protest   21

3. The New Left and the Confrontation at Columbia   39

4. Firestorm in Chicago   63

5. January–June 1969   107

6. The New Mobilization Committee to End the War in
    Vietnam and the Vietnam Moratorium Committee   137

7. Cambodia, Kent State, Etc.   161

8. The End of the New Left COINTELPRO   197

    Selected Bibliography   219

    Index   223

Acknowledgments

I am indebted to a number of individuals who provided me with valuable assistance in the preparation of this book.

Clarence M. Kelley, former FBI Director and Kansas City Chief of Police, provided assistance and expert commentary based upon his extraordinary law enforcement career. Edward S. Miller, Deputy Assistant FBI Director (Retired), read portions of the text and provided commentary.

The Franklin D. Roosevelt Library at Hyde Park, New York, provided information and documents regarding the initial authorization to develop FBI domestic counterintelligence programs.

Information on the actual beginnings of the New Left COINTELPRO and the crucial National Security Council deliberations within the Eisenhower administration came from the Dwight D. Eisenhower Library in Abilene, Kansas.

William C. Davidon, Professor of Mathematics at Haverford College; Professor Thomas E. Ingerson, Tucson, Arizona; Reverend Edwin Edwards, United Church of Christ in New Haven, Connecticut; Dennis G. Kuby, Ministry of Ecology in Berkeley, California; and Eugene Kaza of Portland, Oregon, were all helpful in providing their firsthand impressions of selected New Left COINTELPRO operations.

Gary M. Stern, research associate at the Center for National Security Studies gathered data for me as did Fred L. Lee, a political scholar living in Kansas City.

Jan Shinpoch, Director of Administrative Operations at the National Security Archive in Washington, D.C., researched archive files and made hundreds of FBI counterintelligence documents available to me in manageable form.

I am also indebted to John M. Pfeffer, Librarian with the Data Base and Newspaper Center of the Free Library of Philadelphia.

Carl Stern, originally the law correspondent with NBC News, was the first journalist to pursue the COINTELPRO story. Mr. Stern provided me with a great deal of information and documents, including his first-hand knowledge of the New Left COINTELPRO.

Joan Murray and the staff of Inform at the Minneapolis Public Library kindly fulfilled many requests for newspaper and periodical data. I also received help from Steve Binns of the Linda Hall Library in Kansas City, Missouri, and from the government documents librarians at the Miller Nichols Library located on the University of Missouri at Kansas City campus.

Background information for much of the text was provided by the many capable librarians at the Inter Library Loan Department, Kansas City Public Library.

John T. Elliff, a political scholar based in Washington, D.C., read portions of the text and gave me the benefits of his many years of study. Professor Tony G. Poveda at the State University of New York in Plattsburg, an expert in the study of the FBI, was very helpful.

I am particularly indebted to an extraordinary group of government, history and English professors at Michigan State.

Susan Cowlback, an editorial assistant at the *New Times* in Phoenix, researched files for background data on a selected COINTELPRO target as did Reann Lydick, Research Librarian at Monroe County Public Library in Bloomington, Indiana.

Manuscript typing and end note editing were very capably handled by Nevey Patterson Butler, Mylene Larson Brinson, and Margaret R. Bates. Captain Tom Moore, U.S. Marine Corps (Retired), Gregory D. Black, Professor of Communications Studies at the University of Missouri, Kansas City, and Whitney Anne Kirkpatrick Davis Kretsinger all made several excellent suggestions for the book. Many thanks to James R. Dunton, my editor at Praeger Publishers.

The 279th Meeting of the National Security Council

"The atmosphere at the meeting was that the FBI had given a good account of itself."
—*Attorney General Herbert Brownell*

THE WHITE HOUSE
March 8, 1956

In 1956, President Dwight D. Eisenhower had as much reason as ever for concern about the security of the United States. The Soviet arms buildup continued to threaten the world's balance of power, and Soviet rhetoric grew more belligerent each month.

At 9:00 A.M. on March 8, 1956, these and other matters almost certainly preoccupied the general as he left the Oval Office and made his way to the White House Cabinet Room to preside over the 279th meeting of the National Security Council (NSC).

It was, however, the threat of internal subversion, perhaps even more sinister and more threatening to the United States than Soviet armies massed in various parts of the globe, that would concern the council on that day.

Those who met that day included the president, the vice president, the attorney general, the secretaries of state, defense, and treasury, the chairmen of the Joint Chiefs of Staff and the Atomic Energy Commission, the directors of the Federal Bureau of Investigation, the Central Intelligence Agency, the Bureau of the Budget, and the United States

Information Agency.[1] The meeting was the most significant ever held up to that time regarding the course of American domestic counterintelligence.

J. Edgar Hoover, director of the Federal Bureau of Investigation since 1924, came carefully prepared to present the strongest possible arguments for authority to intensify and expand FBI domestic counterintelligence operations. His standing in 1956, after serving as FBI director for thirty-two years and for sixteen of those years as the chief administrator of the nation's internal counterintelligence operations, was formidable.

It was in June of 1939 that President Roosevelt, faced with the prospect of the nation's involvement in two major wars, issued a secret directive to the FBI which advised that the bureau was responsible for the investigation of subversion virtually anywhere in the United States. This June memo was the closest instruction to a formal charter for FBI domestic intelligence operations.[2] A later Roosevelt directive, issued in September of 1939, instructed all law enforcement agencies and officers in the United States to provide the FBI with any information relating to sabotage, espionage, and subversive activities.[3]

In keeping with Roosevelt's intention, the domestic wartime FBI counterintelligence programs had two general purposes. The first was to provide the president and others in the executive branch with "pure intelligence"—the necessary data to make decisions and develop government policies. The second purpose was to provide preventive intelligence data for future use in wartime.

The wartime performance of the FBI was quite remarkable. The bureau was extraordinarily effective in preventing foreign-inspired subversive activities. It investigated nearly twenty thousand cases of alleged sabotage. Special agents proved quite skillful in intercepting Japanese and German spy rings.

However, FBI domestic intelligence actions went considerably beyond the investigation of actual crimes to include largely unwarranted surveillance of law-abiding organizations and individuals. The most intrusive investigations—justified perhaps, to some degree, by wartime requirements—led to postwar electronic surveillance, mail openings, and surreptitious entries.

By 1945, the FBI budget was almost 43 percent of that of the entire Justice Department.[4] Hoover's actions after World War II included a "massive public relations campaign to exploit cold war fears that eased the bureau's transition from wartime to peacetime and allowed it to maintain its wartime gains.">⁵ With its experience in monitoring the Communist Party during World War II, the FBI was the nation's acknowledged expert on both the international and internal communist threat to the United States.

In 1945, the Communist Party USA (CPUSA) had between seventy-five thousand and eighty-five thousand members.⁶ The CPUSA maintained a hard party line, in keeping with its concept of Stalinist Soviet Communism.

On March 7, 1946, Hoover advised Attorney General Tom C. Clark that the FBI was intensifying its investigation of the Communist Party nationwide.⁷ The bureau already had substantial programs to monitor groups identified with the CPUSA, as well as those whose objectives might be consistent with communist objectives. Instructions were issued to FBI field offices to expand surveillance of individuals who might be detained by the FBI in the event of a national emergency—those listed in the bureau's "Security Index." Later instructions created a new "Communist Index," which would be ancillary to the Security Index. This new index would include virtually all known CPUSA members.⁸

The next year, President Truman approved the Loyalty and Security Program, which authorized government boards of inquiry to investigate the loyalty of federal employees. The Loyalty and Security Program provided authority for a very broad definition of the threat of subversive influence.

In 1950, the Emergency Detention Act became law. This act stated again that the FBI was the agency with congressional authority to investigate individuals who might be detained in the event of a true national emergency.

In 1950, Congress established the Subversive Activities Control Board and confirmed that communist-front and action groups must register with the government. During the postwar period the rest of the Justice Department knew almost nothing about the true scope and depth of FBI counterintelligence activities. Selected programs, such as the preparation of the Communist Index, were deliberately kept secret by the bureau. The Justice Department had no knowledge of FBI programs aimed at "Marxist-type or other revolutionary groups not controlled by the Communist Party."⁹

By the time President Eisenhower took office in January of 1953, the FBI, in an enormous effort, had completed checks on more than six million citizens for possible disloyalty. In this effort the bureau had employed about sixteen hundred special agents and five thousand paid undercover informants.[10]

By 1956, the CPUSA was weak. Forty-two indictments under the Smith Act were brought against it between 1953 and 1956. Additionally, congressional antisubversion committees, together with federal deportation actions against party members, had been effective.

The FBI, of course, knew the actual size of the Communist party. By 1956, membership had declined from its postwar high of seventy-five thousand to eighty-five thousand to only twenty-two thousand. The bureau also knew that the CPUSA was no longer used for espionage by the Soviets.

In 1956, however, the Supreme Court in effect reduced the ability of the government to investigate and prosecute alleged subversives under the authority of the Smith Act. The Smith Act, passed in 1940, made it a crime to advocate in any way "the overthrow of any government in the United States by force of violence."[11] In a new interpretation, the Court held that simple advocacy alone of ideas was not, in and of itself, punishable. The government would now have to prove advocacy of actual violent actions in order to obtain convictions.

Hoover announced that the new ruling would probably reduce the FBI's ability to investigate communist subversion. During the numerous operations against the CPUSA, the confidential covers of a number of FBI undercover informants had been destroyed. In Hoover's opinion, this reduced the bureau's ability to infiltrate the CPUSA. Hoover, of course, wanted to continue to take advantage of conflicts the bureau knew already existed within the CPUSA.

The NSC meeting of March 8, 1956, began with a lengthy reappraisal of the Eisenhower administration's policy regarding shipments from Soviet bloc countries that were provided with United States diplomatic immunity. This review was followed by a directive to the U.S. Communications Security Board to study the matter further and report back to the council with specific recommendations.

At 10:00 A.M., Dillon Anderson, special assistant to the president, announced to the council that J. Edgar Hoover would make a presentation regarding the covert status of communist subversion within the United States.

The title of his presentation was "The Present Menace of Communist Espionage and Subversion." Printed highlights of the talk were distributed to the members of the council. The director reviewed his assessment of the current internal threat posed by the CPUSA. He next discussed successful efforts against the party that were made possible by the provisions of the Smith Act, now weakened by the Supreme Court's reinterpretation. The information presented by Hoover made CPUSA appear far more threatening than it actually was.

After the formal part of his presentation, President Eisenhower "observed that segments of the American people may now feel that there is no domestic communist problem in view of the fact that a number of leading communists have been prosecuted for conspiracy to overthrow the government."[12] The president said that in keeping with his own thinking, domestic communism was still a matter of concern to everyone on the council.

Hoover asked for approval from the president and the council to use every means available to pursue and disrupt the CPUSA. He failed, however, to mention that many of the means he had in mind had already been in use for some time.

Eisenhower asked him to explain the counterintelligence techniques he wished to use.

"Sometimes," Hoover said, "it is necessary to make a surreptitious entry where on occasion we have photographed secret communist records and other data of great use to our security."[13] Additional counterintelligence methods were listed: safecracking, mail interception, telephone surveillance, microphone plants, trash inspection, infiltration, IRS investigations. In short, "Every means available to secure information and evidence."[14]

When Hoover finished the president said nothing but seemed to nod in approval. The cabinet room evidently fell silent. For all practical purposes, no one inside or outside of the cabinet room, in or out of the government, had any meaningful information about these FBI operations. Former Attorney General Herbert Brownell, one of those in attendance, recalls, "The atmosphere at the meeting was that the FBI had given a good account of itself."[15]

Following the NSC meeting the director met with the FBI's domestic intelligence experts to expand and improve the bureau's secret domestic counterintelligence operations. These secret operations would be known within the bureau by the code name COINTELPRO—an acronym for counterintelligence program. The CPUSA COINTELPRO was to be the first of the five main domestic programs—the others would be authorized at later dates.

The first COINTELPRO memorandum, dated May 18, 1956, instructed special agents in COINTELPRO-designated field offices to furnish FBI headquarters with the names of individuals who had been active in the CPUSA.[16]

From this date on, the FBI's principal effort in the CPUSA COINTELPRO was to monitor, analyze, infiltrate, and ultimately destroy the CPUSA. There were in all, over a fourteen-year period, 1,850 separate CPUSA COINTELPRO proposals submitted by FBI field offices; 1,388 were approved for action by headquarters, with documented results achieved in 222 situations.[17]

These efforts devastated what was left of the CPUSA. By 1971, the figure was down to about 3,000 members, a considerable number of those being undercover FBI informants.[18]

In 1956, it was ordered that counterintelligence proposals submitted for COINTELPRO headquarters approval must originate from selected field offices, or from special agents attached to FBI headquarters in Washington. Indeed, selected field offices had to submit COINTELPRO suggestions to headquarters on a quarterly basis. Every COINTELPRO document contained a direct warning to all FBI field offices and special agents: "No counterintelligence action can be initiated by the field without specific bureau authorization."

Each incoming COINTELPRO proposal from the field would be given to the Intelligence Division at headquarters and then to one of the seven section chiefs operating within the Intelligence Division.

In most situations, the individual section chief would send the field office proposal to the COINTELPRO supervisor assigned to each of the programs. Probably the section chief would make no recommendation regarding the proposal; it was the program supervisor who made the first decision to approve or disapprove the proposal. If the supervisor's review was favorable, the proposal would be sent, together with the supervisor's recommendation attached, to the branch chief. If the branch chief approved, it would be sent up the chain of command—to Assistant Director William C. Sullivan in the Domestic Intelligence Division. Sullivan would study the proposal and then take it to the director for final review.

Approximately 30 percent of the COINTELPRO proposals were turned down. Hoover would not permit the FBI to become involved in activities that might be exposed to the public.

Field office progress reports were submitted every ninety days to section chiefs. About 40 percent of the actions in the five main COINTEL-

PROs involved sending anonymous, inflammatory material to target groups or to individuals within the selected target groups. The bureau would also make news announcements of derogatory information available to friendly media in order to expose the activities of target groups. In addition, selected investigative information (sometimes untrue) would be deliberately leaked to local media to reveal target group activities. Agents would also advise local, state, and federal authorities of any civil and criminal violations by target-group members. In other situations, special agents would contact a target-group member's employer, prospective employers, or credit bureaus with information of that person's politics. In a number of instances, special agents even contacted target-group members to let them know that the FBI knew of their questionable activities—a particularly intimidating technique. Sometimes, fictitious organizations were created, complete with forged signatures and documents, membership cards, and so on—all to create and disrupt target groups. Pressure was brought to bear on colleges, universities, and other institutions to remove known communists from teaching positions and other positions of authority. The COINTELPRO techniques, primarily covert, had the main purpose of disrupting and neutralizing targets.

The Socialist Worker's Party (SWP) was the next target. SWP CO-INTELPRO, the second COINTELPRO to be created by the bureau, was authorized by a Hoover memo dated October 12, 1961.[19] A headquarters follow-up letter dated October 17, 1961, was sent to five selected field offices. It said that "a disruption program along similar lines [to that against CPUSA] could be initiated against the SWP on a very selective basis."[20] This second COINTELPRO was a smaller program with only forty-six actions directed against SWP targets and its subsidiary group, the Young Socialist Alliance.

On September 2, 1964, a headquarters memorandum was sent to seventeen selected FBI field offices creating the White Hate COINTEL-PRO.[21] The field offices were to target seventeen Ku Klux Klan (KKK) organizations as well as the American Nazi Party, the National States Rights Party, and other such groups. Four hundred and four White Hate proposals were submitted to the headquarters. Two hundred and eighty-five were approved, with documented results obtained in 139 actions. The KKK was, to all outward appearances, decimated by the end of 1968. By 1971, KKK membership had declined from a 1964 high of approximately fourteen thousand active members to forty-three hundred.[22]

An August 25, 1967, memorandum initiating the new Black Hate

COINTELPRO was sent to twenty-three field offices with instructions to "establish a control file" immediately and to assign responsibility for following and coordinating this new counterintelligence program to all experienced and "imaginative" special agents "with experience in working with black nationalists, hate-type groups and organizations."[23] The purpose of the new COINTELPRO was to "expose, disrupt, misdirect, discredit or otherwise neutralize" such specified groups as the Congress of Racial Equality, the Nation of Islam, the Student Nonviolent Coordinating Committee, the Deacons of Defense and Justice, and the Southern Christian Leadership Conference. In total, bureau headquarters received 540 Black Hate COINTELPRO proposals from forty-one field offices. Of these, 301 actions were implemented, with documented results obtained in seventy-six separate actions.[24]

The last of the original group of COINTELPROs was the New Left program, which began on October 28, 1968, and lasted until April 27, 1971. The FBI launched the COINTELPRO-New Left operation primarily to stem the tide of extreme anti-Vietnam War protest across the nation. In total, bureau headquarters received 381 New Left proposals from approved field offices. Of this total, 285 actions were implemented, with documented results obtained in seventy-seven actions.[25]

By the end of February 1971 the various COINTELPRO operations had been in operation for over fourteen years. During this period 3,247 counterintelligence proposals were submitted by selected field offices to FBI headquarters; 2,370 proposals were implemented, with documented results achieved in 572 actions. The methods in use during the entire period were those outlined by Hoover at the 1956 NSC meeting.

On the night of March 8, 1971, the fifteenth anniversary of that meeting, the security surrounding FBI domestic counterintelligence operations was shattered.

In an astonishing act, a small group of burglars—almost certainly anti-Vietnam War activists of the New Left—went to the corner of Front Street and South Avenue in the Philadelphia suburb of Media, Pennsylvania. They focused their attention on the local resident office of the Federal Bureau of Investigation.

The office's senior resident, Thomas F. Lewis, supervised the work of four special agents assigned to the Media office. One special agent, Jim O'Connor, was a specialist in surveillance of the New Left and was the author of the bureau's *New Left Notes*.

The burglars, undoubtedly working from information received from a source inside the bureau, broke into the FBI offices. They emptied desks and filing cabinets containing an extraordinary selection of highly classified domestic intelligence documents. The burglars, who later identified themselves as the Citizens' Commission to Investigate the FBI, removed about one thousand classified documents, most of which dealt with the secret FBI intelligence operations—the COINTELPRO operations.

The burglary of an FBI office was an astonishing violation of federal law. Nevertheless, the Citizens' Commission obviously felt that the FBI's secret intelligence operations, particularly against the anti-Vietnam War New Left, were quite intolerable. Thus, they no doubt felt it was necessary for them to break the law in order to expose a program that was probably itself a violation of the law.

The FBI's investigation of the Media episode was among the largest it had ever conducted. Members of the New Left, including the Catholic left, campus radicals, antiwar protesters of every description, and selected members of the academic community were targets. This investigation, which carried the code name "Medburg," however, was not successful. The case was never solved.[26]

On March 11, 1971, Haverford College physics professor William C. Davidon, a peace activist, *Boston Globe* reporter Michael Kenny, a reporter who covered war protest issues for the *Boston Globe*, and the Philadelphia FBI office all received letters from the Citizens' Commission. Professor Davidon read his letter to a group of about one hundred persons assembled for a regular meeting of the Swarthmore Ministers Association. It said that intelligence documents had been stolen from the Media office so that FBI surveillance activities directed against entirely lawful political and social protest organizations could be made public. The Citizens' Commission was concerned about FBI surveillance activities that were being conducted against "groups and individuals working for a more just, humane, and peaceful society." FBI files would be studied to determine "how much of the FBI's efforts are spent on relatively minor crimes by the poor and powerless against whom they can get a more glamorous conviction rate, instead of investigating truly serious crimes by those with money and influence which cause great damage to the lives of many people."

Professor Davidon said that he approved of the raid because "the FBI is increasingly engaged in activities which are contrary to the best principles of this country." Davidon chose to read the letter at this particular meeting because, "insofar as he knew, there had been no mention of the FBI raid in the newspapers up to that time."[27]

Davidon remembers the spring of 1971 as a very tense time, since he played a key role in helping to make the Media documents public. "My home telephone was tapped," he recalls, "and I later discovered my name on a number of FBI domestic intelligence documents. The whole value of the Media exposure was to provide some documentation of the extent to which the FBI was infiltrating perfectly legal groups. The FBI under Hoover was becoming dangerously insensitive to people's rights."[28]

The Citizens' Commission letter also announced that COINTELPRO documentation would be sent to "the people in public life who have demonstrated the integrity, courage, and commitment to democratic values which are necessary to effectively challenge the repressive policies of the FBI." The letter concluded by saying that the FBI had betrayed the trust of the American people. In addition, the FBI spent insufficient time and effort in combating "war profiteering, monopolistic practices, institutionalized racism, organized crime and the mass distribution of lethal drugs."[29]

Ten days later, copies of twenty of the stolen documents were sent to Congressman Parren J. Mitchell of Maryland and Senator George S. McGovern of South Dakota. Both men were Democrats and both had been publicly critical of the FBI. McGovern returned the material to the bureau immediately, saying that he "refused to be associated with this illegal action by a private group. Illegal actions of this nature only serve to undermine reasonable and constructive efforts to secure appropriate public review of the FBI."[30]

Congressman Mitchell also denounced the Media burglary. He, too, returned the materials to the FBI. In a speech on March 12, Mitchell said that "burglary is a crime and should be dealt with as such." However, he added, "the investigation and surveillance of individuals and peace groups and black student groups as indicated by the files, was also a crime."[31]

On March 23, copies of fourteen of the documents were sent to well-known journalists and newspapers, including *New York Times* columnist Tom Wicker, Betty Medsger of the *Washington Post*, and the *Los Angeles Times*. Enclosed with each mailing of COINTELPRO documents was a letter which stated: "We have taken this action because we believe that democracy can survive only in an order of justice, of an open society and public trust, because we believe that citizens have the right to scrutinize and control their own government and because we believe that the FBI has betrayed its democratic trust."[32]

It seems certain that both Attorney General Mitchell and Director Hoover discussed the matter with President Nixon. In a public announcement on March 24, Mitchell said that the FBI documents were "highly confidential and should not be published, for this could endanger the lives or cause other serious harm to persons engaged in investigative activities on behalf of the United States."[33]

Ben Bagdikian, The *Washington Post*'s national editor at the time, received a call directly from Mitchell. Nevertheless, Bagdikian recalls, "the *Post* thought it was a significant matter of public controversy and once we confirmed that the documents were authentic, we decided to go ahead. It was an insight into something the public needs to know."[34]

The *Post* editorialized that "this revelation of FBI activity in the name of internal security seems to us extremely disquieting." It recommended that "an appropriate committee of the Congress ought to look much more thoroughly into what the bureau is doing."[35] When the *Post* published parts of the documents (withholding individual names and locations), the *New York Times* and *Los Angeles Times* immediately followed with publication.

In the Nixon administration's view, these documents were released in a manner that was out of context. The Citizens' Commission had obviously chosen to release only those particular memos that exposed the bureau's highly questionable methods of surveillance. "Actually," one Justice Department official remembers, "a full examination of the stolen documents reveals that the FBI showed restraint rather than over-zealousness."[36]

One of the memos included in the March 23d Citizens' Commission release directed FBI agents to monitor activist students. Another document, dated September 16, 1970, contained special agent O'Connor's newsletter *"The New Left Notes*—Philadelphia," which instructed agents to intensify contacts with radicals and dissidents in order to enhance "the paranoia endemic in these circles and to further serve to get the point across that there is an FBI agent behind every mail box."[37]

One document discussed the activities of Dr. William Bennett, a philosophy professor at Swarthmore College. Bennett was suspected of being sympathetic to the Black Panther Party and was known to be quite active in the "Radical Circus," a radical New Left group of college students and faculty who were active in the civil rights and anti-Vietnam War movements.[38]

A memorandum dated July 13, 1970, gave the unlisted telephone number of Muhammad Kenyatta, a vice president of the National Black Economic Development Conference (BEDC).[39]

A six-page memo dated June 18, 1970, concerned the FBI's use of Daniel McGronigle, a cashier at Southeast National Bank, to monitor the BEDC checking account.[40]

A memo regarding the War Resisters Conference at Haverford College on August 1, 1969, made several inquiries aimed at determining "its scope and whether or not there are any indications it will generate any anti-US Propaganda."[41] Also included were instructions on infiltrating the 1970 National Association of Black Students Convention, to be held at Detroit's Wayne State University. In still another memo, there was a Swarthmore Police Department report of black militant activities at Swarthmore College.[42]

In an article in the *Philadelphia News*, it was revealed that the bureau knew, after the Media burglary, that copies of the government case against the anti-Vietnam War Harrisburg Six had been stolen. As the article said, the "crux" of the government case had been removed. Sources said that one of the primary functions of the FBI Media office had been to investigate conspirators in the Harrisburg Six case and thus build a stronger case against Reverend Berrigan and his people. These particular files were kept in Media to enable special agents to refer to documents that were already a part of the government investigation.

On March 26, a Philadelphia reporter received a letter from the Citizens' Commission that read: "In a few days we will contact a first group of these previously undercover agents and suggest they cease their repressive actions if they have not already done so. We will then inform those individuals and any organizations against whom these agents were operating. Following that we will make the names of the first group of agents public."[43]

The Citizens' Committee's second release named seven FBI informants. One mailing was sent to an organization in Cambridge, Massachusetts, known as Resist, a group that raised funds for organizations protesting the Vietnam War. Resist, in turn, made these new documents available to the *New York Times*. Among these materials, the *Times* discovered an FBI memo in which an informant, a lay brother at a monastery, reported that a Villanova University priest had borrowed a monastery car for the entire weekend prior to the bombing of the U.S. Capitol.

This second release also revealed a selection of COINTELPRO memoranda mailed to field offices that proposed the development of a network of paid FBI undercover informants. Every FBI special agent would be required to develop one "racial informant." Additionally, according to the documents, all information obtained through recruited informants "should be recorded by memo—with copies for the files on any individuals or organizations mentioned."[44]

A memo dated September 16, 1970, instructed special agents to be certain that informants "should not become the person who carries the gun, throws the bomb, does the robbery or by some specific violative, overt act becomes a deeply involved participant." It added, "There have been cases where security informants assault police, etc."[45]

A new set of Media documents was received on April 8 by Michael Kenney of the *Boston Globe*. These documents revealed that the daughter of a member of Congress had been targeted by COINTELPRO. The FBI had conducted surveillance of Jacqueline Reuss, daughter of Wisconsin Congressman Henry S. Reuss, a critic of the war in Vietnam. Another COINTELPRO document from this mailing contained a report on the internal rivalry between leaders of the Philadelphia Black United Liberation front.

On April 21, the Black Student Union at Pennsylvania Military College in Chester, Pennsylvania, received copies of six FBI COINTELPRO documents from the Citizens' Commission—documents explaining that the Black Student Union was under surveillance by the FBI and informants. The black students wanted the information to be made public so that the country would be aware of the FBI's "flagrant use of investigation."[46]

A fourth mailing revealed surveillance of the Union for National Draft opposition. This report also concluded that the Black Student Union at Pennsylvania Military College was "a somewhat disorganized group of students, possibly having a membership and/or following of no more than thirty students."[47]

By May of 1971, the Citizens' Commission had released a total of sixty domestic intelligence documents. A final mailing included a study of the Jewish Defense League, a report on the surveillance of Klavern 10 of the Ku Klux Klan in Upper Darby, Pennsylvania, and a surveillance report on a peaceful demonstration held in Philadelphia to protest chemical warfare. It was also revealed that the Bell Telephone Company of Pennsylvania had furnished the FBI with "all unlisted telephone subscribers, including the names and addresses, a service not available to ordinary citizens."[48]

In its final act, the Citizens' Commission released, together with copies of the final group of documents, a summary of all the stolen FBI documents. According to the Commission's letter, "30 percent of the materials in the Media files were manuals, routine forms and similar procedural matter." The remainder was comprised of "40 percent political surveillance and other investigation of political activity." The letter broke down the types of cases involved: two were right wing, ten concerned immigrants, and over two hundred were on left or liberal groups. Twenty-five percent were bank robberies, 20 percent murder, rape, and interstate theft. Seven percent were draft resisters, including refusal to submit to military induction. Seven percent concerned leaving the military without government permission. One percent discussed organized crime, mostly gambling.[49]

Fred Graham of the *New York Times* was one journalist who followed the story. On May 27 he wrote: "At week's end there was a feeling that the other shoe was yet to drop in the case of the pilfered papers. The question that no one could answer was which side would drop the shoe—the thieves, who obviously have more documents, or the FBI, which has a reputation for producing the facts that give the last word."[50]

The objective of the Citizens' Commission had been achieved. J. Edgar Hoover became so alarmed over the possibility of having to endure even more national exposure that he canceled all COINTELPROs on April 28, 1971.[51]

The actual term "COINTELPRO," however, was still unknown to the public at this point. The only use of the term appeared in one of the original fourteen documents released to the *Washington Post*. This particular document was captioned "COINTELPRO-New Left" and was dated September 16, 1970.[52] This memorandum was the document which led ultimately to the release of more than fifty-two thousand previously classified intelligence memorandums—full documentation of the bureau's massive assault on the New Left.

The man who led the effort to have the entire COINTELPRO operation revealed to the nation was Carl Stern of NBC News. Stern was a lawyer and an expert on the Freedom of Information Act. In 1972 he was responsible for reporting and analysis of the Senate Committee on the Judiciary, as well as matters relating to the Justice Department.

During a routine visit to Judiciary Committee headquarters in January of 1972, Stern noticed a document on a staff member's desk that was entitled "COINTELPRO-New Left." He remembers being immediately curious. "What does 'COINTELPRO-New Left' mean?" he asked some staff members. The staffers simply didn't know.

"These people were very experienced and capable members of the Committee staff and they were as interested as I was in determining what COINTELPRO-New Left actually meant." Stern remembers: "They could see from the document itself that FBI agents had evidently gone beyond their normal investigative functions, but had no idea that CO-INTELPRO was as extensive or elaborate as it turned out to be. I decided to look into the matter."

Stern next called the Justice Department's Public Information Office for further information. "Again," he remembers, "I was contacting people that I knew well. They couldn't provide any information at all."[53] Stern then called the assistant FBI director, Thomas Bishop. Again, no information was forthcoming. The newsman made other calls to contacts within the Justice Department. His calls were not returned.

Stern then consulted with Congressman Moorhead's Government Information Subcommittee, the University of Missouri's Freedom of Information Act Center in Washington, and the American Civil Liberties Union. Members at these organizations urged him to make a Freedom of Information Act request for data regarding COINTELPRO-New Left.

Then, on March 26, 1972, he wrote to Richard Kleindiest, the deputy attorney general, and requested access to the following:

1) Whatever letter authorized the Federal Bureau of Investigation to establish and maintain its counterintelligence program denominated "COINTELPRO-New Left."
2) Whatever letter, if any, terminated such program.
3) Whatever letters, if any, ordered or authorized any changes in the purpose, scope or nature of the program.[54]

On April 25, Kleindiest wrote back: The information you seek is exempt from disclosure pursuant to 5 USC 552(b)(1) in that it is specifically required by Executive order to be kept secret in the interest of the national defense or foreign policy. In addition, 5 USC 552(b)(5) exempts from disclosure inter-agency or intra-agency memorandums or letters which would not be available by law to a party other than an agency in litigation with the agency."[55]

On June 30, Stern wrote to the new deputy attorney general, Ralph E. Erickson, renewing his request for information. This second request was denied by letter on August 21.[56] His third request was denied by letter on September 29, a fourth on January 12, 1973.[57]

In late July of 1972 Stern had lunch with L. Patrick Gray, III, then the acting director of the FBI. Stern requested information from Gray on COINTELPRO-New Left in a letter dated September 6, 1972. His request for information was again denied on September 18, 1972.[58]

On September 25, 1973, Civil Action No. 179-73 was filed in the United States District Court for the District of Columbia, appealing the Justice Department's numerous rulings. Stern wanted two documents under the Freedom of Information Act. The first was a letter dated May 10, 1968, addressed to a field official from FBI headquarters in Washington, officially authorizing the "COINTELPRO-New Left" action. The second—a communication from headquarters to all field offices—canceled all existing COINTELPRO operations as of April 28, 1971.

On July 16, 1973, the FBI delivered copies of the two documents in question to U.S. District Judge Barrington D. Parker. After reviewing them, the judge decided, in a nine-page opinion, that the documents should be given to Stern.

Clarence M. Kelley—then director of the FBI—had issued a memo to all special agents-in-charge. He mentioned the anticipated publicity surrounding the developing of COINTELPRO disclosures and how they might produce concerns over possible violations of individual liberties. FBI employees, he emphasized, were to refrain from engaging in investigative activity that could abridge in any way the rights guaranteed by the Constitution.[59]

During that same week in July, Kelley also issued a press release defending the purpose, but not necessarily the methods, of the CO-INTELPRO operations. "The FBI's intent," he noted, "was to prevent dangerous acts against individuals, organizations, and institutions—public and private—across the United States. FBI employees in these programs had acted in good faith and within the bounds of what was expected of them by the president, the attorney general, Congress, and, I believe, a majority of the American people."[60]

On December 7, Kelley received from Carl Stern a letter in which Stern requested additional COINTELPRO documents, including the following: Whatever documents authorized and defined the programs COINTELPRO-Espionage; COINTELPRO-Disruption of White Hate Groups; COINTELPRO-Communist Party, U.S.A.; Counterintelligence and Special Operations; COINTELPRO-Black Extremists; Socialist Workers Party-Disruption Program. On that day, reporter Fred Graham of CBS News also requested access to documents relating to CO-INTELPRO-New Left and to all documents relating to any other CO-INTELPRO programs.[61]

Director Kelley answered Carl Stern's letter and advised him that the documents he requested were in the bureau's confidential investigatory files for law enforcement purposes; therefore, they were exempt from public disclosure.

Attorney General William B. Saxbe, in responding to a new request from the NBC reporter, agreed on March 6, 1974, to supply "part, but not all" of the requested materials. Stern received a document from the FBI COINTELPRO files dealing with White Hate groups, two documents on black extremists, one regarding the Socialist Workers Party, and three memoranda under the general classification "Counterintelligence and Special Operations."

Over the next few years several government committees and departments investigated the still secret FBI domestic counterintelligence programs. The Senate and House Select Committees on Intelligence Activities, headed by Senator Frank Church and Representative Otis Pike, conducted history's most extensive study and analysis of the U.S. intelligence establishment. Some information on COINTELPRO became public during the hearings. The *New York Times*, in an editorial on June 28, 1975, said that "the FBI's counterintelligence programs seemed to have been almost too crude to believe."[62] By July 23, 1975, Church Committee investigators had access to the "full unexpurgated file on COINTELPRO."

"For a number of years," Clarence Kelley now remembers, "controversy over the COINTELPRO operations had gone on with seemingly no end in sight. I decided to issue another public statement in hopes of putting the entire matter behind us."[63] He addressed the issue directly in a speech at Westminster College in Fulton, Missouri, on May 8, 1976:

> During most of my tenure as director of the FBI, I have been compelled to devote much of my time attempting to reconstruct and then to explain activities that occurred years ago.
>
> Some of those activities were clearly wrong and quite indefensible. We most certainly must never allow them to be repeated. It is true that many of the activities being condemned were, considering the times in which they occurred, the violent sixties, good-faith efforts to prevent bloodshed and wanton destruction of property.[64]

On November 21, 1977—more than six years after the burglary in Media, Pennsylvania, and five years after Carl Stern began pursuing the COINTELPRO story—the FBI released some fifty-two thousand pages related to COINTELPRO, virtually the entire file. More than six thousand of these documents revealed the efforts to "infiltrate, disrupt, and otherwise neutralize" the New Left. To understand the extensiveness of this secret assault, we must begin in 1962.

NOTES

1. Minutes of the 279th meeting of the National Security Council, Cabinet Room of the White House, Mar. 8, 1956, 9:00 A.M.; Herbert Brownell, testimony before U.S. District Court, Southern District of New York, June 2, 1981.

2. Senate Select Committee to Study Governmental Operations with Respect to Intelligence Activities, "Intelligence Activities and The Rights of Americans," Book II, 94th Cong., 2d Sess. See Confidential Memorandum of the President, 1939, at p. 27.

3. Senate Select Committee to Study Governmental Operations with Respect to Intelligence Activities, "Intelligence Activities and The Rights of Americans," Book II, 94th Cong., 2d Sess., Apr. 14, 1976, p. 27.

4. Ibid.

5. Tony G. Poveda, "FBI and Domestic Intelligence," *Journal of Crime and Delinquency* (April 1982): p. 197.

6. David A. Shannon, *The Decline of American Communism* (Chatham, N.J.: Chatham Booksellers, 1959), p. 3.

7. FBI Memorandum, J. Edgar Hoover to Attorney General Tom C. Clark, Mar. 7, 1946.

8. FBI Memorandum, Headquarters to Field Offices, Mar. 15, 1948; Special Agents-in-Charge letter, No. 57, Ser. 1948. Apr., 10, 1948.

9. FBI Memorandum, F. J. Baumgardner to A. H. Belmont, June 8, 1951.

10. Morton H. Halperin, Jerry J. Erman, Robert L. Borosage, and Christine M. Marwick, *The Lawless State: The Crimes of U.S. Intelligence Agencies* (New York: Penguin Books, 1976).

11. Sanford J. Unger, *FBI: An Uncensored Look Behind the Walls* (Boston: Little, Brown, 1975), p. 131.

12. Minutes of the 279th Meeting of the National Security Council.

13. Ibid.

14. Ibid.

15. Ibid.

16. FBI Memorandum, Alan H. Belmont to Special Agents, May 18, 1956.

17. House Committee on the Judiciary, Civil Rights and Constitutional Rights Subcommittee, *Hearings on FBI Counterintelligence Programs*, 93d Cong., 2d Sess., Nov. 20, 1974, p. 12.

18. Unger, *FBI*, p. 125.

19. FBI Memorandum, J. Edgar Hoover to Special Agents-in-Charge, New York field office, Oct. 12, 1961.

20. FBI Memorandum, J. Edgar Hoover to Special Agents-in-Charge, Oct. 17, 1961.

21. FBI Memorandum, J. Edgar Hoover to Field Offices, Sept. 2, 1964.

22. House Committee on the Judiciary, Civil Rights and Constitutional Rights Subcommittee, *Hearings on FBI Counterintelligence Programs*, 93d Cong., 2d Sess., Nov. 20, 1974, p. 12.

23. FBI Memorandum, Headquarters to Field Offices, Aug. 25, 1967.

24. House Committee on the Judiciary, Civil Rights and Constitutional Rights Subcommittee, *Hearings on FBI Counterintelligence Programs*, 93d Cong., 2d Sess., Nov. 20, 1974, p. 12.

25. Ibid., p. 156.

26. W. Mark Felt, *The FBI Pyramid* (New York: G. P. Putnam's Sons, 1979), pp. 87–99.

27. "Davidon Unveils Plot Against FBI," *Delaware County Daily Times*, Mar. 12, 1971, pp. 1–2; "Group Claims It Stole FBI Files in Media," *Evening Bulletin*, Philadelphia, Mar. 12, 1971, p. 17.

28. Prof. William C. Davidon, Dept. of Mathematics, Haverford College, telephone interview with author, July 26, 1989.

29. "Davidon Unveils Plot," pp. 1–2.

30. Unger, *FBI*, p. 485.

31. "Mitchell Issues Plea on FBI Files," *New York Times*, Mar. 24, 1971, p. 24.

32. "Group to Publicize FBI's Informers," *New York Times*, Mar. 26, 1971, p. 27.

33. "Security Matters," *Facts on File*, Mar. 24, 1971, p. 15.

34. "Radicals, Ripping Off the FBI," *Time*, Apr. 5, 1971, p. 15.

35. Ibid.

36. Betty Medsger and Ken W. Clawson, "Thieves Got Over 1,000 FBI Papers," *Washington Post*, Mar. 25, 1971, p. 1.

37. "Media FBI Records Show Informants," *Delaware County Daily Times*, Mar. 24, 1971, p. 1.

38. Paul F. Levy and Kitsi Burkhart, "Professor Not Upset by FBI Surveillance," *Philadelphia Bulletin*, Mar. 27, 1971, p. 1.

39. FBI Memorandum, Special Agent Thomas F. Lewis to Philadelphia Special Agent-in-Charge, July 13, 1970.

40. FBI Memorandum, Special Agent Thomas Lewis to Philadelphia Special Agent-in-Charge, June 18, 1970.

41. Katrina Dyke, "FBI Papers Tell of Watch on Blacks," *Sunday Bulletin*, Philadelphia, Mar. 28, 1971, p. 1.

42. FBI Memorandum, All agents from Special Agent Kenneth K. Smythe, June 17, 1970.

43. "Group to Publicize Informers," *New York Times*, Mar. 27, 1971, p. 32.

44. Bill Kovach, "Stolen Files Show FBI Seeks Black Informers," *New York Times*, Apr. 8, 1971, p. 22.

45. Ibid.

46. Charlene Canape, "FBI Data Released at PMC," *Delaware County Times*, Apr. 22, 1971, p. 1.

47. William Greider, "Analysis of Stolen FBI Documents Provides Glimpse of Bureau at Work," *Washington Post*, July 4, 1971, p. A1.

48. Paul Cowan, Nick Egleson, and Nat Hentoff, *State Secrets: Police Surveillance in America* (New York: Holt, Rinehart and Winston, 1974), p. 116.

49. *The Complete Collection of Political Documents Ripped Off from the FBI Office in Media, PA, March 8, 1971* (Rifton, NY: Win Peace and Freedom Through Non-Violent Action, 1972).

50. Fred P. Graham, "Waiting for the Other Shoe to Drop," *New York Times*, May 28, 1971, p. 9.

51. FBI Memorandum, J. Edgar Hoover to Field Offices, Apr. 28, 1971.

52. FBI Memorandum, "The New Left Notes—Philadelphia," Philadelphia Special Agent-in-Charge, Sept. 9, 1970; FBI Memorandum, "COINTELPRO-New Left," Headquarters to Field Offices, Sept. 6, 1970.

53. Unpublished letter, Carl Stern (law correspondent, NBC News) to author, Jan. 15, 1991.

54. Letter, Carl Stern to Deputy Attorney General Richard Kleindiest, Mar. 20, 1972.

55. Carl Stern, NBC News, Washington DC, telephone interview with author, Jan. 4, 1991.

56. Letter, Carl Stern to Deputy Attorney General Ralph E. Erickson, June 26, 1972; Letter, Deputy Attorney General to Carl Stern, Aug. 21, 1972.

57. Letter, Deputy Attorney General Ralph E. Erickson, Sept. 29, 1972; Letter, Deputy Attorney General to Carl Stern, Jan. 12, 1973.

58. Letter, Carl Stern to Acting Director of the FBI L. Patrick Gray, Sept. 6, 1972.

59. FBI Memorandum, Director Clarence M. Kelley to All Special Agents-in-Charge, Personal Attention Memorandum 56–73, Dec. 5, 1973.

60. Statement of FBI Director Clarence M. Kelley, Nov. 18, 1974.

61. Letter, Carl Stern to FBI Director Clarence M. Kelley, Dec. 7, 1973.

62. "Disruption by Stealth," *New York Times*, June 28, 1975, p. 34.

63. Clarence M. Kelley, former FBI director, interview with author, Nov. 16, 1995.

64. "Apology Is Given by Head of FBI," *New York Times*, May 9, 1976, p. 26.

2

The New Left and the Emergence of Anti-Vietnam War Protest

"They are half way citizens who are neither morally, mentally or emotionally mature."

—Director John Edgar Hoover

In the summer of 1962, the fledgling Students for a Democratic Society (SDS), the student arm of the League for Industrial Democracy, released to the nation what became "the most widely distributed document on the American left in the sixties."[1] The 66-page text, officially known as the *Port Huron Statement of the Students for a Democratic Society*, was drafted during an intensive five-day meeting held at the FDR Camp in Michigan, on the southern shore of Lake Huron.

Eight colleges and universities were represented among the fifty-nine individuals in attendance. There were a number of non-SDS members, groups including the Student Peace Union, the Campus Americans for a Democratic Action, the National Student Christian Foundation, and the Student Nonviolent Coordinating Committee. Those in attendance tended to be idealistic, bright, and well-read, with varying activist experience. Most were from white, privileged backgrounds. Kirkpatrick Sale found them to be an extraordinary group of people.[2]

In preparing the Port Huron Statement, the SDS writers, primarily Robert "Al" Haber and Tom Hayden, were attempting to develop an entirely new ideology for what was to become the New Left movement. The New Left, a term coined by C. Wright Mills in 1961, was applied to an advocation of an *evolution* in American politics rather than the revolution advocated by the Old Left for so long with so little success.

The Old Left was considered by the New Left to be out of date and out of step with the new student-based political radicalism of the sixties. The working class, the traditional vanguard for change within the Old Left political philosophy, was seen as simply not up to the task of fostering radical changes in the sixties. The New Left was in large measure a generational rebellion, a rebellion of the young.

The Port Huron Statement was a call to political action. "As a social system we seek the establishment of a democracy of individual participation; governed by two central aims; that the individual share in those social divisions which determine the quality and direction of his life; that society be organized to encourage independence in men and provide the media for their common participation."[3]

Although advocating a student-based multi-issue, multi-organizational social and political evolution across the nation, the document at one point was cautious: "We have no sure formulas, no closed theatre—but that does not mean that values are beyond discussion. . . . If we are correct in believing that the social order is systematically—not just occasionally—unjust, then we should be able to illustrate our belief by systematically pointing to the faults of American life."[4]

Individual Americans, according to the statement, were living lives that were alienated from the very government they were paying taxes to support. Individual citizens, living in the world's richest country in the world's oldest republic, were unable to control their own lives. The power to make social, economic, and political decisions must be made by citizens directly affected by those decisions. There must be a true participatory democracy. The nation's enormously overgrown power apparatus should be the object of reform at every level. The document advocated a total evolution in the nation's social, economic, and political machinery to more directly benefit individual citizens.

On global matters, the Port Huron Statement opposed the unyielding anti-communism of the United States while also castigating the aggressiveness of the Warsaw Pact nations. It urged rapprochement among the major powers and expanded assistance to the Third World.

The New Left concept of action was by no means new in 1962. Protest activities occurred across America well before the Port Huron Conference. Demonstrations with varying degrees of coordination and effectiveness had been directed against racial segregation in the South, against the arms race, against atomic testing, against the growing American military industrial complex, against war, and against the intrusiveness of the House Committee on Un-American Activities.

But Port Huron was epochal in the history of American radical politics. It marked, as scholar Howard Taylor has said, "a turning point in American political history, the point at which a coalition of student movements had become possible and a radical student movement had been formed."[5] The SDS would, before the decade was over, include pacifist, religious, civil rights, and disarmament groups as well as elements of the Old Left.

Tom Hayden recalled more than twenty years later, "when the New Left suddenly emerged, it was a group of very intelligent people, very humanistic people but suddenly we were asked to do things that adults would normally do, like lead an overdue civil rights revolution, stop a war, and poverty."[6]

Activist Todd Gitlin remembers reading the Port Huron Statement for the first time and thinking, "My God, this is what I feel." Delegate Paul Booth recalled, "We really thought we had done a great job. We knew we had a great document." Delegate Bob Ross said, "It was a little like starting on a journey."[7]

During that same summer of 1962, American forces in South Vietnam numbered twelve hundred. John F. Kennedy was then in the second year of his presidency and he was the third American president to be concerned about the future of Vietnam. It had been seventeen years since the first American was killed there and three years since the killing of the first American on military assignment.

By 1962, J. Edgar Hoover had been director of the Federal Bureau of Investigation for thirty-eight years. Although the official authorization for domestic counterintelligence operations against the New Left would not be issued for another six years, it seems certain that he was informed of the Port Huron meeting from the beginning.

In the early sixties, the New Left was most conspicuously represented by a few active SDS chapters on college campuses. These early chapters, having almost no influence on a national scale, were loosely associated with a dozen or more similar types of domestic-based political action groups. By the end of the decade, however, the New Left would be associated with literally hundreds of protest organizations with hundreds of thousands of active participants. The anti-Vietnam War crusade, spearheaded by the New Left influence, came to represent a political and sociological phenomenon almost certainly unmatched in the history of American politics.

In 1963, the New Left—a term often used synonymously with "the movement," or "student movement," or "student New Left," or "student protest," or vaguely, as a general and somewhat inaccurate term referring to any organization or campaign opposed to the war in Vietnam—was still a cause in formation. In order to understand the political dynamics of these years it is important to see, as Kim McQuaid has written, "the antiwar coalition as a whole and of the New Left within the coalition." McQuaid also notes that it is perhaps accurate to describe the New Left as "an impulse or thrust of energy rather than as a description of a structure of thought or action."[8]

The first small protests against American involvement in Vietnam appeared in 1963. The Student Peace Union carried signs against the war during the Easter Peace Walk in New York City. In August 1963, American pacifists displayed signs condemning America's Vietnam involvement during the annual ceremony commemorating the Hiroshima-Nagasaki atomic bombing of 1945. That summer in Philadelphia, members of the Student Peace Union carried signs in front of the city's downtown federal building. In September, the executive board of the Committee for a Sane Nuclear Policy issued a national press release urging "disengagement" in Vietnam. In October, the Friends Committee on National Legislation (the Congressional Quaker Lobby) opened the Vietnam Information Center in Washington, D.C. The first campus demonstrations occurred at several colleges during the fall 1963 speaking tour of Mme. Dinh Nhu, the sister-in-law of Ngo Dinh Diem, the president of South Vietnam.

By the end of 1963 there were over 15,000 American military advisors serving in Vietnam. American aid to Vietnam in 1963 exceeded $500 million. By March of 1964, U.S. troops had been increased to more than 20,000, and over 500 U.S. servicemen had been killed while acting as advisors to the South Vietnamese Army.

In April of 1964, over two hundred members of the Women's International League for Peace and Freedom met in Washington to discuss Vietnam. The organization issued a press release which called for an immediate withdrawal of American forces and a convening of the Geneva Conference at the earliest possible date. Soon after, the *National Guardian* carried a large advertisement signed by almost one hundred college students saying flatly that they would refuse military service in Vietnam. In late May a similar advertisement was carried by the *New York Herald Tribune*.

The maneuverings of the Johnson administration in Vietnam were approved by seven out of ten Americans. Most antiwar dissidents, still very small in number, thought that a much larger American involvement was simply a matter of time. They viewed the conflict as a civil war that could not be "won" by the United States by any rational definition of the word.

While Vietnam was still coming into focus, other matters concerned the New Left.

In May of 1961, a year before the release of the Port Huron Statement, the first of the Freedom Rides began. Student activists went south to attempt to integrate public transportation facilities. The FBI maintained a surveillance of these trips but provided no help whatever in physically protecting the Freedom Riders. In the bus terminals in Anniston and Birmingham, Alabama tensions were especially high. Special agents were there but did nothing. Kenneth O'Reilly, an eyewitness, recalled: "In Birmingham a mob of about forty Klansmen and members of the National States Rights Party greeted the Freedom Riders. Most carried baseball bats or clubs. A few had lead pipes. The FBI looked on."[9]

In September of 1961, the black Student Nonviolent Coordinating Committee, with the help of northern white student activists, began voter registration drives in Mississippi.

In February of 1962, the nation's capitol was the site of a joint demonstration against the testing of atomic weapons, organized by the Student Peace Union and the Students for a Turn Toward Peace. Later that spring, pacifists attempted to interfere with U.S. atomic testing in the Christmas Islands.

In April of 1962, the FBI began its campaign of arranging for Internal Revenue Service (IRS) investigations of left-wing organizations and individual organization members. These targets were selected for investigation because of their political activity and not because they had necessarily violated tax laws.

In 1963 the FBI, utilizing undercover informants, began its systematic infiltration of student organizations. During the period 1964–1968, the bureau gathered enormous amounts of non-criminal "political intelligence" data on protest groups. More than eight hundred members of the Northern Student Movement, displaying considerable physical courage as well as astonishing political naiveté, moved into the Deep South in 1964—for the Mississippi Freedom Summer Project, a voter registration campaign. The FBI did nothing to help the situation. J. Edgar Hoover made it quite clear "that the FBI would not be offering protection to the out-of-state civil rights workers."[10] Over four hundred acts of violence took place that summer against black and white activists. Three were slain in June of 1964. It was this triple murder that prompted the FBI's formation of the White Hate COINTELPRO on September 2, 1964.

The intense political emotions of the civil rights movement set the stage for a student rebellion at the University of California at Berkeley. On September 14, 1964, university officials announced that the solicitation of funds on campus for off-campus political causes would be banned. Students had been raising money to support civil rights initiatives, and they were alarmed at what they saw as the university's attempt to stifle the right to speak freely on any subject. Thus, the Free Speech Movement was born. On January 3, 1965, university officials acknowledged defeat. It was announced that soliciting funds for off-campus political activities would be permitted on campus in the normal areas.[11] However, Clark Kerr, Berkeley president, took the opportunity to say that the campus activists were associated with "persons identified as being sympathetic with the Communist Party and Communist causes."[12]

The students at Berkeley were the first students of the sixties to commit civil disobedience against their own university. As Kirkpatrick Sale has written, Berkeley represented "the most direct confrontation ever seen in an American educational institution up to that time."[13] The Berkeley Free Speech struggle addressed many of the issues of concern to the New Left movement and also the philosophical influence of the Port Huron Statement.

The University of California drama established the pattern for direct action that would characterize student protest throughout the nation for much of the decade. The emotional impact of Berkeley on students nationwide was electrifying. Students realized, probably for the first time, that they had power, and that power could make a difference.

On May 2, 1964, a group of about one thousand students, most of whom had attended a war protest conference in March at Yale University, held two demonstrations in New York. The larger contingent marched to the United Nations Plaza to hear speeches denouncing the U.S. involvement in Vietnam. Police broke up both demonstrations and arrested about fifty students. This group, known as the May 2 Committee, included members of the Progressive Labor Movement, who were extreme in their opposition to the war. The FBI had been monitoring the committee. In late April, special agents and customs officials raided the headquarters of the PLM and seized a "Vietcong propaganda film."

Activist Dave Dellinger organized an antiwar demonstration on July

3, 1964, in Lafayette Park, across the street from the White House. Those taking part included, among others, Joan Baez, Reverend Phillip Berrigan, Reverend Daniel Berrigan, A. J. Muste, and Rabbi Abraham Feinberg. At the conclusion of the demonstration the group walked across the street. Dave Dellinger remembers, "We walked to the fence and kneeled down in front of the White House. It was supposed to be an act of civil disobedience but they didn't arrest us."[14]

Several days later, on July 10, 1964, a petition signed by more than five thousand college instructors was hand delivered at the State Department. It called for the United States to make every effort to secure a neutralized North and South Vietnam "protected by international guarantees."[15]

The administration was not listening. On July 14 an additional three hundred Special Forces advisors were sent to Vietnam. Two weeks later five thousand more U.S. troops were sent. On August 2, 1964, the White House announced that two American destroyers on patrol in the Gulf of Tonkin had come under attack by North Vietnamese torpedo boats. The Americans returned the fire. Two days later there was another attack. The United States retaliated with air strikes against "oil and naval facilities"[16] in North Vietnam. Shortly thereafter, Congress authorized the president to protect American forces in Vietnam and prevent additional Vietnamese aggression.

By late summer, 72 percent of the American people supported Johnson's handling of the Vietnam issue, and fully 85 percent supported the American air strikes against North Vietnam.

In November of 1964 one radical group, the War Resisters League, publicly demanded the fastest possible withdrawal of all American "forces from Vietnam."[17] In early December, members of the National Committee for a Sane Nuclear Policy (SANE) picketed the White House and called for an immediate negotiated peace. On December 19, three protest groups—the War Resisters League, the Committee for Non-Violent Action, and the Fellowship of Reconciliation—joined their small forces to sponsor a series of antiwar rallies in nine American cities.

These early protest activities, although small, sporadic, and sometimes poorly organized, nevertheless revealed a subtle but continuing New Left shift in emphasis and objectives. Many blacks were tending to resent white participation in the civil rights movement. White activists were shifting from civil rights to antiwar protest.

By mid-1964 the FBI was stepping up the investigation of Communist party influence within the antiwar movement. Hoover later instructed special agents "to intensify through all field offices the instructions to endeavor to penetrate the Students for a Democratic Society so that we will have proper informant coverage similar to what we have in the Ku Klux Klan and the Communist Party itself."[18] Late in 1964, members of the SDS met in New York and decided to commit their resources to a consistent campaign against American involvement in Vietnam. This meeting is considered by many to represent the birth of the antiwar movement. The SDS was more radical in its opposition to the war than other groups. At this meeting members planned a protest march to be held in Washington in the spring. They anticipated, quite wrongly, a small turnout.

On February 7, 1965, a small band of well-organized Vietcong guerrillas changed, in one swift surgical stroke, the nature of American involvement in Vietnam—and thus, the course of the domestic antiwar movement in the United States. The Vietcong, operating under cover of darkness, bombarded the American military base at Pleiku with 81-mm mortar rounds. Eight Americans were killed, 126 were wounded, and ten U.S. aircraft were destroyed. In less than a month the United States began a systematic campaign of aerial warfare, called Operation Rolling Thunder.

On February 17, faculty members from a number of New England colleges placed a display ad in the *New York Times* that called for immediate negotiations to end the war. Demonstrations were held in front of the United States mission to the United Nations and on Wall Street.

The U.S. 9th Marine Expeditionary Brigade came ashore on March 8 to guard the American installation at Da Nang, in South Vietnam. It was only a matter of time until American military patrols were engaged in fire fights with the Vietcong.

As the pace of American involvement in Vietnam increased, the American public seemed of two minds. Two-thirds supported the air strikes against North Vietnam. However, the air escalation also revealed that far more Americans were outraged by their government's deeper involvement than anyone imagined. Students and nonstudents alike, many of widely differing political persuasions, were becoming attracted to the ideas of the student New Left and the antiwar movement. The size of the student New Left by the end of March 1965 is indicated by the number of SDS chapters—fifty-two in operation nationwide.

The *New York Times* took notice of the fact that a movement was developing from a quite remarkable patchwork of political action groups. On March 15 the *Times* published its first full-length feature on the New Left with the headline "The New Student Left: Movement Represents Serious Activists in Drive for Change." A number of dissident groups were mentioned, including the SDS, the Student Nonviolent Coordinating Committee, and the Northern Student Movement. The movement was described as "a new, small, loosely bound intelligentsia that calls itself the new student left and that wants to cause fundamental changes in society." According to the article, the New Left's focus of political attention was on "conscription, academic freedom, the war in South Vietnam, disarmament, and poverty."[19]

Todd Gitlin has written that after the *Times* article student radicalism was "certified as a live national issue."[20] The pace of antiwar protest quickened as SANE sponsored a "March on Washington for Peace and a Negotiated Settlement in Vietnam." Two days later, on March 24, a new form of antiwar protest appeared for the first time in the American political arena: "Teach-Ins."

The first teach-in was organized by faculty members at the University of Michigan to provide lectures, debates, and seminars on American policy in Vietnam. It was an all-night session that attracted the astonishing number of three thousand college students and professors. A thesis of the first teach-in, and those that would follow, was that the Johnson administration, in a hideous distortion of the national interest, was moving the United States in the direction of national catastrophe, possibly nuclear war. President Johnson had misled the people of the United States before the 1964 election by asserting that the Vietnam involvement would not involve American combat troops. The teach-in concept spread rapidly to include more than sixty major colleges. A *Newsweek* editorial said that the teach-in concept represented "a splendid new way of communicating wisdom from scholars, through students, to the benighted general public."[21]

The administration was stunned.

The Johnson administration and the FBI took notice of the teach-ins. Thirteen bureau undercover agents attended one sponsored by the Universities Committee on Problems of War and Peace. Members of the SDS, the Young Socialist Alliance, the W.E.B. Du Bois clubs, and many others were identified by name and political affiliation. Also, the names of twenty-three speakers, including university instructors and members of the clergy, were identified. These data were quickly forwarded to headquarters for review, analysis, and placement in the appropriate FBI counterintelligence files. The first FBI report on this event totaled forty-one pages. Copies were sent to the White House, to the Justice Department's Internal Security and Civil Rights Divisions, and to military intelligence. There seems little doubt that President Johnson read the report.

Secretary of State Dean Rusk and others in the administration were extremely critical of the whole teach-in concept, wondering at the "gullibility of educated men."[22] Nevertheless, as one scholar said at the time, "What is perfectly clear is that we have the support of a substantial portion of the academic community."[23]

On March 4, 1965, in testimony before the House Appropriations Committee, J. Edgar Hoover said that the wave of protest against American bombing in Vietnam demonstrated "how unified, organized, and powerful an element the Communist movement is in the United States today."[24] Within days of this testimony, a college professor at an eastern university, doing research on McCarthyism, came under FBI surveillance by the New York field office because he contacted the American Institute of Marxist Studies.

In 1965, the antiwar movement escalated in direct proportion to the escalation of the war itself. Sidney Lens has said that the New Left "movement grew more spontaneously than any leftist force I have ever known, perhaps more so than any in American history."[25]

Hoover ordered intensified infiltration of the SDS in April of 1965 so that the bureau's intelligence division would "have proper coverage similar to what we have on the Communist Party."[26] Large-scale "interviewing"—a traditional FBI method of intimidation—was conducted with as many members from as many SDS chapters as possible.

Another SANE protest march followed, attracting more than three thousand demonstrators led by Dr. Benjamin Spock in New York. During Easter recess, April 17, 1965, the SDS's march on Washington took place with over seventy thousand marchers—the largest single antiwar effort up to that time. This march "suddenly became the projected outlet for protest not just by outraged students but by many of the older generation as well."[27] Within three months the number of SDS chapters grew to more than one hundred.

Hoover and President Johnson met on April 28, 1965. Johnson expressed extraordinary anxiety over the New Left movement and what it was doing to the country. He told Hoover that, according to intelligence reports reaching him, the North Vietnamese and Red Chinese felt that intensified antiwar agitation in the United States would eventually create a traumatic domestic crisis leading to a complete breakdown in law and order. Thus, according to this line of reasoning, U.S. troops would have to be withdrawn from Vietnam in order to restore domestic tranquility. Quite simply, the president felt that the New Left movement was giving encouragement to the enemies of the United States. Hoover advised Johnson that the SDS and accompanying groups were planning to demonstrate against the war in eighty-five U.S. cities between May 3 and May 9, 1965—the largest antiwar demonstration to date. The bureau, Hoover said, would prepare "an overall memorandum on the Vietnam demonstrations and communist influence in the same."[28]

The next day, April 29, Hoover issued instructions for a report to be prepared on "what we know about the Students for a Democratic Society." In the memo he stated, "What I want to get to the president is the background with emphasis upon the communist influence therein." The final report, titled "Communist Activities Relative to United States Policy on Vietnam," proved that the president and the director were completely off the mark. The report said that CPUSA *wanted* to influence antiwar activity but that their influence on the antiwar movement was quite negligible.[29]

A thirty-six–hour marathon teach-in was held at the University of California's Berkeley campus over May 21–22. This event, organized by the Vietnam Day Committee, attracted more than twenty thousand students and professors.

The Nation observed that "few realize just how deeply the teach-ins are reaching into campus life. Trouble is brewing in the most unlikely places."[30]

On June 8, 1965, SANE held an antiwar rally at Madison Square Garden. In July members of Women Strike for Peace, meeting in Indonesia, made the first formal contact between an American antiwar group and representatives of the Democratic Republic of Vietnam and the National Liberation Front. In mid-August the Oakland, California, SDS Chapter, and the Vietnam Day Committee attempted on three separate occasions to block troop transport trains from leaving the Oakland Army Terminal. Later in August the National Coordination Committee to End the War in Vietnam was formed. This umbrella organization of thirty-three different protest groups was the first of several to play a significant role in the movement's nationwide attempt to bring the war to a halt.

On the weekend of October 15–16, a panoply of different groups supporting the movement staged the largest antiwar effort to date. More than a hundred thousand people, in eighty U.S. cities and in several other countries, marched, picketed, and attempted to block troop transports and to occupy induction centers. They provoked furious counterdem-onstrations. Many were arrested.

On November 1, J. Edgar Hoover, speaking in Washington, said that antiwar demonstrators were, for the most part, "half-way citizens who are neither morally, mentally or emotionally mature."[31]

On November 11, the bureau, using the COINTELPRO technique of anonymous mailings, printed copies of an article titled "Rabbi in Vietnam Says Withdrawal Is Not the Answer." They were mailed in plain envelopes to individual members of the Vietnam Day Committee to "convince" the recipients of the correctness of U.S. policy in Vietnam.

There were public draft card burnings in November. On November 2, activist Norman Morrison burned himself to death before horrified onlookers at the Pentagon.[32] The following week, Roger LaPorte fol-lowed this example at the United Nations Plaza.

Before the end of the year, Attorney General Katzenbach "warned that there were Communists in SDS."[33] Senator John Stennis demanded that the administration uproot the anti-draft movement and "grind it to bits."[34]

A 235-page Senate Internal Subcommittee report was issued by Con-necticut Democrat Tom Dodd which said that the anti-Vietnam War movement was, in large measure, "under Communist control."[35]

This type of institutional thinking led to some bizarre activities. For example, on January 22, 1966, more than a year before the official cre-ation of the New Left COINTELPRO, special agents from the Boston field office contacted an editorial cartoonist at an area newspaper. They asked the artist to prepare a cartoon to ridicule a group of antiwar pro-testers who were traveling to North Vietnam. The cartoon was to "depict (the individuals) as traitors to their country for traveling to Vietnam and making references against the foreign policy of the United States."[36]

In February, the Senate Foreign Relations Committee, chaired by Sen-ator J. William Fulbright, held hearings to review an administration re-quest for $415 million in additional aid for Vietnam. The hearings, which were public, went beyond the aid request to include a televised discus-sion of the Vietnam involvement. Millions of television viewers discov-ered that a respectable opinion against the war did exist beyond the protests in the streets. Nevertheless, that month Director Hoover said that the SDS was "one of the most militant organizations" in the country. He added: "Communists are actively promoting and participating in the activities of this organization."[37]

A March 2, 1966, memorandum from the Philadelphia FBI field office reported on an undercover investigation at an area teach-in sponsored by the Universities Committee on Problems of War and Peace, which was attended by antiwar protesters, plus representatives of the Episcopal, Catholic, Methodist, and Unitarian churches. In this action, the bureau was attempting to establish a connection between the antiwar movement and the Communist party.[38]

Informants alleged that a Communist Party official had "urged all CP members" in the area to attend. One speaker was identified as a communist, another as a socialist "sympathizer," another as a conscientious objector, and still another according to the bureau had worked to abolish the House Committee on Un-American Activities. This FBI assignment, utilizing the data provided by thirteen informants and sources, resulted in a forty-one-page intelligence report prepared by the Philadelphia field office.[39] The final document was submitted to headquarters in Washington for analysis.

In the late spring of 1966, William Divale, an FBI undercover informant and college student at Pasadena City College, successfully infiltrated the area SDS chapter. At this same time Gerald Wayne Kirk, also an FBI informant, began his surveillance of the SDS chapter at the University of Chicago. Another FBI informant, Tommy Taft, began to spy for the FBI at Duke University. The student government at Wesleyan College protested the presence of FBI special agents and informants on campus. Their feelings were made known to Hoover, who in a scorching letter of reply said that "Your statements that the FBI investigation is extremely hostile to the goal of academic freedom is not only utterly false but is also so impossible as to cast doubt on the quality of academic reasoning or the motivation behind it."[40] In Hoover's view, the need for additional civilian disturbance intelligence was of paramount concern. Thus, in a letter to the special agents-in-charge at all field offices the director advised, "National, state and local government officials rely on us for information so they can take appropriate action to avert disastrous outbreaks." Field officers "were told to intensify and expand their 'coverage' of demonstrations opposing United States foreign policy in Vietnam."[41]

In the summer of 1966, three soldiers at Fort Hood, Texas, announced that they would refuse to go to Vietnam. Pledges to refuse to serve in Vietnam were made by students at Yale. The slogan "We won't go" was becoming a symbol of resistance.

In October, the FBI made efforts "to discredit and neutralize" a college professor and his association with the Inter-University Committee for Debate on Foreign Policy. FBI headquarters authorized the Detroit field office to send a fictitious-name letter to political figures in Michigan, the media, selected college officials at the University of Michigan, and the college's Board of Regents. The letter accused the instructor of "giving aid and comfort to the event" and asked if his purpose was to "bleed the United States white by prolonging the war in Vietnam."[42]

The San Antonio field office, working with the support of FBI headquarters, attempted to have a Democratic Party fundraising event raided by the Texas Alcoholic Beverage Control Commission. This function was targeted because of two Democratic candidates then running for office. One, a member of the Texas legislature running for reelection, was an active member of the Vietnam Day Committee. The other, campaigning for a seat in Congress, had been visible in his objection to the manufacturing and use of napalm. He had also played a role in sponsoring the National Committee to Abolish the House Committee on Un-American Activities. The FBI saw them as antiwar protesters, and hoped, by publicly embarrassing them, to sabotage their campaigns. In a San Antonio field office memo dated November 14, 1966, it was reported that a prior raid on a local fire department fundraiser had angered the local district attorney. Thus, the Texas Alcoholic Beverage Control Commission decided against the action because of "political ramifications."[43]

By the end of 1966, there had been protests against the war at more than two hundred major universities. Twenty-six percent of all colleges had experienced some form of war protest. More than a dozen "free universities" were established to show "what a radical and non-establishment educational exposure might be." All were operating under intense FBI scrutiny.

In December, the Student Mobilization Committee to End the War in Vietnam was created from an amalgamation of many radical groups. The committee, because of its almost immediate national status, advocated "large mass actions."

In late 1966 and early 1967, *New York Times* reporter Harrison Salisbury filed a series of dispatches that analyzed the developing situation in Vietnam. These articles were written in Hanoi and documented for the first time the civilian damage and casualties created by the American bombing missions.[44]

The antidraft movement gained momentum throughout the spring of 1967. A number of U.S. antiwar protesters visited North Vietnam. The Spring Mobilization to End the War in Vietnam began on April 15. More than fifty thousand marched in San Francisco and fully two hundred thousand protesters descended on Central Park in New York—the largest such demonstration to date.

By 1967, Lyndon Johnson was reviewing bureau reports on antiwar activists several times a week. He found them to be very disturbing. A White House announcement confirmed that the FBI was "keeping an eye" on antiwar demonstrators for the White House. Secretary of State Dean Rusk said that "antiwar demonstrators were supported by a communist apparatus and were prolonging the war."[45]

The FBI surveillance network was growing more extensive every month. Special agents had no difficulty in working directly with some college administrators. At Brigham Young the president of the university recruited students to monitor the antiwar efforts of several liberal professors. Six were fired. At a number of major universities—Illinois, Indiana, Kansas, Ohio State, Michigan State and Texas among them—administrators worked with the FBI by providing the bureau with the results of on-campus undercover surveillance work of antiwar demonstrations.[46]

By mid-1967, the spectrum of the New Left movement, comprised of hundreds of enormously diverse activist groups, were collectively marshaling their radical energies to end the war. Although most groups had different political agendas, which created internal friction and turmoil within the overall effort, they were somehow able to march together under the New Left banner for the peace cause. The total antiwar effort, however, functioning in large measure without a true national blueprint for action went beyond the vanguard New Left to include a broad spectrum of nonradical citizens from every conceivable walk of American life. Almost one hundred antiwar vigils took place weekly during late 1967. In an effort to reach the nerve center of the war effort, thousands marched on the Pentagon and a few actually forced their way inside but were quickly subdued. Robert Wall, then an FBI special agent, remembers, "When the march on the Pentagon took place in October, the FBI was there en masse, watching, listening, photographing and recording the events of the day." The names of arrested demonstrators were then quickly forwarded to the appropriate FBI field offices. These would become part of the FBI data base in Washington and the appropriate field office. "Hundreds of citizens became the object of FBI surveillance," according to Wall.[47]

In late 1967, Attorney General Ramsey Clark established the Inter

Divisional Information Unit of the Justice Department to coordinate and "make use of available intelligence."[48] The IDIU received about 85 percent of its intelligence information from the FBI.

On December 1, 1967, a memorandum from Hoover to twenty-three selected FBI field offices reflected the bureau's increasing uneasiness with the developing antidraft movement. The memo, almost certainly reflecting immense White House pressure, said that "individual cases are being opened regarding leaders of anti-draft organizations and individuals not connected with such organizations but who are actively engaged in counseling, aiding and abetting the anti-draft movement."[49]

Shortly thereafter, thousands of antiwar, antidraft protestors stormed the military induction center in Oakland, California, during "Stop the Draft Week." Other protesters gathered on Boston Common and dramatically burned their draft cards. Dow Chemical, a war materials supplier, became a special antiwar target. Dow recruiters were targeted and harassed during "Dow Days" at Harvard as well as the universities of Illinois, Wisconsin, and Minnesota. On November 15, 1967, another million protesters marched against the war.

In the chronology of the war in Vietnam, the year 1968 was traumatic. The Tet offensive beginning on January 3, a surprise attack by nearly seventy thousand North Vietnamese and Vietcong forces, stunned the American public. Millions came to see that there was no light at the end of the tunnel. The war could not, according to any rational definition of the term, be won. Antiwar violence continued to increase. Ten college campuses were fire-bombed between January and May of 1968. As a means of protest, a million students boycotted classes on April 26. The following day, one hundred thousand marched in New York City. More than 221 demonstrations occurred at 110 colleges between January and June of 1968. An astonishing 3,463 separate acts of campus protest were reported during the same period. Student rebellion was spreading faster than authorities could monitor, intercept, or prevent it. But of all the violence, all the demonstrations, all the chaos and disorder throughout the country, the drama that unfolded at Columbia, a university older than the American republic itself, was the most significant. The events at Columbia, following five years of escalating protests against the war, proved to be the catalyst that led to the FBI authorization for the New Left COINTELPRO.

NOTES

1. Kirkpatrick Sale, *SDS* (New York: Vintage, 1974), p. 69.

2. Ibid., pp. 42–70.

3. Theodore H. White, *The Making of the President 1968* (New York: Atheneum Publishers, 1969), p. 215.

4. Ibid.

5. Sale, *SDS*, p. 70.

6. Nancy Zaroulis and Gerald Sullivan, *Who Spoke Up? American Protest Against the War in Vietnam 1963–1975* (Garden City, NY: Doubleday, 1984), p. 29.

7. Sale, *SDS*, pp. 58–59.

8. Kim McQuaid, *The Anxious Years: America in the Vietnam–Watergate Era* (New York: Basic Books, 1989), pp. 153, 161.

9. FBI Memorandum, Student Nonviolent Coordinating Committee (FBI file No. 100-43140).

10. Sanford J. Unger, *FBI: An Uncensored Look Behind The Walls* (Boston: Little, Brown, 1975), p. 414.

11. W. J. Rorabaugh, *Berkeley at War: The 1960s* (New York: Oxford University Press, 1989), pp. 10–123.

12. "A Campus Uproar That Is Blamed on Reds," *U.S. News & World Report*, Dec. 14, 1964, p. 12.

13. Sale, *SDS*, p. 163.

14. Zaroulis and Sullivan, *Who Spoke Up?*, p. 20.

15. Ibid., p. 21.

16. Ibid., p. 22.

17. Ibid., p. 26.

18. FBI Memorandum, Headquarters to Field Offices, Apr. 28, 1965.

19. Fred Powledge, "The Student Left: Spurring Reform," *New York Times*, Mar. 15, 1965, p. 1.

20. Todd Gitlin, *The Whole World Is Watching: Mass Media in the Making and Unmaking of the New Left* (Berkeley; Los Angeles; London: University of California Press, 1980), pp. 32–77.

21. Kenneth Crawford, "Egghead Souffle," *Newsweek*, May 31, 1965, p. 30.

22. Zaroulis and Sullivan, *Who Spoke Up?*, p. 42.

23. Erwin Knoll, "Revolt of the Professors," *Saturday Review*, June 19, 1965, pp. 60, 61, and 70.

24. "From J. Edgar Hoover: A Report on Campus Reds," *U.S. News & World Report*, May 31, 1965, p. 84.

25. Sidney Lens, *Unrepentant Radical: An American Activist's Account of Five Turbulent Decades* (Boston: Beacon Press, 1980), p. 292.

26. FBI Memorandum, Headquarters to Field Offices, Apr. 28, 1965.

27. Sale, *SDS*, p. 174.

28. Senate Select Committee to Study Governmental Operations with Respect to Intelligence Activities, Book III, 94th Cong., 2d Sess., Apr. 14, 1976, p. 484.

29. Ibid., pp. 484–485.

30. Arnold S. Kaufman, "Teach-Ins: New Force for the Times," *The Nation*, June 25, 1965, pp. 666–670.

31. Fred Halstead, *Out Now! A Participant's Account of the Movement in the U.S. against the Vietnam War* (New York: Pathfinder Press, 1978), p. 90.

32. "War Critic Burns Himself to Death Outside Pentagon," *New York Times*, Nov. 3, 1965, pp. 1, 8.

33. Zaroulis and Sullivan, *Who Spoke Up?*, p. 60.

34. Ibid., p. 60

35. Ibid., pp. 59–60.

36. FBI Memorandum, Boston Field Office to Headquarters, Jan. 22, 1966.

37. Hoover testimony, House Appropriations Subcommittee, Feb. 10, 1966.

38. FBI Memorandum, Philadelphia Field Office to Headquarters, Mar. 2, 1966.

39. FBI Memorandum, Philadelphia Field Office to Headquarters, Mar. 2, 1966.

40. Frank J. Donner, *The Age of Surveillance* (New York: Alfred A. Knopf, 1986), p. 157.

41. FBI Memorandum, Headquarters to Field Offices, May 2, 1966.

42. FBI Memorandum, Detroit Field Office to Headquarters, Oct. 11, 1966; Headquarters to Detroit Field Office, Oct. 26, 1966.

43. FBI Memorandum, Headquarters to San Antonio Field Office, Nov. 14, 1966.

44. Halstead, *Out Now!*, pp. 266–268.

45. "Draft Card Burning Is Backed at Parley," *New York Times*, Apr. 9, 1967, p. 22.

46. Sale, *SDS*, pp. 275–276.

47. Paul Cowan, Nick Egleson, and Nat Hentoff, *State Secrets: Police Surveillance in America* (New York: Holt, Rinehart and Winston, 1974), p. 254.

48. Ibid., pp. 14–15.

49. FBI Memorandum, Headquarters to Field Offices, Dec. 1, 1967.

3

The New Left and the Confrontation at Columbia

"The New Left embraces philosophic dicta from every point in the left spectrum—communists, socialists, nihilists, Castroites, Maoites—all mixed together with political screwballs of every description."

—*Special Agent-in-Charge*
FBI New York Field Office

At 4:30 A.M. on May 1, 1968, Grayson Kirk, the exhausted president of Columbia University, stood amid the wreckage of his office. A sign had been placed on his window ledge: "LIBERATED AREA. BE FREE TO JOIN US." "My God," he wondered, "how could human beings do a thing like this?"

Columbia, one of America's oldest educational institutions, was in a state of revolt, which began on April 23 and had involved more than a thousand students led by the SDS. A police officer who had accompanied Kirk to his office after calm had been restored picked up a book from the floor. "The whole world is in these books," he said. "How could they do this to these books?"

David B. Truman, the university vice president, had another question: "Do you think they will know why we had to do this, to call in the police? Will they know what we went through before we decided?"[1]

Tensions had been escalating at Columbia and other colleges for months. Anxiety at the highest levels of the nation's largest investigative agency had reached a fever pitch. The cause, of course, was Vietnam. J. Edgar Hoover did nothing to calm the situation. On February 22, he stated to the House Appropriations Committee, "If anything definite can be said about the Students for a Democratic Society it is that it can be called anarchistic." He went on to say that "the SDS is infiltrated by Communist Party members who attempt to develop discord among the youth of this country."[2]

On March 13, more than thirty-five hundred students and almost a hundred members of the Columbia faculty refused to go to class as a protest against the draft and the war in Vietnam. Other protests followed at Trinity College, Bowie State College, Colgate, Michigan, and Howard University. On March 26, a letterhead memorandum from Hoover to field offices instructed special agents to immediately report any information regarding New Left activities via teletype to bureau headquarters "for immediate dissemination to the White House and other interested Government agencies."[3] He asked that any such communication from the field to headquarters be put under the caption VIDEM (Vietnam Demonstration). Hoover had been critical of special agents for incomplete reporting of the New Left—failure to report the number of protesters at demonstrations, failure to determine the names of the organizations involved and the identities of individual students.

On April 23, Mark Rudd, a twenty-year-old Columbia undergraduate and president of the area SDS chapter, directed the extraordinary student revolt which led to the occupation of Columbia's Low Memorial Library, and Hamilton, Mathematics, Fayerweather, and Avery halls for seven days. The campus, virtually without outside police assistance, was shut down. Acting Dean Henry S. Coleman was barricaded in his office for twenty-four hours as Mark Rudd announced, "Mr. Coleman had been selected as the group's hostage." Dean Coleman evidently took his imprisonment in stride, for he recalled that he had been "treated very nicely. We had more food than we could possibly eat."[4]

Many students who did not take part in the protest were unsettled by the events. Mike Kogan, then a twenty-five-year-old Columbia graduate student, recalled thinking at the time: "The target at the SDS was the university itself. Their main enemy is the power structure of the United States. They see the university as part of this power structure."[5]

A New York Times editorial dated April 25 said, "Whatever causes these students claim to be supporting have been defiled by vandalism."[6]

The drama of Columbia, which electrified students throughout the nation, was aimed at a number of university policies. The SDS opposed the presence of military and Dow Chemical recruiters on campus and Columbia's association with the Institute for Defense Analysis which "works on military projects aimed at the oppression of the people of Vietnam."[7] They were also protesting the construction of a new gymnasium that would displace some residents of Harlem, and they were defying the university's policy of punishment for students involved in political protest activities.

On April 26, more than one million students participated in the first national student strike at more than a thousand schools—the largest single student demonstration in history. On April 27, fully eighty-seven thousand antiwar protesters assembled for a huge rally in Central Park. At Columbia, after the seventh day of student occupation, after considerable vandalism and fruitless negotiations, the university officials had had enough. They called the police.

At 2:30 A.M. on April 30, one thousand New York police officers moved on Columbia. The academic complex was cleared of students, building by building, in an assault by officers that lasted nearly to dawn. Inside Low Memorial Library a doctor from Cornell Medical College was with the demonstrating students when the police arrived. The fact that he was wearing a white lab coat and carrying a medical bag made no difference. He was thrown to the floor, beaten, and handcuffed. In spite of this he asked to be allowed to treat others who were injured. "That's not necessary," the arresting officer told him. "We will take care of the injured."[8]

Some students did not resist arrest; others threw bottles, flashlight batteries, furniture, and anything else they could get their hands on at the oncoming police. Many resisted arrest by biting, scratching, punching, and even kicking police officers. At the mathematics building students barricaded stairwells and hallways with broken furniture. Others poured drums of liquid soap on stairs, making it more difficult for police to come up after them. Many students staged a counterattack. A janitor, who had the extreme misfortune of being in the mathematics building, was physically picked up by several enraged students and thrown bodily down a flight of stairs to impede the progress of the lawmen.

In total, 711 students were arrested, resulting in the highest number of arraignments ever recorded in a single day by the New York Police Department. Of those arrested, 239 were students at Columbia, 111 were students from Barnard College, and the remaining were from other area schools. Three faculty members were also arrested. A total of ninety-two students and seventeen police officers were injured, and the New

York Police Department received the highest number of complaints ever received for a single police action. This was also the largest police action in the history of American universities.

An uneasy truce followed. In an effort to let the dust settle, administrators closed the university for a week. The radical elements of the student body almost immediately began planning more protests. On May 21, students placed a poster in Ferris Booth Hall which warned of "Showdown No. 2." SDS members, working with other groups, began distributing leaflets which read, in part, "Can an administration which helps make weapons for Vietnam, steals people's land and homes discipline anyone . . . ?"[9]

On May 22, the campus exploded again. Students quickly occupied Hamilton Hall. Other radicals set fires in various parts of the campus. A force of about one thousand police officers moved onto the campus once again. They were in no mood to be pushed around by rowdy college students. Students threw bricks, rocks, and bottles at the lawmen. The police gave no quarter. It was a bloody, wild fight. The lawmen, many of whom were injured, again routed the huge crowd of students. There were almost two hundred arrests.

Jacques Nevard, a deputy police commissioner and an eyewitness, saw something on the Columbia campus that night that he would never forget. "Those fantastic kids linked arms and marched on the police and then the look that went over their faces when the front row realized what they had done. . . ."[10]

David Bell, professor of sociology at Columbia, later wrote, "In a few hours, thanks to the New York City Police Department, a large part of the Columbia campus became radicalized."[11] Dr. Bell, however, underestimated what had happened. The events at Columbia radicalized students throughout the entire nation. Physical violence became a weapon in the expanding protest against Vietnam. Indeed, the New Left's national slogan became "Two, Three, Many Columbias." More students than ever before mobilized for action at colleges large and small, public and private.

In April of 1968, at the time of the Columbia student rebellion, the FBI employed 8,700 special agents nationwide. The great majority of them were assigned to one of the fifty-nine FBI field offices and 516 smaller resident offices throughout the country. A number of offices had special squads involved entirely in gathering political intelligence, that is, security work. The gathering of data on political action groups of the New Left had been in operation for a number of years. As opposition to Vietnam increased, FBI surveillance of the New Left increased substantially.

An FBI investigation of the so-called Boston Five—Marcus Raskin, director of the Institute for Policy Studies, Mitchell Goodman, Yale Chaplin, William Sloan Coffin, Dr. Benjamin Spock, and Harvard graduate student Michael Ferber—led the Justice Department to indict the group in January of 1968 for conspiring "to counsel young men to violate the draft laws."[12]

Hoover was increasing the pressure on the antidraft movement. In a headquarters memorandum dated January 17, 1968, he directed twenty-three field offices "to advise the names of leaders presently under investigation and the names of individuals of the investigations being instituted by your office."[13]

A January 29th memorandum from the Philadelphia field office to headquarters demonstrated the bureau's willingness to see the most minor protest activity as a clue "to potential subversive activities." It advised that Detective Sergeant John Scanlon of the Haverford, Pennsylvania, Police discovered individuals distributing leaflets "against the war in Vietnam and the draft" outside Haverford Senior High School. The memo also reported on a Temple University professor who was a member of the faculty Draft Counseling Board.[14]

That same month, the director created the bureau's Key Agitator Index which would list antiwar groups and leaders who "were extremely active and most vocal in their statements denouncing the United States." The memo explained that "because of their leadership and prominence in the 'new left' movement as well as the growing militance of this movement, each office must maintain high level informant coverage."[15] A later follow-up memo mentioned that "the New Left has on many occasions viciously and scurrilously attacked the Director and the Bureau in an attempt to hamper an investigation." It recommended that "a new Counterintelligence Program be designed to neutralize the New Left."[16]

Hoover had by this time come to the conclusion, perhaps quite reluctantly, that the New Left was not under the influence of or associated with the Old Left—the CPUSA or the SWP. Since this was now Hoover's official opinion, it was the official opinion of the FBI. The director would authorize the development of a New Left COINTELPRO when he felt compelled to do so. The fast-moving and turbulent events of 1968—a year in which Americans faced, in Theodore White's words, "a war we could not win"[17]—were rapidly moving J. Edgar Hoover in that direction.

From the beginning, the bureau had a difficult time providing a precise definition of the term "New Left." Special agents were told that the New Left represented a "subversive force" operating within the United States. It had "no definable identity," but it was, nevertheless, dedicated to destroying America's "traditional values." The New Left, according to official FBI thinking in 1968, "had strong Marxist, existentialist, nihilist, anarchist overtones," and it amounted to "a threat to the security of the United States." Other headquarters memos said that the New Left did not refer to a definite organization, but to a "loosely-bound, free-wheeling, college oriented movement" which encompassed the "more extreme and militant anti-Vietnam war and anti draft organizations." A headquarters-based New Left supervisor said many years later that he did not recall "any document that was written defining the New Left as such." It was his impression that the movement "more or less grew," and it was "more or less an attitude, I would think."[18]

An April 2, 1968, headquarters letter to special agents-in-charge specified that "anti-Vietnam or peace group sentiments" were not, without further justification, supposed to "justify an investigation."[19] In actual practice, this admonition was ignored. A few days later COINTELPRO approved field offices were instructed to initiate "a comprehensive study of the whole movement" for the purpose of "assessing its dangerousness." In-depth reports were to be prepared by special agents and "sub-files" opened under headings that included the following:

Organizations ("when organized, objectives, locality in which active, whether part of a national organization");

Membership (special agents were to use "best available informants and sources");

Finances (including identity of "angels" and funds from "foreign sources");

Communist Influence;

Publications ("describe publications, show circulation and principal members of editorial staff");

Violence;

Religion ("support of movement by religious groups or individuals");

Race Relations;

Political Activities ("details relating to position taken on political matters including efforts to influence public opinion, the electorate and Government bodies");

Ideology;

Education ("courses given together with any educational outlines and assigned or suggested reading");

Social Reform ("demonstrations aimed at social reform");

Labor ("all activity in the labor field");

Public Appearances of Leaders ("on radio and television" and "before groups, such as labor, church and minority groups," including "summary of subject matter discussed");

Factionalism;

Security Measures;

International Relations (travel in foreign countries, "attacks on United States foreign policy");

Mass Media ("indications of support of the New Left by mass media").[20]

At the completion of these wide-ranging reports, requiring thousands of hours of investigative and surveillance work by special agents, the bureau intended to discover and understand "the true nature of the New Left movement." Before these reports were completed, Columbia University exploded into the national limelight on April 23.

It was the very next day, April 24, that William C. Sullivan, assistant director of the FBI in charge of the Domestic Intelligence Division since 1961, made a most curious statement. Sullivan—second only to Hoover in the management of U.S. internal intelligence and one of the architects of the COINTELPRO operations—said that "the trouble at Columbia came as a surprise to the FBI." He claimed that "before we read the headlines and saw the pictures of Mark Rudd smoking a cigar with his feet up on Grayson Kirk's desk, we didn't know the New Left existed."[21]

It is all but impossible to imagine that the bureau's number two man in domestic intelligence was completely unaware of the growing New Left surveillance of the last four years. Sullivan went on to say: "There was no question which division of the FBI would investigate the New Left. It was the job of the Domestic Intelligence Division."[22]

Other government agencies—the Central Intelligence Agency, the Office of Naval Intelligence, the National Security Agency, the Internal Revenue Service, and others—had been paying very careful attention to protesters of the war in Vietnam. But the FBI, under the day-to-day "hands-on" administration of Hoover, was, by far, the lead agency and the most invasive in its efforts to disrupt and neutralize targets.

After Columbia, tensions within the bureau, particularly in Washington, were very high. The special agent who would ultimately supervise the New Left COINTELPRO at FBI headquarters remembers the pressure. "I can't classify it exactly as an hysteria but there was considerable interest (and concern) . . . it would be my impression that as a result of this hysteria, some government leaders were looking to the Bureau."[23]

On May 9, C. D. Brennan, a top intelligence official working directly with Hoover and Sullivan, wrote the memo that created the New Left COINTELPRO. "Our nation is undergoing an era of disruption and violence caused by various individuals generally connected with the New Left," it said. The New Left urges "revolution in America and calls for the defeat of the United States in Vietnam." All COINTELPRO designated field offices were required "to submit an analysis of possible counterintelligence operations on the New Left and key activists by 6/1/68." The purpose of this new COINTELPRO was to "expose, disrupt, and otherwise neutralize the New Left."[24]

The next day, Hoover instructed all special agents in approved field offices to "immediately open an active contact file" and to "assign responsibility for this program to an experienced and imaginative special agent."[25] The director warned, as was his custom, that he would hold each special agent-in-charge directly responsible for the success of COINTELPRO-New Left operations in their respective field offices. In a follow-up letter dated May 21, 1968, he wrote, "It cannot be too strongly emphasized that all offices are expected to develop and maintain adequate sources to enable the Bureau to determine in advance agitational activities."[26] The director was particularly annoyed by the handling of the Columbia crisis where, in his opinion, college administrators committed the cardinal sin of not calling for police help until the situation was out of control.

Hoover issued the New Left COINTELPRO directives on May 23. Special agents had to take action to "counter the widespread charges of police brutality." Field offices had to make every effort to depict "the scrurrilous and depraved nature of the New Left activists." FBI personnel were required to explain "the value of college administrators and school officials taking a firm stand." Hoover closed by saying that "every avenue of possible embarrassment must be vigorously and enthusiastically explored," and that "an imaginative approach by your personnel is imperative."[27] The next day the bureau requested IRS tax returns on sixteen antiwar activists for 1966 and 1967. This information would be used, with other intelligence information, as part of the overall COIN-TELPRO operations to disrupt the lives of individual New Left activists.

After Columbia, the New Left, in Sanford Unger's opinion, was pursued "with a vengeance almost unknown in FBI annals."[28] Hoover demanded and received—within his rigid parameters of complete secrecy—all-out action from field offices nationwide.

A memo from the Newark field office, dated May 27, 1968, reported that the New Left was "difficult to actually define, although it was clear it had a complete disregard for generally accepted moral and social standards." New Left activists exhibited "neglect of personal cleanliness, use of obscenities (printed and uttered), publicized sexual promiscuity." They wore filthy clothes, experimented with drugs, and, as evidenced by the student revolt at Columbia and elsewhere, wanted nothing less than complete destruction of American society. The New Left had to be "destroyed or neutralized from the inside." The memo recommended background checks on as many members as possible, as well as the classic "snitch jacket" technique that had been so effective against other COINTELPRO targets. In this "snitch jacket," key activists such as Dave Dellinger and Tom Hayden would become "the object of a counterintelligence plot to identify them as government informants"; they would be suspected within the movement as "government informants," which would label them as "informants or Government Finks."[29]

The Newark FBI field office moved quickly against the SDS at Princeton University. A memorandum from the director dated June 21, 1968, authorized Newark to print a pamphlet for an anonymous mailing to Princeton University trustees, major benefactors, prominent alumni, and members of the Conservative Club. The memo notes that the pamphlet would feature "photographs of six of the dirtiest and most unkempt SDS demonstrators" who had been previously arrested at Princeton, and onto these photos would be drawn the bodies of apes. A caption would read, "Princeton is not the planet of the apes." The pamphlet would also state, "The above students of the SDS do not and will never represent the student body." It would be published "using commercial, store stationery utilizing maximum care that it will not be traced to the FBI."[30]

The New York field office advised Hoover that the New Left wanted "the absolute destruction of the government of the United States in its present form." It found that most students were from the upper middle class and had a basic contempt for and distrust of what they perceived to be the establishment—the military-industrial government complex of power in the United States. Many, according to the New York memo, expressed admiration for Chairman Mao, Fidel Castro, Ho Chi Minh, and Che Guevara. It reported on "approximately 17 organizations" identified with the New Left: "Included are youth organizations affiliated with the 'Old Left' such as the W.E.B. Du Bois Clubs of America (DCA), a youth organization of the Communist Party (CP), Youth Against War and Fascism (YAWF), the youth arm of the Workers World Party (WWP), and the Young Socialist Alliance (YSA), the youth section of the Socialist Workers Party (SWP). In addition, the Progressive Labor Party (PLP) has been active in its support of the NL through PLP members working within the Students for a Democratic Society (SDS)."[31] A later memo from New York updated Hoover on New Left activity at twenty-two area schools and said that "informant coverage of New Left organizations—particularly the SDS—has been limited to off campus informants and sources."[32]

On July 3, 1968, New York received authorization to mail out copies of an inflammatory letter written by SDS activist Mark Rudd to Grayson Kirk, president of Columbia University. The letter appeared in the May 1, 1968, issue of the *Guardian* newspaper with the headline "Activist answers Columbia prexy."[33] Rudd wrote the letter in response to a speech Kirk had given which, according to Rudd, "complained about youthful antiauthoritarianism." Rudd's letter condemned almost every sentence in Kirk's speech and ended with a particularly harsh obscenity. Copies of the letter were mailed, in plain white envelopes, to college officials throughout the New York area and to members of the Columbia Board of Regents and several of the university's major financial contributors. The last paragraph in the letter, which contained the obscenity, was circled in red. A cover note was included in each envelope:

> We wonder—after you read this letter—if you will consider the Students For A Democratic Society to be a legitimate campus organization in the American University tradition.
>
> —Concerned Alumni[34]

The parents of students arrested during the Columbia riot also received the same anonymous mailing, but with the note shown below included in the envelope:

> So your son or daughter got "busted" during the so-called "student revolt" at Columbia? The attached letter will introduce you to Mark Rudd,

student leader of SDS and the instigator of the whole disgraceful mess. It's your child and your money. Help throw SDS off the campus. Action for a healthy change is up to you.

—Father of a "busted" ex-student[35]

New York was also authorized to prepare a pamphlet that featured a photo montage of the most outlandish-looking members of the New Left, the message reading, "We are the SDS. If we lead will you follow?"

The New York special agent-in-charge also recommended this fraudulent invitation to the parents of arrested students:

Attend The Cultural Bag of The Year
1968 SDS Crap Out
• Do your thing
• Bring your own grass, pot, whatever
• Music by "The Mothers."
• Columbia Students—Free
July 5–6 (All nite, baby) 6:00 PM 'till—
4th Floor, 17 East 17th Street, NYC (SMC Office)
Auspices: SDS, 50 East 11th St.
NY Region
Extra: Meet and gas with Mark Rudd!

This proposal was not approved by Hoover, "due to the possibility of embarrassment to the bureau."

In a memo dated June 13, 1968, the Boston special agent-in-charge informed Washington of the career of one enterprising informant. This individual, who had proven to be quite trustworthy, reported that in one Boston area New Left enclave the living conditions were appalling. Members might wear clothing for weeks and even months without washing. Matters relating to personal hygiene were generally ignored. Eating and drinking habits were abominable. The informant witnessed a number of meetings about antiwar activity where both men and women were sitting in the living room completely without clothes. Men and women lived and slept together, and it was not at all unusual for students to change relationships as easily as moving from one room to the next. This sort of information tended to infuriate Hoover. He considered the moral standards of the student activists to be quite beneath contempt and often said so.

Another COINTELPRO campaign, beginning almost immediately after Columbia, concerned Morris Starsky. Dr. Starsky, an assistant professor of philosophy at Arizona State University, acquired the very dubious distinction of being a target of two COINTELPROs—the SWP and the New Left programs. Starsky, a member of the faculty since 1964, was known to support the SWP. He was also involved in antiwar teach-ins and was not shy about his opposition to the war in Vietnam. Starsky knew he was "a very controversial figure" on campus. At one point he expressly allowed his students to miss class in order to attend an antiwar rally at the University of Arizona in Tucson.

The Phoenix FBI field office took very careful notice of him. A May 1968 memorandum from Phoenix to the director advised that he was "one of the most logical targets for counterintelligence action."[36] Hoover agreed. In the next two years a total of twenty-two counterintelligence memoranda were exchanged between Phoenix and Washington—most of which concerned Morris Starsky. On June 11, 1968, Phoenix received permission to provide Starsky background data to several area news-papers. After having speculated that Starsky "may have falsified atten-dance records or something of that sort," which could conceivably be used to encourage his "dismissal from the ASU faculty," Phoenix was able to report on October 1 that Starsky and his wife "were both named as presidential electors, by and for the Socialist Workers Party."[37]

On October 8, the field office advised that Governor Jack Williams was aware of the situation at Arizona State.[38] On October 25, 1968, it reported that an FBI special agent had been in contact with a member of the state Board of Regents who was curious to know "if the FBI or another source could somehow provide the Board of Regents with facts that would permit them to separate Starsky from the ASU faculty."[39] A January 6, 1969, memo reported that Starsky had been observed in a heated dispute with a young SWP worker over funds and supplies.[40]

Next, with Hoover's full approval, the Phoenix field office mailed, on May 6, 1970, inflammatory anonymous letters to all five members of the Arizona State Faculty Committee on Academic Freedom and Tenure. The letter contained a furious attack on Starsky and his involvement with radical causes—by implication the SWP and the New Left. At one point it asked, "Is this an example of academic socialism? Should the ASU student body enjoy the guidance of such an instructor? It seems to me that this type of activity is something that Himmler or Beria could accept with pride." The letter was signed "A Concerned ASU Alum."[41]

The faculty committee came out in favor of retaining Starsky, but the university Board of Governors disagreed. In its opinion, Starsky had created far too much controversy. A June 30, 1970, memo from Phoenix to the director confirmed that Starsky had agreed to take a one-year sabbatical.[42] The damage to Dr. Starsky's career was, by June of 1970, permanent. "Morris knew he was on a blacklist," Mrs. Starsky now recalls. "Over the years he made hundreds of applications. But he was never able to get another decent job in teaching."[43]

The fact that the FBI had played a major role in the Starsky dismissal was not known until many years later, when fourteen pages of COINTELPRO documents were made available to him under the Freedom of Information Act. A federal court ultimately decided that the professor had actually been fired illegally. He was awarded fifteen thousand dollars. Finally, as a result of the Starsky episode, Arizona State University was censured by the American Association of University Professors for almost ten years.

The Philadelphia field office accelerated its New Left investigations almost immediately after Columbia. A Philadelphia memorandum to Hoover, dated May 29, 1968, advocated an FBI seizure of "every opportunity to capitalize upon organizational and personal conflict of the New Left leaders." Promoting factionalism was the most powerful strategy available to bureau special agents, it said. It discussed the techniques of news leaks, anonymous letters, and derisive cartoons, specifically cartoons that would highlight the anarchistic aims of the New Left by labeling them "mobocracy." They could be "distributed anonymously or through established sources in each division." The memo noted that a leading member of the CPUSA Youth was "neutralized when the Philadelphia office publicized his homosexual activity," and recommended the exposure of other "weaknesses and deficiencies" of individual New Left members. Anonymous letters to the parents of individual New Left members "might very well serve the purpose of neutralizing them through parental discipline." The memo closed by saying that further recommendations for "specific counterintelligence action will be submitted to the bureau."[44]

An eleven-page letterhead memorandum to the director on July 8, 1968, reported on surveillance at Penn State, the University of Pennsylvania, Temple, Lehigh, Bucknell, Franklin and Marshall, Swarthmore, Haverford, Bryn Mawr, and Villanova. Each campus report reflected the FBI's traditional reliance on well-placed undercover informants. Two persons originally recruited as Black Hate Group COINTELPRO informants were "found to have great potential for coverage of New Left activity."[45] Individual New Left groups in Philadelphia under surveillance included the SDS, the W.E.B. Du Bois Clubs of America, the Progressive Labor Party, the Philadelphia Antidraft Union, and the Student Club of the Communist Party of Eastern Pennsylvania and Delaware.

The Philadelphia SDS had distributed a pamphlet which made the rather startling claim that the University of Pennsylvania's City Science Center "was performing research and development work in direct compliance with the American war of aggression in Vietnam."[46] About thirty SDS members at Penn State presented a petition to Charles Lewis, vice president in charge of student affairs, that condemned the institution's alleged relationship with the Institute for Defense Analysis. There was no disorder at that demonstration or at a later, larger one at the City Science Center, where many carried a large sign which read, "Science is for helping people, not removing them in Vietnam and West Philadelphia."[47] The Philadelphia special agent-in-charge believed that "the lack of violence was due primarily to the lack of forceful leaders in the movement." However, if indeed a forceful leader did materialize, the Philadelphia field office would develop "counterintelligence action to disclaim him" and render him "ineffective."[48]

Philadelphia, as did other offices, distributed to college administrators reprints of an article from *Barron's* entitled "Campus or Battleground? Columbia Is a Warning to All American Universities." The writer of the piece called for firmness in dealing with student rebels; Hoover believed that the mailings would be an excellent occasion to contact college administrators. The vice president for general administration at Temple University read it and saw a direct comparison between Columbia and Temple. He planned to pass the article along to other administrators, to "awaken them to the need for immediate firmness in dealing with rebel students." Philadelphia saw the reprint mailings as "an entree to meet and develop other college administrators who are not established sources."[49]

On May 27, 1968, the Cleveland field office advised bureau headquarters that the area New Left was represented by the SDS, which had chapters at Oberlin College, Bowling Green State University, and at an off-campus location in Toledo. Other area antiwar groups, it reported, included the Cleveland Draft Resistance Union and the Kent Committee to End the War in Vietnam.[50]

Special agents monitored an area antiwar demonstration on April 27, 1968. In addition to noting that participants were "long-haired, filthy, hippie types who seemed to have more interest in fraternization with each other than in protesting the war," they identified Case Western Reserve faculty member Sidney Peck as a leader in the Cleveland-area antiwar movement. A copy of Peck's "work paper," which provided tactical recommendations for antiwar activity, was obtained by an undercover source and forwarded to bureau headquarters. A source also provided information on the friction within the New Left between the SDS/Cleveland Draft Resistance faction and the Socialist Workers Party/Young Socialists Alliance faction. Cleveland recommended that these internal conflicts be aggravated whenever possible. The field office also recommended the use of contacts with friendly media to discredit the reputation of Sidney Peck. "Efforts should be made," the memo said, "to demean Peck during organizational meetings and in contact with individual members of the New Left."[51]

A June 27 Cleveland memo reported on a confrontation near the Oberlin College campus. Approximately a hundred antiwar students blockaded a car being driven by a U.S. Navy recruiting officer who was, in effect, held hostage for about four hours until police intervened with tear gas and a fire hose. The college trustees were greatly embarrassed by the incident and demanded a more "stringent attitude toward militant student activities."[52]

The San Francisco field office reported in a May 31 memo to bureau headquarters that the area news media, including radio and television, resorted to outright sensationalism when covering the New Left: the coverage often focused on strange living conditions, drug usage, sex, and nudity among the young people. Most activists, the memo stated, "seemed to enjoy the attention." Thus, in following a familiar theme, San Francisco reported that trying to expose the "moral depravity" of the New Left would not be productive. It went on to report that "the New Left, at least in this area, seems to be a rather disorganized federation of many types of groups." There seemed to be no main target or group that "the counterintelligence program can be directed against." Special agents would, however, remain alert for any possible actions that could be used for disruption. Interestingly, the memo also suggested the possibility of utilizing as informants "hippies," who may or may not use drugs, but might be in an excellent position to furnish the FBI with information of value. Indeed, since the counterintelligence objective was disruption, "it would not be necessary for the informant to have a clean background." Additionally, it was noted that increasing informant payments from $200 to $400 would put the amount on par with the racial informant program.[53]

A June 27 San Francisco memorandum to Hoover reported on a sit-in by approximately four hundred militant students at San Francisco

State College. In this situation, the antiwar students demanded, among other things, the rehiring of a controversial left-wing social science instructor and a ban on the Air Force ROTC program. Police were called in to clear the campus and the administration building. A wild, club-swinging fight broke out. Several were injured and twenty-six were arrested. College president John Summerskill gave in to virtually all student demands. He was excoriated by State College trustees for "yielding to pressure" and was fired. This same communication also reported on an incident in May of 1968 at Berkeley. Several students and faculty members had demanded that the Campus Draft Opposition (CDO) be permitted to hold a "Vietnam Commencement" at the university's Greek Theatre to honor and recognize "individuals, students and faculty who refused to cooperate with the military draft."[54] Though the administration refused, the CDO did conduct a commencement of its own in the form of a rally on the Sproul Hall steps on campus on May 17, 1968.

The Houston field office advised headquarters on May 22 that the New Left in the area was still comparatively small but seemed to offer "excellent potential for counterintelligence activity." Houston further advised that student activists were using marijuana on a regular basis at "pot parties." The Houston office was making strenuous efforts to obtain photographs of all students involved in antidraft activities. The photos, together with the letter below, were mailed anonymously to the students' parents.

Dear Mr. and Mrs. Jones:
    I feel you should be advised that your son, who is a fellow student at the University of Houston, has recently become engrossed in activities which are not only detrimental to our country, our efforts in Vietnam and our common desire for justice, but are extremely detrimental to himself. Many of the people your son has been associating with are confirmed "Left Wingers" and some brazenly advocate communist ideology. While you may be somewhat unconcerned about your son's activities, I am sure you are cognizant of the fact that he is establishing for himself a stigma which soon he may not be able to erase. Although I would like to sign my name to this letter I do consider your son a friend of mine and I would hate to lose his friendship.
    For your information also I am enclosing a photograph of your son which I managed to obtain from [deleted] the University of Houston which shows your son passing out leaflets in front of the draft board in Houston, Texas.[55]
                                                            Very sincerely yours.

On June 25, 1968, Houston reported that an active SDS member was seeking a teaching position in Los Angeles. This young woman, according to the field office, wore outlandish clothes, participated in "SDS-sponsored anti-American activities," used marijuana, and had a generally promiscuous personal life. The letter below was sent to officials of the Los Angeles Board of Education. The signature was fictitious and the address was a vacant apartment where the target had once lived.

Dear Sirs:

It has come to my attention that [*name deleted*] who was a former resident of this apartment complex is enroute to Los Angeles, California to obtain a teaching position.

While I am in complete agreement with her leaving Houston, I feel it my duty to inform you of the background of this girl as she is completely unsuitable in my estimation for teaching youngsters. She was well-known as a radical and trouble-maker while a student at the University of Houston. She appears to be proud of the fact that she has been affiliated with a group calling themselves Students for a Democratic Society and also that she has been involved in many demonstrations against the Vietnam War and other anti-American activities. She is extremely promiscuous in her personal life besides being a user of marijuana. She has had numerous beatnik type persons spend the night in her apartment. Also during the time she was taking practice teaching I understand that she got the officials at the school upset by her wearing mini-mini skirts. She was told she would have to wear more appropriate clothes and she thereafter came to school wearing ankle length dresses. Obviously she merely wanted to cause trouble rather than become educated.

As you can see this girl certainly is not the proper person to be in charge of and teaching youngsters in yours [*sic*] or any other school system.

It is suggested that you might want to thoroughly check this person before offering her a teaching position.

Yours truly
Ann Hill
Resident
1549 Lombardy
Houston, Texas[56]

A June 3, 1968, memo from the Albany field office reported no key activists in the territory. There were, however, active SDS chapters at Cornell, Syracuse, Hooper State College, the Universities of Courtland and Oswego, Colgate, and Albany State. New Left activists of most chapters, it said, were known to smoke marijuana and use hallucinogens such as LSD. Special agents reported that most student activists did not live in campus housing but rather in off-campus apartments described as "slovenly hovels" in which "male and female students are living in open cohabitation."[57] A June 14 memo reported on student efforts to physically block the on-campus recruiting of the CIA, the armed forces, and Dow Chemical at Hamilton College, Syracuse, and the State University at Albany. Police were called in all three situations to restore order.[58]

The Los Angeles field office, in a lengthy memo to headquarters dated May 29, 1968, advised that the New Left COINTELPRO required an entirely different approach from previous efforts "directed at the Communist Party, USA (CPUSA) and other groups." Los Angeles reported that New Left groups in their territory were largely unstructured and poorly organized, and had memberships in constant transition. Meetings were generally chaotic: "The student who shouts his idea the loudest has his plan adopted."[59]

In a familiar theme, Los Angeles suggested that the most effective counterintelligence action against New Left activists would be for college administrators to take firm action against demonstrators from day one. Administrative weakness only encouraged more forceful demonstrations. The bureau should advise friendly school administrators of impending demonstrations on their campuses, and identify for them the leaders of the demonstrations. The field office also advocated providing Selective Service officials with information on draft-eligible students who participate in New Left actions resulting in violence.

On July 3, Los Angeles reported that most New Left organizations at UCLA had merged with the SDS. The same memo reported on a fire bombing at Los Angeles Valley Junior College and an on-campus demonstration in support of the nationally held "Ten Days of Protest and Resistance." At Cal State College, Long Beach, militant students, acting with some faculty members, held demonstrations on May 28, 29, and 31, June 3 and June 4. Most actions focused on the campus administration building which was occupied briefly during each demonstration. Over fifteen hundred participated and forty-two were arrested.[60]

On June 13, Denver reported to headquarters on the status of New Left activity at three area colleges. In April, six University of Colorado SDS members had been arrested during a demonstration at the New Custom House, the local armed forces induction center. Over a hundred antiwar militants converged on the center and refused to leave when ordered to do so. Police responded with force and used chemical Mace to clear the area. Later that same day about 75 students returned to the induction center and loudly protested police brutality. In fact, they carried signs referring to Denver police as "Armed and Dangerous." On April 25, special agents observed about eighty protesters again marching and picketing the induction center in Denver. On the instructions of assistant U.S. attorney Milton C. Branch, all doors to the facility were locked. A stand-off followed with students chanting, carrying signs, and milling around at the center entrance. U.S. marshals later moved in and four demonstrators were arrested for disorderly conduct on federal property.

At the University of Denver about 250 SDS members occupied the registrar's office. They sat down, locked arms, and chanted "We shall overcome" and "We are not afraid."[61] They also took control of the university switchboard. Director of security Wayne Littrell, speaking on behalf of chancellor Maurice Mitchell, told students that if they did not leave immediately they would be subject to suspension, arrest, or both. Some students left voluntarily. Of those that remained, thirty-nine were physically carried to waiting patrol wagons.

At Colorado State University, the SDS chapter merged into a new group called the Peace Action Now Committee (PANC). Membership consisted of eighty students, five university professors, and a few local people from Fort Collins. PANC began holding silent weekly vigils, the first of which was interrupted by a very spirited group of counterdemonstrators who shouted epitaphs and hit the crowd with a barrage of flying missiles. At a March 4 PANC march, about five hundred demonstrators made their way into downtown Fort Collins, where there were speeches against the war. There were no arrests.

These examples of direct field office actions against the New Left undertaken immediately after Columbia may serve to represent what the FBI was doing across the nation. FBI special agent case loads involving the New Left increased exponentially as Vietnam War protests increased.

In the process, the bureau was developing an enormous library of background information on thousands of individual activists. The most exhaustive records were developed on the SDS. In time, the FBI worked with an extensive group of undercover informants to monitor the entire spectrum of the New Left. It is important to note that, aside from vandalism, the great majority of dissidents had not been directly involved in criminal behavior. As Frank T. Donner has written, the New Left COINTELPRO represented "an undisguised assault by the self-appointed defenders of the American way of life."[62] This COINTEL-PRO involved the highest number of actions aimed at the prevention of free speech. The use of "dangerous, degrading, or blatantly unconstitutional techniques" was far more common than in the preceding COINTELPROs.

In the late spring and early summer of 1968, headquarters was asking approved field offices to provide additional suggestions for counterintelligence actions. The responses were analyzed by Hoover, Sullivan, and top intelligence officials. The following headquarters-approved suggestions, almost certainly written with the impending Chicago Democratic National Convention in mind, were included in a letterhead memorandum to field offices on July 6, 1968:

(1) Prepare leaflets designed to discredit student demonstrators, using photographs of New Left leadership at the respective universities. "Naturally, the most obnoxious pictures should be used."

(2) Instigate "personal conflicts or animosities" between New Left leaders.

(3) Create the impression that leaders are "informants for the Bureau or other law enforcement agencies."

(4) Send articles from student newspapers of the "underground press" which show the depravity of the New Left to university officials, donors, legislators, and parents. "Articles showing advocation of the use of narcotics and free sex are ideal."

(5) Have members arrested on marijuana charges.

(6) Send anonymous letters about a student's activities to parents, neighbors, and the parents' employers. "This could have the effect of forcing the parents to take action."

(7) Send anonymous letters or leaflets describing the "activities and associations" of New Left faculty members and graduate assistants to university officials, legislators, Boards of Regents, and the press. "These letters should be signed 'A Concerned Alumni [sic],' or 'A Concerned Taxpayer.' "

(8) Use "cooperative press contacts" to emphasize that the "disruptive elements" constitute a "minority" of the students. "The press should demand an immediate referendum on the issue in question."

(9) Exploit the "hostility" among the SDS and other New Left groups toward the Socialist Workers Party, Young Socialist Alliance and Progressive Labor Party.

(10) Use cartoons, photographs, and anonymous letters to "ridicule" the New Left.

(11) Use "misinformation" to "confuse and disrupt" New Left activities, such as by notifying members that events have been cancelled.[63]

A very important point is that the absence of any precise definition by the bureau of the term "New Left" led to actions against virtually anyone opposed to the war—indeed, against "anyone demonstrating against anything."

That the FBI was apprehensive about a possible confrontation in Chicago is putting it mildly. Pressure was coming from the White House. Hoover sent a broadside to his special agents-in-charge. On July 23, 1968, he told field offices, "I have reminded you time and again that the militancy of the New Left is escalating daily. . . . [T]his type of activity can be expected to mount in intensity and spread." To ensure that it "not be allowed to happen," he would hold each special agent-in-charge "personally responsible."[64]

NOTES

1. A. M. Rosenthal, "Combat and Compassion at Columbia," *New York Times*, May 1, 1968, p. 2.

2. Murray Schumach, "56 Columbia Rebels Seized Among 117 at Sit-In Here," *New York Times*, May 17, 1968, p. 1.

3. FBI Memorandum, Headquarters to Field Offices, Mar. 26, 1968.

4. "Columbia Closes Campus after Disorders," *New York Times*, Apr. 25, 1968, pp. 1, 2.

5. Sylvan Fox, "Goals of Leftists at Columbia Cited," *New York Times*, May 16, 1968, pp. 1, 3.

6. "Hoodlumism at Columbia," *New York Times*, Apr. 25, 1968, p. 46.

7. "The Radicals Do Their Thing at Columbia," *New York Times*, Apr. 28, 1968, p. 15.

8. FBI Memorandum, New York Field Office to Headquarters, June 6, 1968.

9. Ibid.

10. Jerry L. Auron with Andrew Crane, *Up Against the Ivy Wall* (New York: Atheneum, 1969), p. 273.

11. "Columbia Offers to Meet Leaders of Harlem Gym," *New York Times*, May 2, 1968, pp. 1–4.

12. Fred P. Graham, "Spock and Coffin Indicted for Activity against Draft," *New York Times*, Jan. 6, 1968, p. 1.

13. FBI Memorandum, Headquarters to Field Offices, Jan. 17, 1968.

14. FBI Memorandum, Philadelphia Field Office to Headquarters, Jan. 29, 1968.

15. FBI Memorandum, Headquarters to Field Offices, Jan. 30, 1968.

16. FBI Memorandum, C. D. Brennan to W. C. Sullivan, May 9, 1968.

17. Theodore H. White, *The Making of the President 1968* (New York: Atheneum, 1969), p. 30.

18. Senate Select Committee to Study Government Operations with Respect to Intelligence Activities, "FBI Intelligence Deposition," Oct. 28, 1975, Book III, 94th Cong., 2d Sess., Apr. 14, 1976, pp. 22–27.

19. FBI Memorandum, Headquarters to Field Offices, Apr. 2, 1968.

20. FBI Memorandum, Headquarters to Field Offices, Oct. 28, 1968.

21. William C. Sullivan with Bill Brown, *The Bureau: My Thirty Years in Hoover's FBI* (New York: W. W. Norton, 1979), p. 148.

22. Ibid., pp. 148, 149.

23. Senate Select Committee to Study Government Operations with Respect to Intelligence Activities, "Intelligence Activities and the Rights of Americans," Book II, 94th Cong., 2d Sess., Oct. 28, 1975, p. 23.

24. FBI Memorandum, C. D. Brennan to W. C. Sullivan, May 9, 1968.

25. FBI Memorandum, Headquarters to Field Offices, May 10, 1968.

26. FBI Memorandum, Headquarters to Field Offices, May 21, 1968.

27. FBI Memorandum, Headquarters to Field Offices, May 23, 1968.

28. Sanford J. Unger, *FBI: An Uncensored Look Behind the Walls* (Boston: Little, Brown, 1975) p. 232.

29. FBI Memorandum, Newark Field Office to Headquarters, May 27, 1968.

30. FBI Memorandum, Headquarters to Newark Field Office, June 21, 1968.

31. FBI Memorandum, New York Field Office to Headquarters, May 28, 1968.

32. FBI Memorandum, New York Field Office to Headquarters, July 1, 1968.

33. FBI Memorandum, Headquarters to New York Field Office, July 3, 1968.

34. Ibid.

35. Ibid.

36. FBI Memorandum, Phoenix Field Office to Headquarters, May 31, 1968.

37. FBI Memorandum, Phoenix Field Office to Headquarters, June 11, 1968; Oct. 1, 1968.

38. FBI Memorandum, Phoenix Field Office to Headquarters, Oct. 8, 1968.

39. FBI Memorandum, Phoenix Field Office to Headquarters, Oct. 25, 1968.

40. FBI Memorandum, Phoenix Field Office to Headquarters, Jan. 6, 1969.

41. Nicholas M. Horrock, "Files of FBI Showed It Harassed Teacher," *New York Times*, Jan. 29, 1979, p. 12.

42. FBI Memorandum, Phoenix Field Office to Headquarters, June 30, 1970.

43. Tom Fitzpatrick, "Morris Starsky's Proud Exit," *Valley News and Arts Journal*, Feb. 17, 1989, p. 2.

44. FBI Memorandum, Philadelphia Field Office to Headquarters, May 29, 1968.

45. FBI Memorandum, Philadelphia Field Office to Headquarters, July 8, 1968.

46. Ibid.

47. Ibid.

48. Ibid.

49. FBI Memorandum, Philadelphia Field Office to Headquarters, Aug. 23, 1968.

50. FBI Memorandum, Cleveland Field Office to Headquarters, May 27, 1968.

51. Ibid.

52. FBI Memorandum, Cleveland Field Office to Headquarters, June 27, 1968.

53. FBI Memorandum, San Francisco Field Office to Headquarters, May 31, 1968.

54. FBI Memorandum, San Francisco Field Office to Headquarters, June 27, 1968.

55. FBI Memorandum, Houston Field Office to Headquarters, May 22, 1968.

56. FBI Memorandum, Houston Field Office to Headquarters, June 25, 1968.

57. FBI Memorandum, Albany Field Office to Headquarters, June 3, 1968.

58. FBI Memorandum, Albany Field Office to Headquarters, June 14, 1968.

59. FBI Memorandum, Los Angeles Field Office to Headquarters, May 29, 1968.

60. FBI Memorandum, Los Angeles Field Office to Headquarters, July 3, 1968.

61. FBI Memorandum, Denver Field Office to Headquarters, June 13, 1968.

62. Frank J. Donner, *The Age of Surveillance* (New York: Alfred A. Knopf, 1980), p. 232.

63. FBI Memorandum, Headquarters to Field Offices, July 6, 1968.

64. FBI Memorandum, Headquarters to Field Offices, July 23, 1968.

4

Firestorm in Chicago

"Television magnified the agony of Chicago into a national debacle."

—*Richard M. Nixon*

It was a traumatic week in Chicago. As Theodore White later wrote, "For the first time, the most delicate process of American politics was ruptured by violence, the selection of Presidents stained with blood."[1]

The war cast a shadow over everything. As the Democratic Party held an acrimonious convention, antiwar activists clashed in the streets with the forces of law and order in full view of American television.

Senator Eugene J. McCarthy had been an antiwar darkhorse candidate since the beginning of the primaries in early 1968. McCarthy became—particularly after the death of Robert F. Kennedy—the candidate of choice of thousands of young people. Although the antiwar movement was too diverse to officially support any presidential candidate, the nomination of Vice President Humphrey came as a particularly bitter disappointment. Humphrey was the nominal protege of Lyndon Johnson and thus, by association, the war candidate.

McCarthy had seen the potential for violence in Chicago long before the convention began. Indeed, the senator's staff and campaign workers had contacted organizations across the country "asking them to discourage student leaders and other young people from coming to the Chicago streets."[2]

The senator made a dramatic last-minute attempt to have his candidacy withdrawn from the convention floor in hopes, as he later said, "that this, if publicized, would help to ease tensions in the convention and in the city."[3] It was a forlorn gesture. On August 28, the night of the nomination, thousands of demonstrators chanted, "The whole world is watching." McCarthy, although anticipating problems, was nevertheless deeply troubled by the violence: "I did not anticipate that after Vice President Humphrey had been nominated serious beatings would take place on the street outside the Hilton Hotel and in Grant Park across Michigan Avenue."[4]

On October 8, 1967, the Democratic Party announced that the 1968 national convention would be held in Chicago's International Amphitheatre on August 26–29. This facility, about five miles from the downtown hotels that would house the delegates, was adjacent to the city's poorest ghetto areas.

In the fall of 1967, in spite of Vietnam, it seemed highly probable that President Johnson and Vice President Humphrey would be nominated to run for a second term.

In January of 1968, about sixty antiwar activists met in New York to discuss the feasibility of disrupting the convention. Those in attendance became the administrative committee of the National Mobilization to End the War in Vietnam. They included Rennie Davis, director of the Center for Radical Research; David Dellinger, publisher of *Liberation Magazine*; and Tom Hayden, Carl Oglesby, Professor Sidney Peck, and others. Some felt that no action should be taken. Oglesby was against the idea of any demonstration in Chicago "at all."[5] Others saw the matter differently. Sidney Peck remembers, "There were some who felt that the slogan 'from protest to resistance' meant we should physically prevent it from going on."[6]

A counter-convention idea was discussed and dropped. Jerry Rubin thought that some method should be developed to show the convention as something ridiculous. Sidney Lens pointed out to Rennie Davis, "Unless you think we are on the verge of revolution they could kill every one of us if we choose to make it a contest of violence."[7] Some moderates wanted to support the pro-McCarthy forces. In the end, no strategy decisions of substance were made at the New York meeting. The following month, David Dellinger asked two SDS members, Tom Hayden and Rennie Davis, to operate the new convention planning office at 407 South Dearborn in Chicago. Both advocated a nonviolent approach to the convention.

On February 11, National Mobilization held meetings in Chicago with such black political action groups as the Student Nonviolent Coordinating Committee, the Congress of Racial Equality, and the National Rights Organization. The purpose was "to explore the possibility of synthesizing a national structure of black organizations and predominately white protest groups."[8] This effort to present a united front in Chicago was largely unsuccessful. Although the New Left COINTELPRO had not yet been established by the FBI, it is almost certain that the bureau, working through undercover informants, had full access to meeting notes. The possibility of a black/white protest alliance was of considerable concern to Hoover. Specific COINTELPRO actions would soon be undertaken to keep the two races apart.

On March 16, Senator Robert F. Kennedy, an antiwar senator, announced the beginning of his presidential campaign. On March 20, former Marine Corps Commandant David M. Shoup, appearing before the Senate Foreign Relations Committee, called the Johnson administration's Vietnam policy "unadulterated poppycock."[9]

The National Mobilization Committee planned a March 23 meeting held in a rural wooded area not far from Chicago. Those in attendance included Rennie Davis; David Dellinger; the Reverend Daniel Berrigan, Roman Catholic chaplain at Cornell University; William F. Pepper, executive director of the National Conference for New Politics; Linda Morse, executive secretary of the Student Mobilization Committee to End the War in Vietnam; and activist Tom Hayden. More than one hundred antiwar groups were represented, and there is little doubt that the FBI had well-placed informants among the more than two hundred in attendance.

The letter of invitation noted that "a national election year program could be of tremendous importance in deepening the challenge to the corrupt racist and imperialistic politics of the established order."[10] Ideas among the diverse group of delegates ranged from ignoring the Democratic convention altogether to shutting it down. Rennie Davis remembers thinking that "the delegates should be allowed to come to Chicago, so long as they give their support to a policy of ending racism and the war."[11]

One of the key position papers presented at the meeting anticipated a summer "capped by three days of sustained, organized protest at the Democratic National Convention, clogging the streets of Chicago with people demanding peace, justice and self determination for all people."[12] At the close of the conference David Dellinger spoke to the press and said, "We are not going to storm the convention with tanks or Mace. But we are going to storm the hearts and minds of the American people."[13]

By early 1968, 77 percent of the American people disapproved of the Johnson administration's handling of the war in Vietnam. On March 31, Lyndon Johnson announced that he would not seek or accept the nomination for another term. On April 4, Martin Luther King, Jr. was assassinated in Memphis. Just nineteen days later, the student revolt at Columbia began. This year—1968—reflected, in Theodore White's phrase, "a crisis in the American culture."[14]

On April 28, a Chicago antiwar demonstration march with approximately sixty-five hundred participants ended in a confrontation with police in front of the Civic Center. Several eyewitnesses remembered a tense standoff and then a direct assault by officers to dispel the activists. Many claimed that police used excessive physical force and attacked "demonstrators without provocation."[15]

As it gained momentum, the movement had begun to think in terms of "before Columbia" or "after Columbia." Todd Gitlin later wrote that protest groups, particularly the SDS, "would come to know the Columbia events as a series of mythic media images." Dissidents would try to "replicate Columbia" as, after the 1968 Democratic national convention, they would try to "replicate Chicago."[16]

Assistant director Sullivan later remembered that "it didn't take an undercover investigation for the FBI to learn that there was going to be trouble in Chicago."[17] Wild rumors of impending disaster in Chicago began to circulate: buildings near the convention center would be firebombed, there would be snipers with high-powered rifles firing at delegates as they went to the center, police would be assaulted by youth gangs at every opportunity, and weapons were being stockpiled in several area churches. Later in the summer, there were stories that broken glass and illegal drugs would somehow be placed into food and the city's water supply, and that high-ranking officials such as Chicago's Mayor Daley and Vice President Humphrey were marked for assassination. "In view of the assassinations of Martin Luther King, Jr., John F. and Robert F. Kennedy, this information had to be given serious and constant attention,"[18] Sullivan said.

On May 9, headquarters advised special agents that "the Bureau has been very closely following the activities of the New Left and the key activists." The New Left needed to be neutralized at Chicago: "the importance of this new endeavor cannot and will not be overlooked."[19]

On May 20, a memo from C. D. Brennan to W. C. Sullivan reported that the national secretary of the SDS evidently mailed form letters to members nationwide explaining that the IRS "was making a serious move against the organization."[20] The IRS, on the recommendation of the FBI, had been investigating dissident groups since 1965.

On May 22, a memo to field offices from C. D. Brennan at bureau headquarters referred to "the Director approved memorandum of May 9, 1968 setting up a counterintelligence program" with a follow-up letter dated May 10 requesting "analysis and recommendation on potential actions to be instituted against New Left Organizations and key activists." This new memo requested "detailed information on false allegations of police brutality and/or violence used on police, immorality and actions taken by college administrators when confronted by student disorders." Such information would be provided to friendly media by the bureau "to vividly portray the revolutionary type actions and militant nature of the New Left movement."[21]

Another memo from Brennan to special agents dated May 24, 1968, requested "data regarding informant coverage and trouble potential in the forthcoming school year." This information would be used by headquarters to "set forth the identity of all New Left organizations, its ringleaders and data concerning them."[22]

A memo from Hoover on May 28 reinforced this. Special agents were ordered to immediately advise the bureau regarding "present informant and source coverage on each campus." Additionally, "an evaluation should be made as to the potential for violence on campuses in your territory for the forthcoming school year." This information must "reach the Bureau no later than 7/1/68."[23] The next day, Hoover instructed special agents "to review college campus newspapers" and begin "submitting articles which might be used for appropriate dissemination." The director added that "items submitted should be extremely radical on their face, use profanity or be repulsive in nature." They would be submitted to "responsible individuals, such as state legislators, friendly news media and the like."[24]

Several field offices accelerated the actions against the New Left almost immediately. Cincinnati targeted Antioch College in Yellow Springs, Ohio, and told headquarters, "[F]or a number of years individuals from the college and the town have been part of the New Left vanguard." The Antioch campus was "most often run by a small group of militants that are permitted by college authorities to attack every segment of American Society." Special agents had observed that "the dirty anti-social appearance and behavior of a large number of students can be seen to have the fullest beatnik image."[25]

On June 3, 1968, Cincinnati received bureau approval to mail anonymous letters to legislators and friendly media designed to undermine the academic credibility of the college and disrupt "those students who spend most of their time engaging in anti-social activity, protest demonstrations, and affiliations with subversive groups."[26] Special agents also discovered that an antiwar organization, called Cincinnati Action for Peace, was using a United Campus Christian Fellowship meeting facility across the street from the University of Cincinnati. The UCCF was associated with three prominent area Protestant denominations.

The Cincinnati field office received permission on July 31, 1968, to anonymously mail the letter shown below "to the leaders of the UCCF [United Campus Christian Fellowship] and other Protestant religious groups in the Cincinnati area to block this political use of the Christian facility."

Dear Fellow Christian,

You and a number of other committed Christians are being alerted in this manner because action is needed before the new school year starts to prevent further danger to the minds of our youth.

There is enclosed for your personal examination a copy of a leaflet which was passed out on our streets this last school year. Please examine the wording. You surely recognize it for what it is. Note that it announces a meeting to be held at 2699 Clifton.

We were led to believe the United Campus Christian Fellowship (UCCF) house at 2699 Clifton Avenue was established by Christians to provide a Christian atmosphere in which our youth could meet. What a mockery of our responsibility. Are we providing instead a base for a Godless ideology?

Who is running UCCF? Who supervises activities there? Who authorized other groups to meet there? What is it being used for?

You are urged to request Church authorities to make an immediate thorough review of UCCF structure aimed to insure it is being used to fulfill a Christian purpose.

The youth of the Church need your care and guidance.

—A Concerned Citizen[27]

Enclosure

Cincinnati reported on September 20, 1968: Counterintelligence action against UCCF has "resulted in some disruption of their activities."[28]

A June 7, 1968, COINTELPRO memo from Philadelphia Special Agent William S. Bett demonstrates how extensive FBI and local law enforcement coverage of the New Left could be on any occasion. In this situation, the SDS was holding a protest meeting against "research for weapons used in Vietnam." Only a hundred activists attended and there were no violent incidents. Nevertheless, there were twenty-two law enforcement personnel monitoring the event. They utilized seven police cars and one communications vehicle. The coordinator of the demonstration was Haverford physics instructor William Davidon. The demonstrators carried placards that read, "Science is for helping people, not removing them in Vietnam or West Philadelphia." There was full television coverage. At the bottom of the memo, Bett noted that the "heavy surveillance paid off in fresh material for the dossiers of ten people and two organizations."[29]

On June 1, 1968, Detroit reported on antiwar elements at Michigan's major state-supported colleges and universities. Headquarters was informed that "past student agitation at the University of Michigan has demonstrated that university administrators cannot be expected to react, other than to solve the immediate demands and end the disruption."[30] Detroit explained that pressure from state legislators, alumni, and university governing boards provided the best means of forcing administrators to stand their ground in student confrontations. On June 18, 1968, Detroit received authorization to develop an anonymous letter directed to the university pressure groups "pointing out the weaknesses of school administrators in meeting New Left demands."[31] This same memo also reported on a June 5 confrontation between police and students at Michigan State in which campus and local police attempted to arrest a number of antiwar activists on narcotics charges. More than a hundred sympathizers confronted police. Many were arrested on the spot.

The 1968 SDS national convention was held at Michigan State in East Lansing, Michigan, and attended by 550 delegates. This convention at Michigan State was the last major convention to be held before Chicago. It was infiltrated by FBI undercover informants. Sources reported discussions which included racism, the "Columbia University incident," and the need to recruit "uncommitted students, high school students, workers, hippies, and the American poor."[32]

One panel discussion concerned the idea of "coffee house workshops" for servicemen. These would provide "the excellent opportunity for the SDS to politically orient servicemen." The SDS international secretary stressed the need to combine forces with students from other countries "to allow the movement to continue to move forward in the months to come."[33]

A major floor fight emerged concerning control of the SDS between the Progressive Labor faction and the existing SDS management group. As a result, two different groups formed within the organization. One faction was still formulating SDS radical ideology. The Progressive Labor people, "the action faction," believed that nothing short of the active overthrow of the Establishment was warranted. A June 28, 1968, headquarters memo advised selected field offices that both factions had as their target "the total change of the American way of life." The memo instructed special agents to "make excellent use of pertinent information" by providing details of the SDS national convention to "friendly media."[34]

A Detroit memo dated July 1, 1968, provided headquarters with the details of a bureau-approved press release which provided "friendly media" with details on the director's congressional testimony about the New Left as well as information on the SDS convention.[35] As a result, several Michigan legislators went to the Michigan State campus and were shocked to find what they regarded as pornographic literature on display and "a red banner bearing pictures of Lenin and Trotsky as well as the hammer and sickle insignia."[36] Several legislators criticized Michigan State officials for permitting the university to host this group.

Detroit sent two memos on July 3, 1968. The first reported a scuffle between police, antiwar demonstrators, and counterdemonstrators at Wayne State University in Detroit. Antiwar students raised "a blue and green flag with a gold star in the center identified as a Vietcong flag." There was a good deal of pushing and shoving as counterdemonstrators attempted to pull the flag down. Detroit police and fire engines arrived to break up the fight and lower the flag. Counterdemonstrators "seized the Vietcong flag and burned it nearby."[37]

The second memo described protest activities taking place at the University of Michigan, listing faculty advisors who had worked with student New Left organizations. Campus New Left members looked upon these faculty members "as their dependable campus supporters and or protectors," it noted. One organization in particular which used "publicly supported funds to aid the Viet Cong and engaged in the sale of artifacts of North Vietnamese origin" was named as a prime COINTELPRO-New Left target.[38]

On July 15, 1968, New York reported that one of the "three top leaders of the antiwar movement," Jerry Rubin, had been arrested.

Rubin, with Abbie Hoffman, cofounder of the Youth International Party of yippies, was "arrested in his apartment on June 13, 1968, by the NYPD Narcotics Squad, on charges of Possession of more than an ounce of Marijuana."[39] Rubin, however, as reported on August 12, would be able to attend the Democratic convention while on bond. The same memo reported that the National Mobilization Committee to End the War in Vietnam was then "in the process of coordinating demonstrations in Chicago, Illinois, during the National Democratic Convention." New York also reported that the government in Hanoi, North Vietnam, had released American prisoners of war to the National Mobilization Committee, and activists were on their way "to Hanoi to receive three more American prisoners."[40]

A July 14, 1968, *New York Times* article entitled "Student Peace Group Leaders Charge Trotskyite Take-Over" revealed a dispute within the Student Mobilization Committee to End the War in Vietnam (SMC). The SMC included members of the SWP, the Young Socialists Alliance, the CPUSA, and other New Left organizations. These diverse groups, while joining forces to oppose the war, were nevertheless widely split on many issues, including racism, poverty, campus liberation, and others. The FBI, almost certainly working with knowledge obtained from undercover informants, felt that "this rift appears to hold promise for counterintelligence action."[41]

On August 13, 1968, after receiving headquarters approval, New York mailed the letter below to "68 individuals and organizations in the New Left and peace fields." It was "written in the jargon of the New Left, necessitating the use of a certain amount of profanity."

WHO BUSTED SMC'S ASS?

Events since the disaster on June 29–30, have again demonstrated that everything the YSA touches turns to pure horseshit. [*Name deleted*] and her gang of hypocrites took poor old SMC apart, changed all the pieces around, and put in back in the form of a sterile YSA group. Useless talk and parliamentary procedure is the new name of the game.

We who had served SMC from the beginning shed a few bitter tears, packed our bags and left. [*Name deleted*] had the vision too. She saw through the Trotskyite shit and followed her nose through the door. She wasn't alone either. Many others, including Resistance, WRL, SDS and the Du Bois Clubs, followed her into the clear. So, we formed the Radical Organizing Committee to deal with issues related to the dirty war in Vietnam, the draft, racism and campus complicity. We wonder how long it will be before YSA takes a bead on the ROC?

We admit to a few hangups—mostly financial—but the Trotskyites have had a few for years. There's the street-meeting hangup. We suspect that any SMC activity in the future will be in the form of YSA street meetings—zero contributions to the ending of the Johnson war. While the Trotskyites talk and talk, the war goes on and on.

All of which builds to a fine point—known to most of the independents in SMC for a long time. The old-line organizations haven't completely dried up. . . . nothing but dust between the ears. Let's face it, the contributions of the SWP, YSA and PL to the movement have been minimal to say the least. The CP died of old age several decades ago, although we understand Gus is living real well.

We think ROC has something new to offer—a new approach to the problems of our times, a new light on the rise of radical consciousness within the student movement. This time, baby, the fascist tactics of the YSA are not going to get the chance to wreck the organization. No more committee packing and other high handed crap so neatly done by the Trotskyites. YSA can stick with its own hangups. *We don't want 'em!*

With it all, you have to admire the way YSA operated. [*Name deleted*] and [*name deleted*] were beautiful . . . just beautiful. They stuffed their platform up our collective asses smiling all the while. They were pained when we left. [*Name deleted*] still looks pained.

We'll work for ROC now. Let's see what happens. A final word for YSA: "You busted SMC's ass. You and you alone. Good luck, mothers."

—Peace[42]

In August, 1968, the San Antonio field office took note of an article in the *San Antonio Light*—the student newspaper at the University of Texas at Austin—which was headlined "Free Love Comes to Surface In and Around UT Austin" and was concerned with the atmosphere of "free love and cohabitation" then said to be in existence at the university.[43] In the bureau's opinion, such a lifestyle was a typical and degrading manifestation of the New Left movement.

After obtaining approval from bureau headquarters, San Antonio developed a fictitious letter that was supposed to be from a parent who was planning to send his son to the university. This unsigned letter and a copy of the "Free Love" newspaper article were mailed to Texas State Senator Wayne Connally, brother of Governor John Connally, and also to Frank C. Erwig, chairman of the Board of Regents of the University of Texas.

In reference to this COINTELPRO action, a headquarters memo dated August 27, 1968, noted that "such a communication may be of value in forcing the university to take action against those administrators who are permitting an atmosphere to build up on campus that will be a fertile field for the New Left."[44]

A June 10, 1968, COINTELPRO memo from Newark serves as an example of the bureau's determination to disrupt the lives of individual activists before the Chicago convention. It reported on David Dellinger's checking account at First Clinton National Bank in Clinton, New Jersey—including deposits, balances, and payees.

Special agents also provided the bureau with financial information on Dellinger's magazine, *Liberation*. The FBI also worked with the New Jersey Telephone Company to gain access to Dellinger's unlisted telephone numbers, the size of his monthly telephone bills, the dates of his phone calls, and the individual numbers called. They learned Dellinger's work schedule, the year and make of his car, and when and where his mail was delivered by the Hampton, New Jersey, post office. The FBI also gathered information regarding Dellinger's July 11, 1949, arrest "on a charge of disorderly conduct, Lewd Act in a subway station men's room."[45] All of this information was made available to an FBI contact, a reporter with the *New York Daily News*.

Boston special agents reported two direct confrontations with antiwar protesters in June. The first involved two U.S. Army specialists fourth class who, absent without leave, "took refuge and sought sanctuary in the Arlington Street Church in Boston." The church board of trustees immediately recognized the religious and moral nature of their action and gave notice that "if any confrontation came it would be in the sanctuary of the place of worship." Nevertheless, government officials did enter the church and bodily carried the fugitives to government vehicles. A terrific fight broke out between police and protesters waiting outside. It was only after police reserves arrived that officials were able "to transport the prisoners from the church."[46]

In a similar situation in Providence, Rhode Island, two Selective Service Act fugitives sought refuge in the Church of the Mediator. On June 3, "upon entering the church agents observed approximately 20 to 30 individuals wearing beards and beads sitting around in a circle in what might be referred to as the sanctuary of the church." Protesters gathered in considerable force outside the church, and it was only with great difficulty that special agents transported the prisoners to government vehicles. There was much name calling and pushing and shoving, and a few objects were thrown at officials. Many protesters had to be dragged away from blocking government cars. The Boston memo said "these actions by the protesters were made in an attempt to embarrass the Bureau and Providence Police Department" since television reporters were in "the immediate vicinity of the church."[47]

During the first week in July, Boston reported on surveillance at Boston University, Brandeis, Dartmouth, Franconia College, Harvard, Radcliff, MIT, Tufts, Williams, and the Universities of Maine, New Hampshire, and Rhode Island. Special agents reported that the New Left activity on the Harvard campus involved the May Second Committee, the SDS, and the Progressive Labor Party. One Harvard student, responding to questioning, said, "I consider it honorable to be a revolutionary. . . . This country will cease to be run by men for their own gain."[48]

At Brandeis, sources reported that while the Democratic convention was being discussed by students, the SDS "has not been effective in organizing any formative group on the campus." At Tufts, the SDS "had been active in three demonstrations none of which resulted in any violence." At MIT, one memo said, "students in attendance are all engaged in serious academic pursuits which leaves little time for outside activity."[49]

In Chicago, approximately two dozen New Left political organizations comprised of three main protest groups—the National Mobilization Committee to End the War in Vietnam (National Mobilization), the Youth International Party (Yippies), and the Coalition for an Open Convention (COC)—met to plan protest strategy. The stated goal was to bring "together dissident groups of widely diverse political and social leanings, of various sizes and geographical sites and involving them all in one major antiwar demonstration focused on the Democratic Convention."[50]

On August 1, National Mobilization representatives met with city officials and asked for a permit to allow activists to sleep in city parks during the entire week of the convention, a parade permit for a mile-long demonstration—in front of the International Amphitheatre—after the Democratic candidate had been nominated, and a rally permit in Grant Park the day after the nomination.

On August 6, Rennie Davis, protest coordinator for National Mobilization, announced that demonstrations would focus the world's attention on "the slaughter in Vietnam."[51] David Dellinger told reporters that the antiwar forces would demonstrate in the streets of Chicago no matter who the Democratic nominees might be and, for that matter, antiwar activity would continue throughout the nation "until the United States troops are withdrawn from Vietnam."[52]

On that same day, the Chicago Police Department announced that all 11,900 officers would work twelve-hour shifts for the entire week of convention activity and would provide "the tightest security ever offered a political convention."[53]

The first contingent of protesters began arriving in Chicago on August 18, and they immediately established Lincoln Park as a base of operations. A National Mobilization position paper was given to reporters. Tom Hayden promised that the movement would "reassert the presence and vitality of the antiwar movement."[54]

One activist, a peace movement veteran, remembers thinking: "The spectacle of the Democratic Convention nominating Hubert Humphrey while so many other guys are being nominated for death in Vietnam or for quiet oblivion in the ghetto is just plain grotesque."[55] Nevertheless, National Mobilization's official position was that they were committed to nonviolence and would not try to disrupt the convention itself. As if to underscore the point, Mayor Richard Daley announced, "As long as I am mayor of this city there will be law and order in the streets."[56]

The next day, Governor Samuel H. Shapiro, acting on the request of Daley, ordered 5,659 heavily armed, riot-trained National Guardsmen to active duty in Chicago. Their mission was to "head off threats of tumult, riot and mob disorder." National Guard troops received direct orders to "shoot to kill if disturbance erupts and the troops cannot prevent looting and arson any other way."[57] Over two thousand FBI and Secret Service agents, together with federal marshals, were assigned to the convention area. David Dellinger remembered that "in a setting like Chicago it is never clear who is a paid agent provocateur and who is generally argumentative or sectarian, honestly fearful ('Let's get out of here before someone gets killed!') or violent ('Kill the pigs!')."[58]

There were rumors of assassination plots directed against both Humphrey and McCarthy. Six thousand regular U.S. Army troops, recently trained in riot control and equipped with rifles, flame throwers, and bazookas, were airlifted to Chicago on Monday, August 26. Firemen were stationed at each alarm box within a six-block radius of the convention center.

National Mobilization coordinators Rennie Davis and Tom Hayden charged that the city was "becoming an armed camp in a garrison state."[59] Martin Slade, a rally coordinator, remembers telling "our people not to come to Chicago" and warned that activists would be "taking a chance by walking into a police state." Nevertheless, activists planned to demonstrate "even at the risk of bodily harm to ourselves."[60] The number of antiwar demonstrators actually active in the streets of Chicago during the convention was comparatively small—probably ten thousand—and certainly far less than the fifty thousand originally anticipated.

Well in advance of the convention, the Chicago field office began targeting the most prominent New Left groups—the SDS, the SMC, the National Mobilization Committee, and the Chicago Area Draft Resisters. A May 27 memo to headquarters explained that "the Chicago Office is at present carefully examining all of its New Left informant files to determine if one or more of these informants could be used on a full time basis."[61] On June 10, Chicago received authorization to "cooperate with local authorities and the Chicago Office of the Internal Revenue Service in efforts to disrupt the operations of the New Left." The headquarters memo added that the IRS is "presently conducting an audit of SDS funds at the Bureau's request."[62]

COINTELPRO memos dated June 12, 1968, and June 14, 1968, directed special agents across the nation "to furnish the Chicago office appropriate inserts setting forth all seditious activities sponsored by the SDS."[63]

On June 13, Chicago advised headquarters that area underground newspapers continued to reveal the New Left's "abnormal attitudes toward sex." These could not be directly confirmed, since the informant might be "compromised, his trustworthiness impaired or he might otherwise cause embarrassment to the Bureau."[64]

Chicago was advised by headquarters on June 21 that special agents in East Lansing had obtained a brochure during the SDS national convention at Michigan State entitled "Ham Radio." The brochure explained that the SDS and other protest organizations were "trying to set up a radical ham radio network," which would no doubt be particularly valuable in preparing for the Democratic National Convention. Hoover instructed all approved field offices to find informants who had ham radio experience and could penetrate this communications network. "Your liaison with the Federal Communications Commission could be a source for such individuals," he said.[65]

Chicago reported on June 28 that special agents had made local contact with the IRS to determine if six key New Left activists had filed tax returns "or made fraudulent entries on these returns in previous years."[66]

On July 8, Chicago advised headquarters of protest activities at area colleges including Northwestern, Chicago, Roosevelt, Illinois, Northern Illinois, and the Illinois Institute of Technology. This memo seems to indicate an astonishing lack of detailed information, for it notes that Chicago is developing "informants in the broad organizations."[67]

Hoover advised Chicago on July 16 that National Mobilization in Chicago was $3,600 behind on their telephone bill. This information was to be made public immediately.[68]

With the pressure mounting almost daily, and in light of the fact that 101 colleges had already been rocked by violence during the first half of the year, it is not terribly surprising that bureau memos seem almost obsessive about the potential for violence in Chicago. Special agents were working overtime, and a great many New Left leaders had been identified by name and background. With the help of informants, special agents were reporting on draft card burning, antidraft counseling, antiwar demonstration, campus protests, and picketing of military and CIA recruiting.

Nevertheless, the government's collective intelligence and law enforcement agencies seemed unable to contain the violence. President Johnson and the director were in constant—perhaps daily—communication. The head of the nation's largest investigative agency was in an unenviable position.

On July 23, 1968, Hoover issued a long memo to all special agents-in-charge at approved field offices. The memo, given here, gives some idea of his frustration:

INVESTIGATION OF THE NEW LEFT

—There has been a marked increase in recent months of bombings and burnings of public buildings and other acts of terrorism which could logically have been perpetrated by extremist elements of the New Left. New Left leaders have constantly exhorted their followers to abandon their traditional role of "passive dissent" and resort to acts of violence and terrorism as a means of disrupting the defense effort and opposing established authority. Publications of the New Left are replete with articles proposing the bombings of draft boards and other Government installations, and literature containing detailed diagrams and instructions for making incendiary devices has been widely disseminated among New Left groups.

I have been appalled by the reaction of some of our field offices to some of the acts of violence and terrorism which have occurred, such as those which have recently taken place in certain college towns and in some instances on college campuses. While it is recognized that many of these acts do not constitute violations of law within the primary investigative jurisdiction of the Bureau, it is essential, where the strong presumption exists that acts of violence have been perpetrated by New Leftists or other subversive elements under investigation by the Bureau, that every logical effort should be made to resolve through contact with established sources whether these elements are in fact responsible for such acts. Of course, good judgment and extreme caution must be utilized in this connection so as not to convey the impression to the public or other investigative agencies that we are assuming jurisdiction in those instances where there are not facts which would establish FBI jurisdiction.

It cannot be too strongly emphasized that positive results can be achieved only through the development of adequate high quality informants who are in a position to obtain detailed information regarding the activities and future plans of individuals and organizations affiliated with the New Left movement.

When terroristic acts occur which by reason of the target of the act or by reason of the locale would appear to fit into the objectives of or could have been motivated by subversive elements, particularly New Leftists, I expect an immediate and aggressive response from you in the form of alerting and directing all logical sources and informants into activity to determine if subversive groups could have been responsible.

I have reminded you time and again that the militancy of the New Left is escalating daily. Unless you recognize this and move in a more positive manner to identify subversive elements responsible so that appropriate prosecutive action, whether federally or locally initiated, can be taken, this type of activity can be expected to mount in intensity and to spread to college campuses across the country. This must not be allowed to happen and I am going to hold each Special Agent in Charge personally responsible to insure that the Bureau's responsibilities in this area are completely met and fulfilled.

> Very truly yours,
> John Edgar Hoover
> Director[69]

The bureau wanted tax returns of New Left leaders. On July 26, Chicago was able to report to Washington that a working relationship had been established with a key management official at the Chicago area IRS office. Since this relationship was clearly beyond regulations, Chicago was "placing requests for these returns on a staggered basis so as not to arouse any curiosity among IRS personnel as to the reason for the IRS requests."[70]

Special agents were in almost daily contact with paid undercover operatives. However, William C. Sullivan came to feel that the potential for violence in Chicago was so serious, particularly in light of the King and Kennedy assassinations, that the bureau should break longstanding tradition and utilize disguised special agents as undercover informants. "I wanted our men to be able to infiltrate these groups," he later wrote, "but how the hell can a well dressed man with a handkerchief in his pocket mingle with the Yippies on the streets of Chicago without becoming a laughing stock?" Sullivan unfortunately presented his idea to Hoover, who evidently exploded. "As long as I am director of the FBI," he shouted, "I'll not have any agent wearing old clothes or long hair." Sullivan decided to ignore Hoover's admonition altogether. He contacted Chicago special agent-in-charge Marlon Johnson. "When I offered to give him my own authorization to allow five or six of his agents to stay away from the office long enough to grow some hair, he was willing to take the risk," Sullivan remembered.[71] In Hoover's FBI, such insubordination was an act of considerable courage.

Johnson selected young, unmarried special agents for the assignment. They were able to infiltrate the New Left very quickly. In a number of situations, they gave the Chicago office more balanced reports on the potential for violence. Disguised special agents discovered that one of the more extreme New Left groups was actually planning to seize an entire television network at the Chicago convention hall. The FBI was able to give the Chicago police enough information to prevent it. This undercover effort was not, however, without its moment of high drama. Sullivan and Johnson discovered, to their mutual horror, that one special agent had, as Sullivan remembers, "been selected to attend a top level strategy session. He had just been selected to serve as one of the leaders in an attack on the Convention Hall." Chicago police moved in and arrested the whole group, including the special agent. Fingerprinting—which would be part of the processing at police headquarters—would reveal the man to be an FBI special agent. Hoover would almost certainly hear of the situation, and Sullivan and Johnson would be fired on the spot. Both FBI men, in a state of near panic, enlisted the help of a high-ranking Chicago police official who somehow got the agent out of jail "without arousing anyone's suspicion."[72]

On July 25, two FBI undercover informants from the New York office, known as NYT-3 and NYT-2, reported to headquarters a statement by activist leader Tom Hayden: "The North Vietnamese are shedding blood. We must be prepared to shed blood."[73]

Another New York undercover informant, NYT-6, discovered that the Youth International Party (the Yippies) "plan[ned] to organize a self-defense group" to be known as "the Plague," which, he thought, "might contain an element of the Black Panthers."[74]

An arrested female demonstrator's purse, discovered by Chicago police, contained what was described as "a little blue book." It provided an outline of the "battle plan" to be used by left-wing radical groups. It revealed plans to block all streets leading to the convention hall, thus "forcing ranking Democratic officials to use helicopters to attend the National Convention at the stockyard amphitheater." There would be "mass charges through police lines into the convention hall." Demonstrators, as this extremely radical document revealed, "would split into small groups to raid the city's business district." Further, "the groups were to break hotel and store windows, damage police cars and in general 'raise cain.' "[75]

On August 1, an FBI office, listed in the COINTELPRO documents only as a "Midwest City Field Office," strongly encouraged the IRS to audit an individual listed as a "mid-western college professor" associated with "new left activities."[76] It was known that the professor was planning to attend the Democratic National Convention, and the bureau had hoped to use the audit to neutralize the professor before he went to Chicago. The use of such tax information is unlawful, but the FBI special agent responsible for this investigation felt that the end justified the means: "Any drain upon the time and concentration which [the professor], a leading figure in the Demcon planning can bring to bear upon this activity can only accrue to the benefit of the Government and the general public."[77]

In early August, headquarters advised Chicago that the IRS was evidently having an impact on New Left preparation for the convention. This memo explained that the SDS national staff reported "Internal Revenue Service (IRS) constantly harassing national SDS and IRS contemplating legal action against the SDS to obtain payment of taxes."[78]

An August 3 COINTELPRO memo reported that young McCarthy supporters would realize, after the first few days in Chicago, that "Senator Eugene McCarthy cannot win the Presidential nomination and therefore, will offer an excellent opportunity for possible recruitment into SDS membership." Also, Chicago police would completely surround the convention hall and would use almost any excuse for "a mass bust and arrest of radicals at the convention."[79]

Chicago reported on August 9 that the SMC "presently has an indebtedness of $18,000." Chicago urged creditors to apply pressure for payment. The following week, Hoover was informed that undercover informants would continue to be "alert for any information regarding the possible disruption of the DNC."[80]

On August 6, an undercover informant learned that protest leaders "expected three hundred demonstrators to be arrested before Wednesday (August 28, 1968), and that a total of approximately 1,000 persons would be arrested by the Chicago police and other agencies during the entire period." The informant added that "all persons planning to demonstrate in Chicago should take some kind of protection against mace."[81]

Other findings by informants revealed that thirty-five lawyers, members of the National Lawyers Guild, had volunteered to provide legal services for those arrested. A separate corps of four hundred individuals would be formed to observe police action. National Mobilization marshals would be trained in first aid and self defense.

A memo from headquarters intelligence official C. D. Brennan to William C. Sullivan outlined the use of "disinformation" to further disrupt National Mobilization planning for Chicago. It reported that one of the "major problems facing National Mobilization is that of finding housing for the demonstrators who are coming from outside the Chicago area." The Chicago field office duplicated the blank forms prepared by National Mobilization to solicit housing for out-of-town demonstrators. Special agents filled out 217 of these forms with fictitious names and addresses and sent them to National Mobilization for processing. NMC members made long and useless journeys to locate these addresses.[82] This was accomplished with no possibility of embarrassment to the Bureau.

On August 16, a New York informant advised the bureau that approximately fifteen members of the East Side Service Organization (ESSO) planned to arrive in Chicago on or about August 20. The informant described ESSO as antidraft, antipolice, and antisociety. They were known to possess "rifles, revolvers and molotov cocktails."[83]

New York informants advised the FBI on August 20 that members of the Veterans and Reservists Against the War in Vietnam were going to Chicago. Those members were instructed to bring "a helmet, gas mask, poncho, and medical supplies."[84]

There were three main locations for probable confrontation in Chicago—Lincoln Park, the International Amphitheatre, and the Hilton Hotel across from Grant Park where many delegates were staying.

The battle for the streets began with a series of small skirmishes between Chicago police and activists on Saturday, August 24. The Chicago deputy chief of police in charge of Lincoln Park felt a strong show of force was probably the only message the dissidents would understand. "You can't give in to these people," he told his officers.[85] At the park curfew hour of 11:00, a force of officers cleared the area of about sixty activists, but these young people quickly regrouped and ran south on Wells, the main street of Old Town, chanting "Peace Now! Peace Now! Stop the Democratic Convention!" They created a major traffic jam on North Avenue and stopped. Police reinforcements arrived and went into action again and forcibly cleared the intersection. *Chicago Daily News* reporter Lawrence Green recalls seeing an approaching police officer and holding up his press card and shouting, "Press! Press! Press!" The policeman screamed in the reporter's face, "F—— your press credentials!"[86] and struck the reporter with his nightstick. Squad cars were stoned, and eleven young people were arrested and charged with disorderly conduct.

On Sunday, August 25, the Chicago firestorm—what Norman Mailer called "revolution by theatre and without a script"[87]—began in earnest. At about 1:30 in the afternoon, hundreds of demonstrators, including FBI undercover informant NYT-5, marched south on Clark Street, through the city's downtown loop area. They crossed over to Michigan Avenue, proceeded south nearly to Grant Park, and then back toward Lincoln Park. The march went largely without incident. By 3:00, a crowd of about five thousand had gathered in Lincoln Park.

At about 5:00 there was a direct confrontation between the huge group of demonstrators and about sixty uniformed police officers. The police—stunned by the extraordinary hostility of the demonstrators— retreated under a hail of bricks, rocks, and bottles. Police reinforcements carried out a violent counterattack with nightsticks and Mace. Total confusion followed as hundreds of the demonstrators scattered into the streets of downtown Chicago. The young people staged a series of hit-and-run attacks, smashing car windows and storefront plate glass windows, overturning trash cans, and screaming epitaphs at police. Violent clashes took place on Stockton Drive at the intersection of LaSalle Drive, LaSalle Street, Clark and Eugenie—the Eugenie Triangle—on the Michigan Avenue bridge, and at the Ohio Wabash intersection, the Old Town Triangle, and elsewhere. In clashes with police a pattern developed: there would be a standoff. Police would let the demonstrators begin throwing rocks and bottles and then would mount a furious club-swinging assault. Demonstrators would scatter out and regroup for another skirmish at another location.

Demonstrators launched a counterattack near Lincoln Park, and hand-to-hand fighting erupted. The police fell back, regrouped, and charged with nightsticks in every direction. A volunteer medic who was at Lincoln Park remembers, "When someone would fall three or four cops would start beating him. One kid was beaten so badly he couldn't get up. He was bleeding profusely from the head. The kids scattered to the street."[88]

Many from both sides were treated for injuries. About two dozen police vehicles were severely damaged. Sunday, August 25, ended as if from exhaustion.

At about 5:15 A.M. on Monday, August 26, the FBI learned that demonstrators were planning new tactics in Chicago that might involve turning on fire hydrants, calling area police and fire departments with false alarms, and stringing wire between trees in Lincoln Park to stop three-wheel police vehicles. At about 4:00 P.M. on Monday, demonstrators, accompanied by four FBI informants, clashed with police at Grant Park. Heavily armed officers formed a skirmish line as activists moved toward the Hilton Hotel. Demonstrators hurled rocks, cherry bombs, and bottles at officers. According to the U.S. Attorney's report, they taunted police "with the vilest conceivable language."[89] The police attacked and cleared the area by seven o'clock. By nine o'clock, a dozen or more protest groups ranging in size from one hundred and fifty to two thousand moved up and down Chicago streets chanting, "Ho Ho Ho Chi Minh" and "Hey, hey, LBJ! How many kids did you kill today?"[90]

Another group of about a thousand moved out of Lincoln Park heading south on Clark Street with the intention of reaching the Sherman Hotel, headquarters of the Illinois delegation. Virtually all northwest traffic stopped as police pushed demonstrators out of the area. Still another group was heading south on Wells chanting "Peace Now!" Police again charged, yelling, "Kill! Kill! Kill!" and dislodged the young people. A local attorney on his motorbike accidentally rode into the area and remembers "all the police around me were yelling and waving their nightsticks."[91] Several reporters, including Marv Kupfer of *Newsweek* and James Stricklin of NBC, were injured by police while trying to cover the action in the street. Later that evening, a group of demonstrators that included FBI undercover informants NYT-5 and NYT-8 built a picnic table barricade in Lincoln Park. They were dislodged with a massive "tear gas barrage." There were fifty-five arrests and at least fifty injuries. Other clashes followed near the downtown loop at Eugenie and Old Town Triangle and on Clark Street.

The city seemed to be in complete chaos. One eyewitness remembers, "Cars were stopped, the horns began to honk, people couldn't move, people got gassed inside their cars . . . police were the objects of stones and taunts."[92] In the streets, "violence continued through the early morning hours." Groups of all types, including "locals," stoned police cars, broke windows and stoplights, and shouted epithets at police. Norman Mailer remembers "demonstrators flooded out onto the streets, blocking traffic, fighting with plainsclothes men who awaited our exodus."[93]

The next day, Tuesday, Louise Peck, wife of activist Sidney Peck, arrived in Chicago to find her "worst fears" confirmed: "Everywhere you looked you saw tanks and armored cars."[94]

At about 7:30 that evening, a group of about a thousand demonstrators marched south on Clark Street chanting, "Hell, no, we won't go!" and "Peace Now!" They collided with police at Clark and Barton Streets. Another group of about a thousand marched from Lincoln Park to Grant Park and back without incident. Police cars were stoned at Eugenie and Old Town Triangle and at the Lincoln, Wells, and Clark intersection. Police, heavily outnumbered, fired their weapons in the air to disperse demonstrators. A furious battle followed at Lincoln Park. Seven officers were injured, nine police vehicles were badly damaged, and there were ninety-three arrests. An FBI undercover informant was at Lincoln Park and saw rocks being thrown at the police car, and all car windows were broken. The officers left the scene in a shower of rocks. This action was repeated six times. "Members of the PD were subject to vile obscenity."[95]

Around midnight, a crowd of about three thousand gathered in front of the Conrad Hilton. A city official at the scene remembers, "The crowd became rowdy, missiles were flying, obscenities and filthy taunts were hurled at police. . . . Some police were kicked by members of the crowd." Demonstrators were chanting "Pigs must go!" and "Two, four, six, eight, who do we assassinate?" Police responded with nightsticks, tear gas, and Mace. By two o'clock in the morning, both sides were exhausted. National Guard troops had moved in to relieve the overworked Chicago police force. FBI informant NYT-8 reported that the park was quiet by 2:30 A.M.[96]

Later on Wednesday, a crowd of about ten thousand demonstrators gathered in a public park between Columbia and Lake Shore Drive. A tiny force of about fifty Chicago police officers was present. A violent skirmish began around four o'clock, when demonstrators shouting "Kill the pigs!" assaulted police with such a rain of missiles that the lawmen were forced to retreat. Massive police reinforcements mounted a savage counterattack with nightsticks, Mace, and tear gas. Still later on Wednesday, a force of demonstrators, on their way to the convention hall, ran into police at Columbus and Balbo Drive. National Guardsmen, with rifles and fixed bayonets, moved into the intersection and thwarted the violence.

However, at the intersection of Balbo and Michigan, in full view of television cameras, the conflict between demonstrators and police reached a crescendo. At the corner of the Hilton Hotel, at the intersection of Balbo and Michigan, a "violent street battle" took place between some four thousand demonstrators and three hundred officers. Several officers went down hard under a barrage of flying missiles. Police discipline collapsed. Twenty-one reporters and news photographers were clubbed. Dozens of demonstrators, many bleeding with severe head injuries, retreated. Several demonstrators were thrown through the plate glass window of the Hilton Hotel. FBI informant NYT-8 was in the thick of the action and reported that when the Illinois National Guard relieved police, "no further serious disruption occurred." He admitted that the Chicago police used excessive force against demonstrators even though they were provoked by "name calling and obscenities." In NYT-8's opinion, the Illinois National Guard was far more effective than the police.[97] Other street actions followed on Thursday and Friday, but they were mild compared to the fight at Balbo and Michigan on the night of the presidential nomination.

The costs of that week in Chicago were considerable: 192 police officers injured, 81 police vehicles damaged, one antiwar demonstrator killed, about 425 demonstrators treated at area medical facilities, approximately 200 demonstrators treated by mobile medical teams, probably 400 given first aid for tear gas and Mace, and 668 arrested.

Norman Mailer, in remembering Chicago, called the 1968 Democratic Convention "the bitterest, the most violent, the most discordant, most painful and in certain ways the most uncontrolled" in several generations. Kirkpatrick Sale wrote that "the Democratic National Convention in August was one of the most propelling and influential events of the sixties."[98]

Although demonstrators of the New Left took a savage pounding in the streets, they nevertheless advanced the antiwar cause: by rallying the radical and peace elements—dispirited perhaps by the Johnson withdrawal, by radicalizing thousands of young people who had given the electoral process "one more chance," and by stripping away what they felt to be the "facade of liberal policies from the Establishment" and exposing what they saw as "the raw machinery of repression and force" behind the Establishment. Indeed, Theodore White later wrote, "If the Chicago police won the battle of the streets, the Mobilization, exactly as it planned, won the greater victory—that of public opinion."[99]

For the violence it inspired, the convention has had few equals in American political history. David Dellinger later recalled, "The police attacks helped convince millions of people that the society was falling apart and would not return to normal until the war was ended. Thus, we achieved our immediate objective of increasing public disillusionment with the war."[100]

There was almost universal condemnation of the brutality used by the Chicago Police Department, though certainly not from J. Edgar Hoover. On August 28, the director ordered the Chicago field office special agent-in-charge to "obtain all possible evidence that would disprove these charges"—that the Chicago police used excessive force—and "to consider measures by which the cooperative news media may be used to counteract these allegations." He went on: "When actual evidence of police brutality is not available, it can be expected that these elements will stretch the truth and even manufacture incidents to indict law enforcement agencies. We should be mindful of this situation and develop all possible evidence to expose this activity and to refute these allegations."[101]

In the September issue of *Law Enforcement Bulletin*—a monthly bureau publication that was mailed to every police agency in the nation, Hoover warned that leaders of the New Left planned to "launch a widespread attack on educational institutions." The ultimate aim of the New Left was to "smash first our educational structure, then our economic system and finally our Government itself." It would be "foolhardy for educators, public officials and law enforcement officials to ignore or take lightly the revolutionary terror invading college campuses."[102]

On September 3, 1968, in a memo to sixteen FBI field offices, Hoover instructed special agents "to collect all possible information regarding provocations of police by demonstrators and the reaction thereto." The field offices were to "immediately debrief sources who covered demonstrations at the convention to obtain all information which would bear on these activities." The director made it clear that those sources were numerous: "We authorized recipient offices, exclusive of Chicago, to send 32 informants to Chicago to cover demonstrations at this Convention."[103] A report by the Chicago field office entitled "Demonstration at Balbo Street and Michigan Avenue, August 28, 1968 Chicago Illinois," was completed and sent to Washington on September 6. It was sent directly to Hoover and contained "considerable information regarding provocations against the Chicago Police Department."[104]

On the same day, New York sent the director an in-depth summary of the data gathered at Chicago by undercover informants NYT-1 through NYT-10. An accompanying memo classified the report as confidential: "It is felt that unauthorized disclosure of the information attributed to these sources could compromise them and thus be injurious to the United States."[105]

A September 6 San Francisco memo reveals just how extraordinary the FBI surveillance was in Chicago. An undercover source, working out of San Francisco and assigned to monitor events in Chicago, provided special agents with sixty-two photographs taken during the convention week. These photos, listed below, were forwarded to bureau headquarters to help provide "background for the Bureau in preparation of brief regarding the Chicago situation."

Marchers from Lincoln Park are turned away from entrance to Hilton Hotel by police Monday night while carrying National Liberation Front (NLF) (*center*) and black (*far right*) flags.

Protesters facing a barricade with NLF flag and peace flag.

NBC truck filming Clark Street scene after tear gas was fired in Lincoln Park.

Demonstrators facing light from NBC truck.

ALLEN GINSBERG and others leading chant in front of NBC truck.

GINSBERG and others continuing to demonstrate for benefit of NBC truck.

Arrest of girl after main confrontation in front of Hilton Hotel Wednesday.

Arrest of priest or minister Wednesday after his refusal to move on.

PD officer using Mace on cameraman who refused to turn out light shining in officer's eyes.

West of Hilton Hotel near St. Mary's Chapel. Arrest of demonstrator who joined in setting up barricades on street.

National Guard Line at Hilton Hotel.

"Free Huey" Rally in Lincoln Park Tuesday.

Ministers or priests encouraging demonstrators to sit in Lincoln Park Tuesday night beyond curfew limit.

Priests or ministers and demonstrators taunting police in Lincoln Park Tuesday night. (Police trucks and headlights can be seen in background.)

Demonstrators running after tear gas fired in Lincoln Park Tuesday night.

Policeman dragging fallen demonstrator in Lincoln Park Tuesday night. This policeman, a few seconds later, was hit by a barrage of bricks and bottles from demonstrators and was forced by objects hitting him to drop demonstrator and retreat.

Demonstrators flee Lincoln Park Tuesday night after being gassed.

Entire group who had been hurling objects at police.

Two demonstrators in white T-shirts running laughing just after policeman had been hit with objects in Lincoln Park Tuesday night.

Police car, far left, speeding through crowd after being hit by barrage of objects.

Start of barrage on police car 8845 on Clark Street at Lincoln Park Tuesday.

Crowd from Lincoln Park overflowing into Old Town District of Chicago after being driven from Lincoln Park Tuesday night.

Line of National Guard preparing to stop marchers from leaving Grant Park Wednesday afternoon.

CBS cameraman [*name deleted*] (with bandage over eye), who said he had been hit by a policeman Monday night.

JACK PERKINS of NBC News with demonstrators' flags in background.

Individuals facing camera sometimes acted as leaders in demonstration.

First police charge of demonstrators in front of Hilton Hotel showing pacifist type group seated.

Police dragging girl protester in police wagon in front of Hilton Hotel.

Policeman moving demonstrator in front of Hilton Hotel

Scene approximately two minutes after first police charge at Hilton Hotel Wednesday.

Police dragging demonstrator to patrol wagon.

PETER YARROW (Ph.) and MARY (LNU) of Peter, Paul, and Mary singing group entertaining demonstrators in front of Hilton Hotel, and type of public address system used by demonstrators.

One of the demonstration leaders seated on grass. Note helmet carried by girl.

Group of demonstrators equipped with helmets and gas masks posing for photographers in Lincoln Park Monday.

TOM HAYDEN and other demonstrator in Lincoln Park Monday being arrested by plain-clothes officer.

DICK GREGORY in white cap huddled around apparent leaders of march Thursday afternoon.

DICK GREGORY and line of leaders of march Thursday afternoon.

Speaker helping to lead march Thursday afternoon.

Demonstrators passing police patrol wagon while on march Thursday afternoon. In 8-3 demonstrator is spraying police van with yellow paint.

DICK GREGORY and three other leaders, Thursday afternoon march.

A police official called "Commissioner" by members of the press supervising demonstration Thursday afternoon. This police official was very friendly in relations with demonstration leaders.

Demonstrators running from tear gas after gas was fired Thursday night.

Individuals attempting to repair flat tires from line of cars which had the air let out of their tires.[106]

Five sets of photographs were processed. One set went to Chicago and the additional sets, via air mail special delivery registered mail, were sent to the bureau.

A September 8 headquarters memo ordered special agents in Chicago to inform their undercover informants that many incidents were actually staged by protesters to bait the police into reacting by force. Further, special agents were to determine if the New Left had violated anti-riot statutes. There is nothing in the record to suggest that the bureau was concerned by the fact that the Chicago police had used excessive force.[107] Subsequent memos from Hoover advised special agents to "remain alert for and to seek specific data depicting the depraved nature and moral looseness of the New Left," and "use this material in a vigorous and enthusiastic approach to neutralizing them."[108]

On October 1, the FBI issued a press release that asserted that "Soviet and Chinese Communist espionage and a mushrooming New Left movement on college campuses were posing growing threats to the nation's security." The bureau placed most of the blame on the SDS, "a fore-runner in this nihilist movement."[109]

On October 9, Hoover instructed special agents to focus their attention on students who had been arrested in Chicago, to publicize the arrests to parents, school officials, and local media via anonymous letters. Field offices would be expected to take this and every other opportunity to "destroy this insidious movement."[110] In a confirming memo to Washington, the Chicago office confirmed a pre-convention contact with the Illinois Bell Telephone company regarding National Mobilization's unpaid phone bill of $2,167. Chicago reported that direct contact by special agents had disrupted National Mobilization in its preparation for demonstrations, "since communication between the Chicago office of NMC and NMC offices in other areas of the country were greatly restricted."[111]

Hoover's next memo was on October 28, 1968. He again defined the term "New Left," which he said "does not refer to a definite organization but to a movement which is providing ideologies or platforms alternate to those of existing communist and other basic revolutionary organizations." He asserted that "there is a need to compile a single investigative report, a clear-cut picture of the entire New Left movement." Additionally, Hoover instructed that quarterly reports on the New Left CO-INTELPRO were to be submitted and subfiles were to be opened and monitored by special agents *on a daily basis*.[112]

The White House, stunned by the events in Chicago, demanded intensified efforts against antiwar activists. Thus, while the dust was still settling in Chicago, Hoover moved quickly to continue and even expand COINTELPRO operations against the New Left everywhere.

The Atlanta field office reported to headquarters on October 9, 1968, that the Atlanta Alliance for Peace, a coalition of peace groups, was planning a major march and demonstration on October 27.[113] Through a key undercover source the FBI was able to monitor events in Atlanta on a daily basis. This contact was concerned about the strong local influence of the Young Socialists Alliance and its Trotskyite faction, and was apprehensive about "the New Left as it constituted an increasing danger to the security of the United States."[114]

Special agents, with headquarters' approval, provided the contact with additional information on the New Left that confirmed his apprehension and encouraged his efforts to disrupt the Atlanta Alliance. This material included two pamphlets, "Students for a Democratic Society, Front Runner of the New Left," and "What Must We Do Now? An Argument for Sabotage as the Next Logical Step Toward Obstruction and Disruption of the U.S. War Machine"; a brochure entitled "Campus or Battleground? Columbia Is a Warning to All American Universities"; and a photocopy of an article from the February 19 issue of *The Militant* providing results of the Seventh National Convention of the YSA.[115]

The Philadelphia field office proved to be particularly skillful in the use of friendly media. In the fall of 1968, the *Philadelphia Inquirer* featured an article that was headlined "TO END ANARCHY ON THE CAMPUS" and was based on J. Edgar Hoover's message published in the September 1968 *Law Enforcement Bulletin*. A Philadelphia memo to the director, dated September 6, 1968, suggested that "the Bureau may desire to direct a letter to him [the paper's editor] of approval or appreciation concerning this editorial."[116]

Special Agents working out of the San Diego field office identified four students at San Diego State College as SDS key activists. The letter shown below was mailed to their parents. Information was also provided confidentially to the San Diego police department in hopes of having the students arrested on charges of illegal cohabitation and the local SDS evicted from their 3446 Adams Street quarters.

Dear Mr. ____:

I am writing to you with a great deal of reservation and hesitation over a situation in which your son (daughter) has become involved at San Diego State College. I too have a student at San Diego State and can therefore appreciate your concern over what our children, grown up as they may be, may become involved in once they leave our protective custody and launch out on their own, so to speak.

Your son (daughter) has joined and is active in a New Left movement known as the Students for a Democratic Society (SDS). This organization is basically a college student group. It draws its supporters from a motley variety including beatniks, hippies, disenchanted intellectuals, young faculty members and other students on the campus. The movement is held together by bitter hatred of what is called "the establishment," that is the institutions of democratic society. The SDS is a highly militant group and has even been described as a group that "we have going for us" by GUS HALL, the General Secretary of the Communist Party, USA.

In addition, I am enclosing a copy of the "Teaspoon Door," which is widely read by SDS members, including your son (daughter). As you can see, it strongly attacks all of the democratic institutions and values which we cherish. It also indulges in pornography and openly advocates "liberal love and sex."

I cannot believe that you, as a parent, can condone this type of influence over your children in a state supported school. As for myself, I have written a strong letter of protest to MALCOM LOVE, President, San Diego State College, San Diego, California, and also to Dr. HARVEY J. URBAN, Chairman, College Advisory Board, 233 A Street, San Diego, California 92101.

I sincerely hope that you will feel inclined toward doing the same thing along with having a "heart to heart" talk with your son (daughter) as I also have done.

Sincerely,
T.E. ELLIS
San Diego, California[117]

In December of 1968, the Oklahoma City field office was contacted by the father of a student at Oklahoma State University. The man indicated that his son was planning to join the SDS chapter at the university and "inquired as to whether the SDS was a subversive organization and whether or not his son should join this organization." The special agent told the individual that FBI files were confidential and he should write to the Subversive Organizations Section, Internal Security Section of the Justice Department in Washington for complete information. The individual evidently pondered the matter and "indicated he planned to write to obtain information pertaining to SDS at the OSU campus concerning his son and SDS."

By December 18, 1968, the field office determined that the man did not write the letter as intended. Oklahoma City "recommended Bureau authorize the Oklahoma City office to send an anonymous mailing" to the president of OSU.[118] Hoover agreed by memo on December 31, 1968, and authorized the anonymous mailing of the letter below, together with "xerox copies of the article appearing in the November 14, 1968, issue of the *Stillwater News-Press*, the November 27, 1968, issue of *Oklahoma City Times*, and the July 18, 1968, issue of the *Lawton Constitution*. This letter, Hoover hoped, could result in the individual "forcing his son to withdraw, thereby disrupting the SDS chapter."

Dear Mr. [*name deleted*],

I will introduce myself to you only as a parent of an OSU student which puts us in a common category.

It has come to my attention that your son, [*name deleted*] and [*sic*] one of the active members of the Students For a Democratic Society organization at OSU. You probably have previously read of this organization, which is commonly called SDS, in the local newspapers or magazines which are circulated nationally. If so, you probably also have read of the immoral character of many of these SDS members. Some of their leaders both here at OSU and at the University of Oklahoma have been arrested on dope charges. One of their members at OU, [*name deleted*] was recently sentenced to 15 years in prison for selling dope. A member at OSU, [*name deleted*], was arrested in Chicago during the Democratic National Convention and more recently, in November, 1968, at Stillwater on a dope charge. The immoral character of many of these students plus the subversive features of the organization itself, in regards [*sic*] to its desire to overthrow our government, leads me to believe every parent of these SDS members surely is opposed, as I am, to their activity.

Enclosed are copies of newspaper clippings and a couple of reprints I ran across in looking into this organization.

This information is being furnished to you not to cause trouble in your family but with the fervent hope that you as a parent and government employee will do something about your boy's actions in connection with this organization.

Yours truly,
A concerned parent[119]

On April 8, 1969, Oklahoma City reported that the mailing on behalf of [*name deleted*] was an apparent success and the individual "became inactive in the SDS."[120]

The Butte, Montana, field office received permission to target and disrupt the SDS at the University of Montana. The letter shown below was mailed widely across the state on October 2 and 3, 1968: to the editors of all Montana newspapers, to service clubs, commanders of the American Legion, civic leaders, judges, members of the University Board of Regents, politicians, educators, chiefs of police, and county attorneys.

The Montana press on September 11, 1968, reported the defense of obscenity by the University of Montana President, who says the academic community, not the lay public, must determine whether obscene material has instructional value in the college classroom. We won't argue academic freedom vs. immorality for the moment. We say this despite the fact that Denault M. Blouin, English Instructor at the University of Montana, used "The Student as Nigger" in a *freshman English Composition class*.

Who is [*name deleted*] anyway?

A man by the same name on April 15, 1967, burned a card at a public draft card burning in the Sheep Meadow in Central Park in New York City. We suppose this, too, can be passed off as academic freedom.

But what about [*name deleted*] and the Students for a Democratic Society. Do we want what happened at Columbia University in New York City and at many other college and universities last spring to happen in Missoula—do we really need it.

The Students for a Democratic Society openly and publicly make no bones about their aim and determination to change our democracy to one of anarchy and this is to begin with revolutionary terrorism on the campus. Is [name deleted] a member of the Students for a Democratic Society? Has he already formed, or attempted to form, a Students for a Democratic Society chapter at Missoula?

The Students for a Democratic Society in Portland, Oregon, publish a thing called The Agitator (Want a copy—the address: Box 02032, Portland Oregon, 97202). Page seven of this thing, issued March 31, 1968, has an article by [name deleted], UM." [Name deleted] calls it "Activity in Missoula" and in the article describes all he has accomplished in Missoula since he arrived, which, incidently [sic], was September, 1967. He details his efforts at organizing, not only with the university students, but also with Missoula *High School students*.

He writes, among other things, "We are now ready to organize and help shape—there are things that may happen, but it is probably wise not to talk about them until they have happened—there must be patience and a sense of when to be at the right places when it appears situations are ripe for organizing," and he concludes by writing, "There is a lot of work to do, because there are strong possibilities that we can win some struggles." My, hasn't instructor [name deleted] been busy instructing English!

We all saw pictures taken at the recent Students for a Democratic Society National Convention on the Michigan State campus in June. Did you see the red flag of communism and the flag of North Vietnam being proudly displayed—Did you read the revolutionary statements of the speakers—Did Instructor [name deleted] attend. We don't know, but [name deleted] English Department, University of Montana, Missoula, subscribed to "Anarkos" during the convention. What's "Anarkos"—it's only the publication of the Anarchists, one of the more militant of the Students for a Democratic Society outfits and the name seems self-explanatory. Possibly, Instructor [name deleted] is only seeking more material for his freshman English Composition class.

Instructor [name deleted] can have his academic freedom, but who is supporting him and paying his salary with money to engage in his extra-curricular organizing. We are!

The news media on September 11, 1968, reported in glowing headlines that the Montana University system approved a budget that calls for $74,500,000. of *your* tax money and [name deleted] is urging a bond issue. All of the presidents of the six units of the University system are publicly urging voters to support the six mill levy in the coming November election.

Let's face it—the money out of our pockets is supporting Instructor [*name deleted*] "organizing." We don't like it and we don't need it.

—A group of concerned
tax-paying parents of
Montana[121]

According to a follow-up memo to J. Edgar Hoover, dated December 27, 1968, the letter was a great success. The SDS chapter at the university voted to disband on October 14, 1968.[122] The English instructor's contract was not renewed.

On October 11, 1968, the Cleveland field office reported that it had asked the local IRS office to carefully examine the 1966 and 1967 income tax returns of key activist Sidney Morris Peck. The IRS auditors followed through and advised the Cleveland FBI office that, after a preliminary investigation, it appeared "that substantial recoveries appear in at least four areas of the returns."[123] The IRS office also confirmed that the bureau's anonymity would be fully protected. The bureau would be advised of the results of the audit as soon as possible.

Hoover, in a rare letter of congratulation to Cleveland on October 25, 1968, said "you have taken an imaginative and aggressive approach to this most pressing problem. You are encouraged to continue your efforts to neutralize the New Left."[124]

The Boston field office received permission from headquarters, on September 12, 1968, to furnish "background data on SDS, anti-Vietnam and antidraft activist leaders at Harvard, Radcliff and Boston University" to an area writer with the last name of Hall. The bureau hoped that Hall would "write an article pointing out the possibility of Columbia-type riots occurring at institutions of learning" in the Boston area. The final article was to be released to "friendly media." Included with the material supplied was a copy of the director's message in the September 1, 1968, issue of the *Law Enforcement Bulletin* concerning the possibility of attacks on area educational institutions. A copy of the *Barron's* article "Campus or Battleground? Columbia Is a Warning to All American Universities" was also included with the material. Special agents were instructed to "be most circumspect in dealing with Hall concerning the matter and you should take all necessary steps to preclude embarrassment to the Bureau."[125]

Soon thereafter, Boston managed to irritate the director by evidently paying only "lip service" to the New Left COINTELPRO. "You must," Hoover warned on October 21, 1968, "approach this problem aggressively." The Boston special agents handling key activists "must be alert for any and all situations which hold a possibility for effective counterintelligence actions." For several paragraphs, Hoover broadsided Boston for a less than satisfactory approach to neutralizing the New Left. He closed by saying that "failure on your part to seize the initiative may result in administrative action being taken."[126]

The St. Louis field office, working with an established local source, discovered an SDS plot to infiltrate area high schools. A local special agent contacted a friendly media source at the *St. Louis Globe Democrat* to provide him with this information and explain, from the bureau's perspective, the nature and intention of the SDS. An October 10, 1968, memo to headquarters confirmed that, as a result of the negative SDS publicity appearing in the newspapers, planned speaking engagements were canceled at Lindberg and Webster Grove High Schools in the St. Louis area.[127]

On November 6, 1968, St. Louis advised Hoover that the local SDS chapter was attempting to develop a close working relationship with the Black Liberators, an area black militant group. The field office memo noted that the Black Liberators "have an arsenal of weapons and frequently refer to killings and violence." Charles Koen, the "prime minister" of the black group, evidently a powerful speaker, had planned to give a series of lectures sponsored by the SDS chapter at Washington University. The letter below, obviously designed to disrupt a potential relationship between the two groups, was mailed anonymously to Charles Koen.

Dear Prime Minister:
    We, several members of the SDS at WU have been in attendance at several of your rallies at Whol Center, WU & feel you make an excellent appearance & project your message well. This letter is written as a potentially helpful criticism in the advancement of the movement.
    1. General Dent should not be allowed to speak to college groups. He does not appear too intelligent as witnessed by numerous errors in speaking style. Also he attempts to draw the same magnetism as you attract & fails in his effort. We feel he brings out the "nigger" in the black community in regard to the above.
    2. We feel you should not lecture to the U. campus concerning weap-

ons. We are leftists, not militants. It is proper to use any means necessary to gain your freedom, however, some whites are not responding favorably to militancy & we must gain a semblance of respectability before we can be most effective.

We hope these ideas will be useful in analyzing your future activities.[128]

The Albuquerque field office reported to headquarters that three students had been suspended at the University of New Mexico because of their participation in an anti-ROTC demonstration on September 22, 1968.[129] Shortly thereafter, some students who were concerned about the New Left volunteered their services to the FBI. They collected more than a thousand student signatures in support of the university decision to suspend the three, and they helped with an anonymous mailing to members of the faculty, the university board of regents, members of the state legislature, and administrative personnel at other colleges and universities in New Mexico. The mailed materials included copies of a *Reader's Digest* article, "SDS, Engineers of Campus Chaos," and newspaper articles concerning rioting at San Francisco State College. Attached was a note, "Please don't let it happen here."[130]

Undercover sources in Detroit advised special agents that the SDS used St. Joseph's Episcopal Church on November 29, 1968, to December 1, 1968, for a meeting that advertised "movies, party, dope and sex provided by the Wayne State Chapter FREE!" Headquarters reacted quickly and authorized the anonymous letter and hypothetical meeting schedule below to be mailed to the religious affairs editor at the *Detroit News*. At Hoover's specific direction, it was to be from a parent "who is taking exception to the use of the church premises for such un-Christian activity."

Dear [*name deleted*]

As a parent concerned with the moral atmosphere within which my children are being reared, I am enclosing a copy of a letter circulated on the Wayne State University Campus, advertising an SDS meeting at St. Joseph's Episcopal Church, November 29–December 1, 1968.

I am appalled that the SDS meeting, referred to in the enclosure, apparently met with the approval of the Episcopal Church. Especially am I disturbed regarding the tentative agenda for 8:00 p.m. which reads, "Movies, party, dope and sex provided by the Wayne State Chapter. FREE!!!"

How can we as parents expect our young people to be imbued with Christian ideals when church premises are literally desecrated. Surely a

Christian church should lend neither its name nor its premises for such avowed purposes.

I trust that in the future, through your wisdom, you will not allow such meetings to be held in the Episcopal Churches within your Diocese.

I regret that the atmosphere so widespread today precludes identifying myself. I do hope that under your leadership the prospects for the future will improve.

Sincerely,
A Concerned Parent.

MICHIGAN SDS MEETING

Place: St. Joseph's Episcopal Church on Woodward and King in Detroit. Fathers [*names deleted*] TR 1-4750

Time: Friday, November 29 through Sunday, Dec. 1st.

Note: Bring money (for food and 1 dollar registration fee) and sleeping bag.

TENTATIVE AGENDA:

FRIDAY:

10:00–1:00   Registration Housing & other details will be settled here. Newsreel films will be shown at this time.

2:00–7:00   Discussion of the SDS election program held at a number of campuses on Nov. 4 & 5 and the Mobilization call for a march on Washington on Inauguration Day.

8:00   Rap by Bernadine Dohen, Inter-Organization Secretary of SDS, and a discussion of national student scene.

SATURDAY:

10:00–1:00   Open time for workshops. Might include subjects like High school and dorm organizing, or broad questions like organizing, at working class colleges.

2:00–7:00   Discussion of future programs and the December N.C. Possible topics include co-ordinated regional activities around the resumption of bombing of Vietnam, police repression, etc.

8:00   Movies, party, dope and sex provided by Wayne State Chapter. FREE!!!

SUNDAY:

2:00–6:00   Discussion of regional questions, including mandat-
                     ing of travellers, and discussing what the role of trav-
                     ellers should be.

P.P.S. Give your chapter this information and send it on to anyone else who
might be interested.[131]

A memo from San Francisco to J. Edgar Hoover dated November 22,
1968, provides a good insight into the COINTELPRO-New Left operations at the field-office level during these turbulent times. The memo
discusses the extreme political tension then existing within the SDS itself. SDS national council meetings, according to sources, were often
the scene of furious debates between the Progressive Labor Party (PLP)
faction and the SDS management.

The PLP felt that the entire SDS organization should be restructured
to form a strong central organization with the authority to direct national
SDS operations with a strong hand. Local offices should report to regional offices and regional offices should only report to a strong national
headquarters for policy decisions and direction. Such an organization
would represent the very antithesis of the SDS concept of "participant
democracy."

This concept, according to FBI sources, provided that power would
flow from the bottom up without a strong national office. In effect, the
program was unworkable. The national office almost always deferred to
the local offices in policy decisions. Thus, there was no national, overall
set of goals. The result was often chaotic.[132]

The SDS chapter at San Francisco State College was heavily infiltrated
with PLP members. The PLP urged an area-wide participation of all
SDS offices in Stop the Draft week at the Oakland, California, induction
center. Under the participatory democracy concept, the local offices
could, and did, decide not to participate at all. In effect, any SDS member could act as an SDS spokesman or spokeswoman at any time on any
subject. The memo noted that "San Francisco is of the same opinion as
the Bureau that dissension within the SDS chapters prevents them from
taking more effective action."

At one SDS chapter meeting in Berkeley, California, a fistfight broke
out between PLP leaders and SDS local leaders over a policy decision.
One SDS member, who had been openly critical of the PLP, "claimed

that he had been beaten up by three thugs at gunpoint who told him 'our friends in Progressive Labor don't like what you have been doing and the information you have been putting out.' " Local special agents found it difficult, with leaders and personnel changing at least every semester, to maintain a consistent informant coverage. The memo added that, with the SDS situation constantly in flux, it was "not possible to clearly define the nature or extent of the ideological schism within the SDS even within individual chapters." It was a situation that the San Francisco field office had "neither the informant or personnel in the vicinity of college campuses, to handle at this time."[133]

David Dellinger, reflecting on the Chicago convention and its impact on the antiwar movement, wrote that although "the immediate result of the Chicago police riots was to increase antiwar sentiment, the long-run effect was to make it more difficult for that sentiment to express itself in an organized, effective fashion."[134] There was no doubt, however, that the antiwar efforts would continue, and by the end of 1968 there were more students protesting the war than ever before. Indeed, a *Fortune* magazine poll reported that "an estimated total of 750,000 of the nation's 6.7 million college students now identify with the New Left."[135]

NOTES

1. Theodore H. White, *The Making of the President 1968* (New York: Atheneum, 1969), p. 257.

2. Eugene J. McCarthy, *The Year of the People* (New York: Doubleday, 1969), p. 197.

3. Ibid., p. 212.

4. Ibid., p. 215.

5. Nancy Zaroulis and Gerald Sullivan, *Who Spoke Up? American Protest Against the War in Vietnam 1963–1975* (Garden City, NY: Doubleday, 1984), p. 176.

6. Sidney Lens, *Unrepentant Radical. An American Activist's Account of Five Turbulent Decades* (Boston: Beacon Press, 1980), p. 327.

7. Ibid., p. 327.

8. Daniel Walker, *Rights in Conflict: Chicago's 7 Brutal Days* (New York: Grosset and Dunlap, 1968), p. 9.

9. Zaroulis and Sullivan, *Who Spoke Up?*.

10. Donald Janson, "Leftists Plan Democratic Convention Disruption," *New York Times*, Mar. 24, 1968, p. 64.

11. Ibid.

12. Walker, *Rights in Conflict*, p. 10.

13. Ibid., p. 13.

14. White, *The Making of the President 1968*, p. 190.

15. Fred Halstead, *Out Now! A Participant's Account of the Movement in the U.S. against the Vietnam War* (New York: Pathfinder Press, 1978), p. 390.

16. Todd Gitlin, *The Whole World Is Watching: Mass Media in the Making and Unmaking of the New Left* (Berkeley; Los Angeles; London: University of California Press, 1980), p. 194.

17. William C. Sullivan with Bill Brown, *The Bureau: My Thirty Years in Hoover's FBI* (New York: W. W. Norton, 1979), p. 157.

18. Ibid., p. 158.

19. FBI Memorandum, Headquarters to Field Offices, May 9, 1968.

20. FBI Memorandum, C. D. Brennan to W. C. Sullivan, May 20, 1968.

21. FBI Memorandum, C. D. Brennan to W. C. Sullivan, May 22, 1968.

22. FBI Memorandum, W. C. Sullivan to C. D. Brennan, May 24, 1968.

23. FBI Memorandum, Headquarters to Field Offices, May 28, 1968.

24. FBI Memorandum, Headquarters to Field Offices, May 29, 1968.

25. FBI Memorandum, Cincinnati Field Office to Headquarters, June 3, 1968.

26. Ibid.

27. FBI Memorandum, Headquarters to Cincinnati Field Office, July 31, 1968.

28. FBI Memorandum, Cincinnati Field Office to Headquarters, Sept. 20, 1968.

29. FBI Memorandum, Philadelphia Field Office to Headquarters, June 7, 1968.

30. FBI Memorandum, Detroit Field Office to Headquarters, June 1, 1968.

31. FBI Memorandum, Headquarters to Detroit Field Office, June 18, 1968.

32. FBI Memorandum, Chicago Field Office to Headquarters, July 5, 1968.

33. Ibid.

34. FBI Memorandum, C. D. Brennan to W. C. Sullivan, June 28, 1968.

35. FBI Memorandum, Detroit Field Office to Headquarters, July 1, 1968.

36. Ibid.

37. FBI Memorandum, Detroit Field Office to Headquarters, July 3, 1968.

38. FBI Memorandum, Detroit Field Office to Headquarters, July 3, 1968.

39. FBI Memorandum, New York Field Office to Headquarters, July 15, 1968.

40. Ibid.

41. FBI Memorandum, Headquarters to New York Field Office, July 25, 1968.

42. FBI Memorandum, Headquarters to New York Field Office, Aug. 8, 1968; FBI Memorandum, New York Field Office to Headquarters, Aug. 13, 1968.

43. "Free Love Comes to Surface In and Around UT Austin," *San Antonio Light*, Aug. 11, 1968, p. 14-B.

44. FBI Memorandum, Headquarters to San Antonio Field Office, Aug. 27, 1968.

45. FBI Memorandum, Newark Field Office to Headquarters, June 10, 1968.

46. FBI Memorandum, Boston Field Office to Headquarters, June 13, 1968.

47. FBI Memorandum, Boston Field Office to Headquarters, June 3, 1968.

48. FBI Memorandum, Boston Field Office to Headquarters, July 2, 1968.

49. Ibid.

50. Walker, *Rights in Conflict*, p. 43.

51. Donald Janson, "Militant War Protest Slated Outside Democratic National Convention," *New York Times*, Aug. 6, 1968, p. 2.

52. Ibid.

53. Janson, "Militant War Protest Slated Outside Democratic National Convention."

54. J. Anthony Lukes, "Dissenters Focusing on Chicago," *New York Times*, Aug. 18, 1968, pp. 1, 64.

55. Ibid.

56. Ibid.

57. Sylvan Fox, "Guard Told To Shoot If Defied in Chicago," *New York Times*, Aug. 24, 1968, p. 1.

58. David Dellinger, *More Power Than We Know: The People's Movement Toward Democracy* (Garden City, NY: Anchor Press/Doubleday, 1975), p. 65.

59. Donald Janson, "Guard Is Called Up to Protect Chicago During Convention," *New York Times*, Aug. 21, 1968, pp. 1, 32.

60. Ibid.

61. FBI Memorandum, Chicago Field Office to Headquarters, May 27, 1968.

62. FBI Memorandum, Headquarters to Chicago Field Office, June 10, 1968.

63. FBI Memorandum, Headquarters to Field Offices, June 14, 1968; June 12, 1968.

64. FBI Memorandum, Chicago Field Office to Headquarters, June 13, 1968.

65. FBI Memorandum, Headquarters to Chicago Field Office, June 24, 1968.

66. FBI Memorandum, Chicago Field Office to Headquarters, June 28, 1968.

67. FBI Memorandum, Chicago Field Office to Headquarters, July 8, 1968.

68. FBI Memorandum, Headquarters to Chicago Field Office, July 16, 1968.

69. FBI Memorandum, Headquarters to Field Offices, July 23, 1968.

70. FBI Memorandum, Chicago Field Office to Headquarters, July 26, 1968.

71. Sullivan with Brown, *The Bureau*, pp. 158–159.

72. Ibid., p. 159.

73. FBI Memorandum, New York Field Office to Headquarters, Sept. 6, 1968.

74. Ibid.

75. Ibid.

76. FBI Memorandum, Midwest City Field Office to Headquarters, Aug. 1, 1968.

77. Ibid.

78. FBI Memorandum, Headquarters to Chicago Field Office, Aug. [*date deleted*], 1968.

79. FBI Memorandum, Chicago Field Office to Headquarters, Aug. 3, 1968.

80. FBI Memorandum, Chicago Field Office to Headquarters, Aug. 9, 1968; Aug. 13, 1968.

81. FBI Memorandum, New York Field Office to Headquarters, Sept. 6, 1968.

82. FBI Memorandum, Chicago Field Office to Headquarters, Sept. 6, 1968; FBI Memorandum, C. D. Brennan to W. C. Sullivan, Aug. 15, 1968.

83. FBI Memorandum, New York Field Office to Headquarters, Sept. 6, 1968.

84. Ibid.

85. Walker, *Rights in Conflict*, p. 86.

86. Ibid., p. 87.

87. John Schultz, *No One Was Killed, Documentation and Mediation: Convention Week, Chicago, August 1968* (Chicago: Big Table, 1969), p. 79.

88. Walker, *Rights in Conflict*, p. 92.

89. Ibid., p. 105.

90. Ibid., p. 106.

91. Ibid., pp. 107–108.

92. Ibid., p. 114.

93. Norman Mailer, *Miami and the Siege of Chicago. An Informal History of the Republican and Democratic Conventions in 1968* (New York: World Publishing, 1968), p. 153.

94. Zaroulis and Sullivan, *Who Spoke Up?*, p. 187.

95. FBI Memorandum, New York Field Office to Headquarters, Sept. 4, 1968.

96. FBI Memorandum, New York Field Office to Headquarters, Sept. 6, 1968.

97. Ibid.

98. Kirkpatrick Sale, *SDS* (New York: Vintage Press, 1974), p. 473.

99. White, *The Making of the President 1968*, p. 300.

100. Dellinger, *More Power Than We Know*, p. 125.

101. FBI Memorandum, Headquarters to Chicago Field Office, Aug. 28, 1968.

102. "Hoover Assails Campus Terror Led by New Left," *New York Times*, Sept. 1, 1968, p. 1.

103. FBI Memorandum, Headquarters to Field Offices, Sept. 3, 1968.

104. FBI Memorandum, Chicago Field Office to Headquarters, Sept. 6, 1968.

105. FBI Memorandum, New York Field Office to Headquarters, Sept. 6, 1968.

106. FBI Memorandum, San Francisco Field Office to Headquarters, Sept. 6, 1968.

107. FBI Memorandum, Headquarters to Chicago Field Office, Sept. 8, 1968.

108. FBI Memorandum, Headquarters to Field Offices, Oct. 9, 1968.

109. "FBI Says Threats from the New Left and Spies Increase," *New York Times*, Oct. 2, 1968, p. 44.

110. FBI Memorandum, Headquarters to Field Offices, Oct. 9, 1968.

111. FBI Memorandum, Chicago Field Office to Headquarters, Oct. 20, 1968.

112. FBI Memorandum, Headquarters to Field Offices, Oct. 28, 1968.

113. FBI Memorandum, Atlanta Field Office to Headquarters, Oct. 9, 1968.

114. Ibid.

115. Ibid.

116. FBI Memorandum, Philadelphia Field Office to Headquarters, Sept. 6, 1968.

117. FBI Memorandum, San Diego Field Office to Headquarters, Oct. 31, 1968.

118. FBI Memorandum, Oklahoma City Field Office to Headquarters, Dec. 18, 1968.

119. FBI Memorandum, Headquarters to Oklahoma City Field Office, Dec. 31, 1968.

120. FBI Memorandum, Oklahoma City Field Office to Headquarters, Apr. 8, 1969.

121. FBI Memorandum, Headquarters to Butte Field Office, Oct. 1, 1969.

122. FBI Memorandum, Butte Field Office to Headquarters, Dec. 27, 1968.

123. FBI Memorandum, Cleveland Field Office to Headquarters, Oct. 11, 1968.

124. FBI Memorandum, Headquarters to Cleveland Field Office, Oct. 25, 1968.

125. FBI Memorandum, Headquarters to Boston Field Office, Sept. 12, 1968.

126. FBI Memorandum, Headquarters to Boston Field Office, Oct. 21, 1968.

127. FBI Memorandum, St. Louis Field Office to Headquarters, Oct. 10, 1968.

128. FBI Memorandum, St. Louis Field Office to Headquarters, Nov. 9, 1968.

129. FBI Memorandum, Albuquerque Field Office to Headquarters, Sept. 22, 1968.

130. FBI Memorandum, Albuquerque Field Office to Headquarters, Dec. 12, 1968.

131. FBI Memorandum, Detroit Field Office to Headquarters, Dec. 10, 1968; Headquarters to Detroit Field Office, Dec. 20, 1968.

132. FBI Memorandum, San Francisco Field Office to Headquarters, Nov. 22, 1968.

133. Ibid.

134. Dellinger, *More Power Than We Know*, p. 125.

135. "*Fortune* Poll Finds 750,000 Students Identify with Left," *New York Times*, Dec. 30, 1968, p. 2.

5

January–June 1969

"You know, you see these bums, you know blowin' up the campuses."

—*Richard M. Nixon*

By early 1969, many antiwar organizations were abandoning their moderate political views altogether. The war, in the view of many, simply could not be brought to a halt by any manner of peaceful protest. By this time, almost 40 percent of the nation's colleges and universities had experienced some form of violent protest with little or no impact on the war in Vietnam. The election of Richard M. Nixon signaled little change in Vietnam policy to the antiwar movement.

Civil disorders on a considerably larger scale than anything previously seen in the United States during the twentieth century were spreading across the country. Many felt that, if the war did not end soon, any possibility of restoring domestic peace to American national life might be lost for a generation.

The FBI greatly accelerated its efforts to neutralize the antiwar movement and hopefully reduce the level of violence. Forty-two of the bureau's fifty-nine field offices, utilizing thousands of special agents and undercover informants, were actively involved in COINTELPRO operations against the New Left by early 1969.

One of the first targets for New Left disruption in early 1969 was the inauguration of Richard M. Nixon.

An undercover informant advised the Cincinnati field office that SDS members at Ohio State University were planning to participate in antiwar demonstrations at the Nixon inauguration.[1] On December 27, 1968, Cincinnati received permission to make anonymous phone calls to area transportation companies designed to confuse both the transportation companies and SDS leaders regarding "the cost of transportation and the time and place for leaving and returning." Cincinnati also placed deliberately misleading travel brochures at many campus locations to show "different times and places for demonstration planning meetings," as well as "conflicting times and dates for traveling to Washington."[2]

Soon after the New Year, the National Mobilization Committee (NMC) began making plans for "a series of antiwar activities in Washington around the inauguration of President-elect Nixon on January 20, 1969." The central planners included Rennie Davis, David Dellinger, and Sidney Lens.

"Dave Dellinger and Rennie Davis took the optimistic view; they proposed a counterinaugural to challenge Nixon immediately," Sidney Lens remembers. Lens took the opposite view: "If we try to bring people to the streets for the January inaugural they will be lost in the crowd and attract little attention." There was also considerable risk in "interfering with what is considered a hallowed American ritual."[3] However, the optimistic view prevailed. National Mobilization moved ahead with plans to disrupt the Nixon inauguration.

The FBI Washington field office monitored National Mobilization planning very carefully. On January 9, it submitted to headquarters a copy of the Washington NMC's housing form for out-of-town demonstrators. The next day, it received permission to "reproduce copies of the housing form distributed by the Washington Mobilization Committee (WMC), fill them out with fictitious names and addresses, and return them to WMC."[4]

The Washington field office also determined that NMC marshals were using walkie-talkies to coordinate their demonstration activities and to monitor police and military movements within the city. An undercover informant furnished call letters and frequencies used by NMC organizations. Special agents used the same citizens band to provide the marshals with misinformation and, pretending to be an NMC unit, "countermanding NMC orders." Another informant, posing as an NMC organizer, reported that, as a result of the disinformation campaign, communications simply broke down. The informant also reported that very confusing orders were issued, then changed, then changed again.

In all the confusion "NMC groups were dispatched to areas that had no relevance to the inauguration activities."[5]

Against this backdrop of FBI infiltration and internal political discord, a loose alignment of antiwar groups, including National Mobilization, the New York Parade Committee, the Coalition for an Anti-Imperialistic Movement, and others proceeded with their plans for disruption. The SDS did not support National Mobilization's "call for the inaugural demonstrations." Nevertheless, on Saturday, January 18, activists held a series of preparatory workshops attended by about two thousand. On January 19 a group of about eight thousand, led by David Dellinger, marched peacefully down Pennsylvania Avenue and then to a huge circus tent near the Washington Mall. By evening their numbers had grown to about ten thousand. The "Counterinaugural Ball" featured rock music and a light show.[6]

On Monday, January 20, the day the new president would take the oath of office, about twelve thousand activists were spread up and down the parade route. Many carried protest signs and shouted antiwar slogans. Some tried to physically disrupt the proceedings, but with little success. The group of twelve thousand activists, no matter how determined or energetic, was simply too small to have any impact at all on the huge inaugural crowds assembled in Washington. The planners should have known better. Without a clearly defined purpose or direction and without substantial numbers of participants, it was, as Charles DeBenedetti later wrote, "at best an exercise in ineptitude."[7]

National Mobilization was severely criticized by other elements within the antiwar coalition for leading a demonstration that was poorly planned, poorly attended, and, in the end, an embarrassment. FBI undercover sources immediately reported this friction within the ranks. As a result, the New York field office suggested an anonymous letter that would "ridicule the inaugural activities of the National Mobilization Committee and the work of its Chairman, Dave Dellinger."[8] Bureau headquarters agreed on January 24, 1969, and the letter was sent to New Left organizations and individuals, with the usual precautions to protect the identity of the FBI.

FLASH FLASH FLASH FLASH FLASH FLASH
DESPERATE DAVE DANGLES DINGUS
Murderously Mangles MOBE

Washington, D.C. Jan. 20—Speaking in his usual high pitched voice, Dave Dellinger, National Chairman of the National Mobilization committee

(MOBE), today claimed that the anti-inaugural demonstrations called by his organization had been responsible in getting the Paris peace talks going again.

Dellinger made this startling disclosure before an audience of newsmen in the dingy Hawthorne School which housed many of his followers. A cluster of the latter stood behind their guru sniffling and fingering wilted flowers. Dellinger, looking pale—more fairy-like than ever—tried to control the squeaks in his voice to no avail. "How many demonstrators did MOBE bring to the inaugural?" he was asked.

"At least ten thousand," he answered.

"Bullshit," was heard in several sections of the room.

Dellinger shuffled his notes. "Let's make that five thousand."

"Bullshit."

"Would you believe three thousand?" Silence. Dave rolled his eyes at the ceiling. "I'm not going to play at numbers," he chirped. "What matters is that MOBE accomplished so much. We did get the peace talks going. We did break some windows in the National Geographic Society building. Despite police brutality, our brave people managed to throw cans and sticks at the President." His voice went higher—sounding like glass bells in a soft summer breeze. "We shook the establishment, gentlemen."

Associated Press stood up. "We understand MOBE is broke. That you lost control of the thing. That SDS and many other organizations in the peace movement refused to back you. That you have no idea how MOBE funds were spent."

Dellinger put a finger in his mouth and sucked it reflectively. Some minutes passed before he spoke. "MOBE is solvent, boys. As of this moment, we have $1.54 in the treasury. The price of peace is high." He tried to look grim. "SDS, of course, is just a bunch of dirty college kids with grass for brains. We didn't want them or need them." He formed his lips into a cute bow. "I must go now. We're hitching a ride back to New York today unless we can raise bus fare."

He shoved four fingers into his mouth and was led slowly from the room humming "We Shall Overcome."[9]

Despite the Washington fiasco, the Steering Committee of National Mobilization met in New York on February 7, 1969, to plan a series of spring antiwar campaigns. Planners included David Dellinger, Tom Hayden, Paul Potter, Irving Beinen, Fred Halstead, Eric Weinberger, Sidney Peck, Sidney Lens, Student Mobilization Committee executive secretary Carol Lipman, and Barbara Bick of Washington Women Strike for Peace.[10] Out of this meeting came huge demonstrations in more than forty cities. In the first week of April, one hundred thousand marched in New York, thirty thousand in Chicago, and forty thousand in San Francisco. Earlier, on March 19, a federal grand jury in Chicago indicted David Dellinger, Tom Hayden, Abbie Hoffman, Jerry Rubin, Bobby Seale, Rennie Davis, Lee Weiner, and John Froines. The charges included conspiracy to incite a riot during the Democratic National Convention.

By the spring of 1969, campus protests were more frequent and much more violent than ever before. About one in five involved violence, physical injury, and property destruction. Protests were occurring in the country at the rate of two a day. About one third of the nation's student body had been directly involved. One protester had been killed, and demonstrators began to carry weapons for the first time. By June, at least eighty-four firebombing and arson incidents had occurred on college campuses. Ten firebombings had taken place off campus; some high schools were hit by violence.[11] The message seemed clear: the violence and disorder could not be contained until the nation left Vietnam.

The media and public outcry grew with each passing week. By late spring 1969, there had been at least four thousand student arrests, and one thousand students had been suspended. Seventy-six percent of these springtime actions were punished by arrest, loss of financial aid, or expulsion. A Gallup poll indicated that 82 percent of the American public felt that demonstrators were simply going too far, and that 80 percent of the nation's faculty members felt the same way. In April, J. Edgar Hoover testified before a House subcommittee that the New Left "was a firmly established subversive force dedicated to the complete destruction of our traditional democratic values and principles of free government."[12]

In Los Angeles, the FBI had been working to increase tensions within the SDS chapter at California State College. A November 7, 1968, memo to headquarters reported "constant friction between the Progressive Labor Party and the Communist Party at the SDS Chapter at this school."[13] Hoover saw a great opportunity, and the bureau moved aggressively.

An undercover informant was instructed to start the nasty rumor that the leader of one SDS faction was actually using chapter funds to support his drug habit. Another leader was falsely accused of embezzling similar funds from a chapter at another school. Los Angeles reported that "as a result of actions taken by this informant there have been fist fights and acts of name calling at several recent SDS meetings," and that "members of one faction have made early morning telephone calls to other SDS members and have threatened them and attempted to discourage them from attending SDS meetings."[14]

Los Angeles also advised headquarters that area high school principals and administrators were "totally unaware of the SDS and its aims and objectives." Los Angeles received, on July 7, authority to mail anonymously copies of the article "SDS: Engineer of Campus Chaos," which appeared in the October 1968 *Reader's Digest* and "Campus or Battleground? Columbia Is a Warning to All American Universities," from *Barron's* magazine, to fifty-two area high-school officials. The mailing, in the director's opinion, would make them "more aware of the SDS and its efforts to disrupt the normal educational processes."[15]

The San Diego field office targeted a dissident because he was active in draft counseling at the local Message Information Center. A January 28, 1969, memo reported that "the Message Information Center (MIC), San Diego 100-14427, appears to be operating a 'crash pad' at 4029 Dove Street, San Diego." A follow-up memo explained that the intended target was "sufficiently active in the New Left movement to be targeted in the counterintelligence program."[16]

Soon thereafter, two Selective Service violators were arrested by federal agents at the Message Information Center. By coincidence, the COINTELPRO target was also present. Next, a paid FBI informant, also working at the Message Information Center and speaking at a Center meeting, announced that the target was actually a federal agent. The announcement, of course, was completely untrue, but the damage had been done. San Diego reported that the target had been "completely ostracized by members of the MIC and all the other individuals throughout the area . . . associated with this and or related groups." The San Diego field office had learned the year before that marijuana and other drugs were being used at the Message Information Center.[17] This information was given to San Diego police, who raided the house on Dove Street. Shortly thereafter, the owner, reportedly "fed up" with the whole affair, had the house demolished.

On January 8, 1969, the Chicago field office reported on continuing tension between the Progressive Labor Party and other SDS factions.[18] On January 13, it received permission to produce an inflammatory pamphlet titled "New Laugh Notes," which would "widen the rift between SDS and PLP."[19] Mailings and campus distribution would be handled by the Chicago, New York, San Diego, and San Francisco field offices.

With both cartoons and text, the pamphlet leveled withering criticism at current SDS leaders and accused them of outright misuse of SDS funds. It appeared as if it came from the Progressive Labor faction. A January 23 Chicago memo confirmed that "a source close to the national office of SDS advised that the reaction of several members was that this had been mailed by the PLP faction of the SDS." J. Edgar Hoover congratulated Chicago: "The pamphlet shows a great deal of thought and ingenuity on the part of your office."[20]

A second Chicago pamphlet, "Into the Streets: A Handbook for Revolting Kids," used a children's-book format to present members of the SDS as nothing but a group of spoiled children. It was anonymously distributed to civic groups, PTAs, high school and college officials, and selected moderate student groups. The director hoped that this mailing would point out to the above groups "the absurd activities often resorted to by SDS."[21]

On May 1, 1969, the Chicago field office reported to headquarters that "a potentially strong alliance is forming between SDS and the Black Panther Party (BPP)." This was not an unfounded fear. Panther leader Fred Hampton had said: "We work very closely with the SDS and they help us out in many ways and we try to help them out in as many ways as we can." Such a merger, in the FBI's opinion, would provide the SDS "with the capability to provide major acts of violence through the volatile BPP." A follow-up Chicago memo recommended actions which would depict such a relationship as "an effort on the part of SDS to utilize the BPP as a mercenary group fighting a black war for white liberation."[22] Thus, on May 21, Hoover authorized Chicago to instruct BPP and SDS undercover informants to plant ideas and spread rumors "for use in creating a rift between the BPP and the Students For a Democratic Society."

In addition, the letter shown below was anonymously mailed by the Detroit field office at a later date to Black Power and New Left leaders.

Dear Brothers and Sisters,
    Since when do us Blacks have to swallow the dictates of the honky SDS? Doing this only hinders the Party progress in gaining Black control over Black people. We've been f—ed over by the white facists [sic] pigs and the Man's control over our destiny. We're sick and tired of being severely brutalized, denied our rights and treated like animals by the white pigs.

We say to hell with the SDS and its honky intellectual approaches which only perpetuate control of Black people by the honkies.

The Black Panther Party theory for community control is the only answer to our problems and that is to be followed and enforced by all means necessary to insure control by Blacks over all police departments regardless of whether they are run by honkies or uncle toms.

The damn SDS is a paper organization with a severe case of diarrhea of the mouth which has done nothing but feed us lip service. Those few idiots calling themselves weathermen run around like kids on halloween. A good example is their "militant" activities at the Northland Shopping Center a couple of weeks ago. They call themselves revolutionaries but take a look at who they are. Most of them come from well heeled families even by honky standards. They think they're helping us Blacks but their futile, misguided and above all white efforts only muddy the revolutionary waters.

The time has come for an absolute break with any non-Black group and especially those f—ing SDS and a return to our pursuit of a pure black revolution by Blacks for Blacks.

Power!

Off the Pigs!!!![23]

On June 6, an anonymous FBI letter was sent to top officials at SDS headquarters accusing them of refusing to hold a national convention because of fear of the strength of the pro-Progressive Labor Worker Student Alliance (WSA). A June national SDS convention was planned for Chicago. However, the SDS national office faction walked out, "leaving the WSA to hold its own version of the SDS convention."[24]

Next, the bureau used a friendly media connection, the *Chicago Tribune*, to help disrupt the convention. Special agents supplied *Tribune* reporter Ron Koziol with information regarding the internal struggle for control of the SDS. On June 17, 1969, the paper ran a front-page story headlined "Red Unit Seeks SDS Rule."[25] On June 30, Chicago special agent-in-charge M. W. Johnson advised headquarters that the article "aggravated a tense situation and helped create the confrontation that split the SDS."[26]

In New York, special agents continued their efforts to infiltrate the factional disputes within the SDS. The letter shown below was written as if by a loyal SDS member and was mailed on January 24, 1969.[27] It was designed to "disrupt plans for a peace demonstration sponsored by the YSA, SWP, SMC, and the Fifth Avenue Peace Parade Committee to be held April 5, 1969."

NEWS FROM THE SAND CASTLE

ITEM: Mark Rudd says he's willing to serve in the Army where he would continue his personal agitation on behalf of the "revolution." Aside from the fact that the Army wouldn't touch him with a ten foot pole, Mark is talking from his ass again. We'll give him two days of basic before some DI lifer sticks the butt end of an M-16 in one ear and out the other. Settle down, Mark. The revolution awaits.

Another thing. Give up the quest for bread and return to SDS-Columbia. It needs you badly. 200 clams per lecture may be tough to give up but money isn't everything, pal.

ITEM: Progressive Labor continues to throw the blocks to the NY Region of SDS. Really nothing new. PL has screwed us for years. PL elements within SDS supported the UFT during the recent teachers strike and neatly splintered the Regional office. The Labor Committee was destroyed—resurrected—smashed again and so on. PL is still using the name of the SDS Labor Committee to spread their political crap. Having PL in any radical movement is like having communal syphilis.

ITEM: The SDS Nat'l Council: in Mich. early this year was a disaster— nay—a calamity. Even the dungy Times wrote it up as a farce. ———— managed to save what was left of SDS but PL still rammed the Maoist line down to our gonads. In addition, this meeting was slopped up by the anarchist nuts. Up Against The Wall and allied groups have had it. Let them join the Klan—we don't need them.

ITEM: Where are we headed? Oblivion, pal, that's where. In the near future PL will own SDS—lock, stock and jock—and those of us who *really* worked for the campus revolution will probably re-join the plastic society for self-protection. PL is pushing into revolutionary ideology that borders on sheer insanity. Their worship of Chairman Mao—the Chinese George Wallace—as a divine being shows how sick they really are. To sum it up, kiddies, Mao sucks. . . .

—Bernie
(Sand Castle Class of '70)[28]

In June 1969, New York special agents prepared an anonymous letter designed to ridicule the "National Mobilization Committee To End the War in Vietnam and its leader Dave Dellinger." The letter, approved by Hoover, was also meant to disrupt a planned meeting of various peace groups scheduled for the July 4th weekend in Cleveland. Hoover noted on his memo, "Since this pamphlet may further serve to fragment the New Left, it is being approved."

WHITHER DOTH WE GO DAVY BABY?

Now, that the year of confrontation (such as it was) has jazzed its way into oblivion, perhaps, we should look to the future. Where has the turmoil and strife led us? Is the loss in Vietnam over? Has racism in Amerika diminished? Did we screw up the Nixon inaugural? Are the pigs beating our asses with less energy?

* * * **Hell NO!** * * *

Where, then, are you taking us now, Mr. Dellinger? National Mobe is dead and stinking up the atmosphere. Most of the well-known movement organizations are flat on their ass, financially and otherwise. The student "revolts" at Columbia and City died in the hiss of piss. At City our Black Brothers told us to stick it which we did . . . to the hilt. sds has folded into a limp mass of stringy kids rapping at each other in a jargon devoid of all meaning. The fountain has dried—their minds impotent. They froth at the mouth and wave their fists to the sounds of laughter. Their contribution to the Third World has turned to dog shit.

On the bridge of our sinking ship stands Captain Davy with the wind screaming through his teeth. With the waves of reaction lapping at his knees, Capt. Davy merely smiles and says, "Just wait, fellows. We'll soon have another victory for the S.S. Mobe." He flutters his pinkies like a bird ready for flight. "Just wait 'till we get to Chicago this fall."

Special Bulletin, Dave. When you get to Chicago the pigs will be waiting. They'll kick the shit out of you, buddy. The same goes for any of us nuts who follow you there. I well remember the last time. I've got the bloody shirt hanging in the pad. I look at it every night and cry a little—for the bloodletting was for naught. It was smash, smash and smash.

I humbly suggest it's time for a change. We, who still support the movement, should take our stand on the corpse of Mobe and chuck Davy baby over the side. Give him a nice salute and play the pipes slowly . . . he at least deserves that much.

—Peace
Bernie (Sand Castle Class of '71)[29]

The Detroit field office, reflecting extreme dissatisfaction with the handling of New Left matters at the University of Michigan, sent a scorching letter of dissatisfaction to the director on February 7, 1969.[30] It noted that university officials and president Robbin Fleming were at least giving "lip service" to the demands of the Board of Regents and state legislators for more control of student organizations and demonstrations on campus. It was known, however, that Fleming wanted no law-enforcement representation on the Michigan campus. Police could be summoned only on his "direct authority." Special agents reported that Fleming's own office was virtually destroyed during a student sit-in and he ordered it immediately redecorated so that "the Regents would not learn of it."[31] In other situations, the memo explained, the university administration had actually taken sides in the struggle among the various New Left factions.

During a spring disturbance at the Michigan State campus in East Lansing, an individual grabbed the speaker's microphone and used vulgar language while addressing the crowd. The individual's language was printed word for word on the front page of the *State News*, the official university student newspaper. The main article appeared in the February 12, 1969, issue and in five smaller followup articles.[32] A controversy immediately erupted over the type of journalism being employed by the *State News*. Detroit was authorized, on March 27, 1969, to anonymously mail the letter below to *State News* advertisers:

> As a patron of your store I can assure you that I will be no more tolerant of a store that continues to advertise in such a smut sheet.
>
> A disgusted taxpayer and patron[33]

In another action involving a student at Michigan State, the bureau targeted an undergraduate who was a member of the SWP. The student was a daughter of a brigadier general in the U.S. Army assigned to the Surgeon General's office in Washington. The letter below, together with a copy of a *State News* article headlined "Socialist Group Gains Members," was mailed on April 18, 1969.

> Dear ____
>
> Enclosed is an article which appeared in a local Lansing newspaper on April 5, 1969. For your information your daughter is very active in the Young Socialists Alliance which is dedicated to the overthrow of our government. I don't know if you agree with her activities but I thought I would let you know what she has been up to.
>
> —A Patriotic American[34]

An undercover informant in Atlanta advised special agents that Nelson Perry Blackstock, the head of the Atlanta chapter of the Young Socialists Alliance, worked in the mimeograph room at Shell Oil in Atlanta and was using Shell Oil Company equipment to print literature for the local chapter of the Young Socialists. Some of it was distributed during GI Day in Atlanta on October 27, 1968. It was known that another Young Socialists member named Jerry Heard was working in the same department with Blackstock. After approval from headquarters, the following letter was typed on non-watermarked paper and mailed in a plain envelope to J. H. Hall, personnel department, Shell Oil Company, Atlanta:

> Dear Sirs:
> I was riding on a bus the other night and overheard two hippies talking about a peace demonstration. One of these hippies said that they saved a lot of money by using Shell Oil Company printing presses. They talked about some fellow called NELSON who uses Shell Oil Company printing equipment to print propaganda against the war.
> I am a Shell Credit card holder but do not wish to divulge my name; however, I think if this is true that it should be stopped.
>
> Very truly yours,
> A Shell customer[35]

The letter must have threaded the needle almost perfectly. J. H. Hall advised a bureau source that Blackstock submitted his resignation on April 18, 1969, and that a review of Blackstock's work record found him "far from satisfactory." A COINTELPRO memorandum to headquarters ventured that, in all likelihood, the anonymous bureau letter triggered the review of Blackstock's work record and hence "would have caused his dismissal."[36]

In early March 1969, the Albuquerque field office learned that the SDS, having been refused space by officials at the University of Texas, was planning to move its National Council meeting to Albuquerque. They would secure rooms at the University of New Mexico and rent the civic auditorium from city officials. The meeting was scheduled for March 27–March 30.[37] Special agents quickly contacted the local chief of police, the city manager, and local news media, "in order to acquaint them with the problems that this would entail for the city of Albuquerque." As a direct result, university officials denied the SDS the use of campus facilities, and "the City Manager rescinded their contract for use of the Civic Auditorium."[38]

In January 1969, special agents in the Baltimore field office discovered an interesting article in the *Newark Weekly*, of Newark, Delaware. It was headlined "Creatures in the Dark" and drew parallels between the philosophy and terminology of the New Left and that of Adolph Hitler's "New Order." Both movements, the article said, had no tolerance for opposition. Baltimore received permission to anonymously mail copies to administrators at Johns Hopkins University, the University of Maryland, and Towson State College, as well as the Talmudical Academy, a Jewish theological school, and the Baltimore chapter of B'nai B'rith, "in the hope that it will influence their attitudes toward the New Left."[39]

On April 22, 1969, Baltimore was authorized to take action in an attempt to hinder the growing relationship between the SDS and the BPP. Special agents were to instruct their informants in the BPP to "start a program designed to undercut the SDS by suggesting to BPP members that SDS was a core of elite white chauvinistic students which was exploiting the militant strength of the BPP."[40]

In late 1968, the FBI learned that approximately thirty Oberlin College students were engaged in a hunger strike "as a form of protest against the war in Vietnam." Special agents from the Cleveland field office identified two of the students by name. Then, simply by consulting the Oberlin College student directory, the agents determined the students' home addresses. The letter below was sent to the parents of Oberlin College student John Kaza.

Oberlin, Ohio

Dear Mr. and Mrs. Kaza:

I am writing to you in the hope that, as John's parents, you may be able to persuade him of the lack of wisdom in becoming part of a hunger strike by Oberlin students in protest against the Vietnam war. I also oppose this war but I have tried to convince John that fasting to express opposition can only lead to injury to his health and damage to his academic standing. Obviously my efforts have been unsuccessful and I am concerned to the point where I reluctantly am writing this letter to you.

Another part of my concern for John's present conduct is my strong feeling that the hunger strike is being guided and directed by a group of left-wing students who call themselves the Young Socialist Alliance. I don't know too much about this group but I have made some inquiries and everything I have learned thus far indicates they are cynically using John and others for purposes that go far beyond opposition to the war.

I hope you will understand my reasons for writing without divulging my name. I would like to continue as John's friend and I am afraid that, in his present state of emotional involvement, he would not approve of anyone who brought his actions to the attention of his parents. I hope I am doing the right thing.

Sincerely yours,
An interested student[41]

Oberlin College alumnus Eugene Kaza, John's father, remembers the letter after more than twenty years: "The whole Vietnam thing was going on. Students were demonstrating. My son and some others were fasting against the war which was certainly their right. This letter came to our house and we had no idea who it was from. My wife and I were stunned and angry. We really didn't determine that the letter came from the FBI until 1978 or 1979. It seemed like a childish thing for the FBI to do."[42]

On February 27, 1969, Cleveland was authorized to anonymously distribute the fictional letter shown below which asserts that the Progressive Labor faction of the SDS was infiltrated by the FBI. About one thousand copies of the letter were distributed to delegates attending the National Council meeting of the SDS in Austin, Texas.

Brothers and Sisters,

If you want to know where the FBI is at in SDS, you need not look any further than the nearest PL. Consider that before Milt Rosen, Mort Scheer, Bill Epton, & Co. were expelled from the CP, they were the CP's raucous caucus. Now it stands to reason that any fed [*name deleted*] will gravitate towards the action faction in any left organization, because he will find more material for more sensational reports, resulting in said fed being paid more. Furthermore, he will be better able there to act as a provocateur, and get more credit for assisting in arrests, among the noise boys. Why else would they so loudly advocate super-militant tactics, or take a more-revolutionary-than-thou position, unless they knew they had nothing to fear?

We all know that Philip Abbot Luce was a PL.

We all know that PL analyses this society as if nothing had changed in the past seventy-five years. This says something to their mentality, displaying the naivete of a right-wing zealot masquerading as a radical. A similar naivete is shown by Herb Philbrick and his ilk, but these at least tell you where they're *really* at.

We all know PL did not participate in Chicago. Is this in order to prevent fed heads from getting cracked by Chicago Pigs who weren't in the know?[43]

On March 12, 1969, the Denver field office submitted to Hoover an SDS publication which provided institutions with information on how to make explosive devices for the purpose of sabotage. The same brochure featured a questionnaire captioned "Sex Relationship Inventory."

According to Denver special agents, the pamphlet was distributed to students of a local high school. With the director's approval, the Denver office contacted a friendly media source at the *Denver Post* with a photocopy of the pamphlet so that "he could either prepare an editorial concerning it or publish excerpts from it." Hoover cautioned, of course, "that the Bureau's interest in this matter is to be kept in the strictest confidence and under no circumstances is he [the news contact] to identify the Bureau as the source of this material." He added: "This material is another example of the moral looseness and revolutionary nature of the New Left."[44] Interestingly, the article actually appeared in the April 30 issue of the *Rocky Mountain News* headlined "Allott Rips SDS Bomb Sex Document." The Colorado U.S. Senator Gordon Allott issued a blistering press release which charged that SDS members handed out documents at a recent Denver East High School game telling students "how to make bombs and other explosives" and also distributed a pamphlet entitled "Sex Relationships Inventory."[45] All things considered, this was a very successful COINTELPRO action.

Richmond, Virginia, special agents reported in a memo dated January 11, 1969, that FBI agents handling New Left investigations were "in close, almost daily contact with the Intelligence Squad of the Richmond Police Department."[46] The local police were quite resourceful and cooperative, and had "a very active interest in disrupting New Left activity in Richmond." The main New Left target in Richmond was the Southern Student Organization Committee (SSOC), which maintained a communal living-type house adjacent to the Virginia Commonwealth University campus. The FBI worked with local authorities to bring intense civic pressure which forced the SSOC to move. The memo also reported that "another potential counterintelligence action is related to a current drive being conducted by the Vice Squad of the Richmond PD concerning a crackdown on drug abuse."[47]

In a variation of the anonymous mailings, the FBI occasionally produced anti–New Left literature. When the Indianapolis field office requested permission to produce a newsletter for distribution on the campus of Indiana University, headquarters cautioned, as it did in all such cases, that the office not embarrass the bureau in any way. It was titled the *Armageddon News*. Its purpose was to disrupt the New Left at the school.

Vol. 1, #1   **9/27/68**

PURPOSE

ARMAGEDDON NEWS will be prepared and distributed periodically by a group of concerned IU students who have returned to our school campus this fall to expose at Indiana University the
"CONSPIRACY OF THE NEW LEFT."
We feel the majority at IU abhor the devious and disgusting actions last year of the New Left Hippie Breed. We have spent considerable time and effort to get the straight *"dope"* on these pseudostudents, and we intend to keep you *WELL INFORMED.*

LAST YEAR

In this first issue, we want to highlight last year's activities.

Some will recall that IU had the distinction of being named as organizing Indiana for the March on Washington, D.C. in October, 1967. Mark Ritchey led his dissidents to our capitol where the press reported obscene behavior rarely connected in the past with IU's academic traditions. Encouraged by this support, the Committee to End the War in Vietnam, led by Mark Ritchey and Russell Block, and the Students for a Democratic Society, led by Dan Kaplan and Robin Hunter, and their ilk, stormed the police guard and took over a room of the Business Building where Dow Chemical was interviewing applicants. . . .
. . . SHADES OF COLUMBIA!
Thirty-five hippie leftists were arrested and all convicted.

Not to be dismayed, the very next day, the last day of October, they gave IU its darkest hour with the ill-mannered and obnoxious behavior in "receiving" Secretary of State Dean Rusk at IU Convocation. They, who demand freedom of speech, refused to allow him to present his views. About 300 hissed, booed, and screamed names, and it was very enlightening that many thousands of IU students signed an apology to the Secretary.

In the second semester, Robert Grove and Larry Waxberg, his loyal lieutenant, did not reorganize the DuBois Club. David Colton, a math instructor who went to Canada, insinuated they had formed a Communist Party club at IU to replace it this fall—*WATCH FOR IT!!!!* Grove was able to get James West and Ted Pearson, members of the National Committee of the Communist Party, USA, to come to IU at the end of the semester to help recruit members.

NEXT ISSUE

We have been able to infiltrate members into the *New Left* organizations at IU. We intend to expose officers, members and activities of *all*

New Left organizations at IU. Watch for the next issues for details of the :
   Students for a Democratic Society
   Committee to End the War in Vietnam
   W.E.B. DuBois Club
   Communist Party
   Young Socialist Alliance
"DON'T LET THE NEW LEFT WIN THE ARMAGEDDON AT I.U."[48]

Issues of the *Armageddon News* were mailed to selected students on the campus. A memo to headquarters, dated December 7, 1968, claimed that "this distribution was greatly responsible in limiting the number of curious students which normally follow such organizations during this period."[49]

In Newark, the field office learned through an undercover campus informant that members of the student body at Rutgers University were publishing a newspaper called *Screw*. According to bureau documents, it contained "a type of filth that could only originate in a depraved mind. . . . 'The paper' is being given away and sold *inside* Conklin Hall, Rutgers University, Newark by 'hippie' types in unkempt clothes, with wild beards, shoulder-length hair and other examples of their nonconformity." In the bureau's mind, this type of loose and lurid behavior personified the New Left. Newark took action. A letter mailed to several members of the Senate Education Committee in the New Jersey State Senate read, in part: "Would you want your children or grandchildren, especially young girls, subjected to such depravity? . . . [T]his is becoming a way of campus life. Poison the minds of the young, destroy their moral being and in less than one generation this country will be ripe for its downfall." The letter was signed by "A Concerned Student."[50] A New Jersey Senate Education Committee investigation of the matter soon followed.

Undercover informants for the Houston field office attended a May 14, 1969, SDS planning meeting at the University of Houston, and obtained there a strident single-spaced, seven-page document that explained SDS plans to infiltrate and disrupt business and industrial firms in the Houston area.[51] On May 27, Hoover authorized the Houston field office to contact the local Junior Chamber of Commerce and explain what the SDS had in mind for Houston in the summer of 1969. Special agents provided the Chamber of Commerce and several cooperative area firms with the SDS document, copies of David Dellinger's *Guardian* newspaper, and the SDS "Work-In Organizers Manual." Hoover's memo cautioned, of course, that "your source should understand that the FBI cannot be divulged as the source of this information."[52] The information was contained in a general newsletter mailing of the Texas Manufacturers Association on June 9, 1969; virtually every major industrial and manufacturing firm in the state thus learned of the SDS plans before they were implemented.

In the summer of 1969, the SDS planned to hold a major convention at either Penn State or the University of Pennsylvania. Undercover informants advised officials at both universities that such a conclave would not be in the best interests of either institution. Both schools agreed.[53]

The SDS Labor Committee of Philadelphia made plans to create a disturbance at a local sheriff's sale of tax-delinquent property on December 2, 1968. Such an action, they thought, would force Philadelphia police to arrest them and attract, somehow, the sympathy of the working class. The bureau informants advised the Philadelphia Civil Disturbance Squad, who came in force to the sale.[54] A January 23, 1969, Philadelphia field office memo confirmed that the disturbance failed to materialize because the presence of the Civil Disturbance Squad "dampened the spirit of the SDS members."[55]

On April 9, 1969, the Pittsburgh field office anonymously mailed a letter to the leaders of thirty-five antiwar organizations in the area. It was an obvious attempt to undermine the credibility of the area's leading antiwar publication, *Pittsburgh Peace and Freedom News,* by alleging that the newspaper was being unduly influenced by the Communist Party U.S.A.:

Dear Friend:

I have just finished reading the February, 1969, edition of the *Pittsburgh Peace and Freedom News*. In my opinion and also in the opinions of several friends the P & F News is attempting to cover too broad a scope, e.g. the grape boycott, instead of sticking to matters relative to peace and resistance. If you ask me, it appears that the P & F News is just another publication like the Guardian or the Daily World. Perhaps, there are reasons for similarities between the P & F News and these radical newspapers.

Is it possible that [*name deleted*], the "ramrod" of the Peace and Freedom Center (the publisher of P & F News) and his wife, [*name deleted*], are being unduly influenced by members of the Communist Party in the Pittsburgh area? Apparently this is the case. The [*names deleted*] are pretty closely associated with [*name deleted*] and his wife, [*name deleted*], according to leaders in the Pittsburgh peace movement.

I certainly am not in a position to identify the [couple] as CP members. However, when I participated in a recent demonstration in support of a fellow-resistor at the Federal Building on March 5, 1969, I did see [*name deleted*] in the company of Gus Hall, a leader of the CP in New York.

I'm positive of Gus Hall's identity as I saw him when he appeared on the Ohio University campus as a speaker during the Spring of 1967. Also, I've seen him several times on the TV in New York when I lived there.

Aforementioned edition of the P & F News noted . . ."we've made several important decisions, . . ." I say to you, let's kick out the [couple] and give the P & F News a new look. Maybe the Peace and Freedom Center would have a new look, too. How about it?

—Pittsburgh Resistor
(and protestor)[56]

In early June 1969, the president of the Pittsburgh area ACLU asked the Governor of Pennsylvania to publicly reprimand state police officials for conducting an investigation of Westinghouse High School following the appearance at a high school assembly of two controversial poets known for their efforts in the draft resistance movement. They were invited to the school by David Worstel, a leader in the Pittsburgh movement. This fictional letter was mailed to the two Pittsburgh daily newspapers, the Pittsburgh Board of Education, and Westinghouse High School:

Dear Sirs:

The article in the June 11 "Post Gazette" (Pittsburgh 'Press' where appropriate) says that the State Police assaulted academic freedom by investigating the visit of two poets to an English class at Westinghouse and they should be reprimanded. If anybody should be reprimanded, it should be the teacher who brought the poets there. Both of them are known for being against the draft laws and they preach that these laws should not be obeyed. Also, how come a man, David Worstell, who has been convicted as a draft dodger, can teach our children at Westinghouse and bring in other speakers who are opposed to our country to talk to the students, who are a captive audience? That is where the assault on academic freedom is.

How come the principal at Westinghouse and the Board of Education permit this type of action to go on? And why is such a teacher as this permitted to continue to poison the minds of students?

The ACLU jumped on the wrong people when they blamed the State Police. The State Police should make the complete results of their investigation public so all parents would know what is going on in their schools.

Sincerely,
Arthur Robinson
7720 Flure Way
Pittsburgh, Pa.[57]

On January 22, 1969, the Washington field office received headquarters' approval to target the father of an area antiwar activist, a graduate student instrumental in organizing the SDS chapter at Georgetown. The field office mailed this anonymous letter to the student's father, then living in York, Pennsylvania:

Dear [*name deleted*],

I have been meaning to write you for some time now, but have delayed doing so until now in the hope that the situation would improve. Regrettably, this has not occurred, and on the contrary, the situation has worsened considerably. The matter involves your son, [*name deleted*], and his activities in Washington D.C., in connection with a group called Students for a Democratic Society, and with other radical anti-war and anti-democratic groups.

Most likely you are aware of the fact that [*name deleted*] has been an organizer and leader of the Students for a Democratic Society at Georgetown University and has now "graduated" to become a leader on the regional level for the Students for a Democratic Society. He, in company with three or four other former university students, are living in a community house at 1779 Lanier Place, N.W., Washington, D.C., and [*name deleted*] manages to be actively present at any and every wild type of demonstration going on in Washington. He tries to stir up people and to attack the Government, the war and just about any other issue that his organization can seize upon.

It is of some concern to me that [*name deleted*] is making a mess of what started out to be a promising future. I am sure you will realize the sad consequences of a person bringing himself to the attention of the authorities as being a radical demonstrator and active leader of the Students for a Democratic Society. I have tried to point out to [*name deleted*] the ridiculous and dangerous situation in which he is involving himself, but unfortunately I have met with little or no success. As his father, perhaps you could speak with him and try to straighten him out before he messes himself up completely. I hope and pray you will be successful in doing so.

—A Concerned Friend[58]

A review appeared in the March 31, 1969, Washington *Evening Star* which was highly critical of "An Essay on Liberation," a new book by widely known New Left philosopher Dr. Herbert Marcuse. In the reviewer's opinion, it represented nothing more than an attempt to weaken the moral fiber and accepted values of the nation. With approval obtained on April 30, the Washington FBI field office affixed the logo of the Students for a Democratic Society to the title, reprinted it, and had it distributed on Washington area campuses by established undercover sources.[59]

The San Antonio field office, in an attempt to disrupt the local SDS organization, targeted a Progressive Labor Party member known to be taking narcotics.[60] San Antonio received FBI headquarters approval on February 11, 1969, to send an anonymous letter to Progressive Labor headquarters in an attempt to bring to their attention "the narcotics problem that exists" in the PLP in San Antonio. It was mailed to Progressive Labor, GPO Box 808, Brooklyn, New York 11201.

> Dear [name deleted],
>   You don't know me and my reason for not signing this letter is because, while I am interested in the activities of progressive labor, there are some things I have recently learned that concern me.
>   I think that progressive labor has a good program and there are some good people in the movement; however, I understand that here in Austin, one of the students involved in progressive labor is [name deleted]. I understand he is on "speed" and also might be using heroin.
>   I feel we have enough problems against a common enemy without having to tolerate people within our midst who use narcotics.
>   If this is the type of person you tolerate within your organization, I want no part of it.[61]

On January 30, 1969, San Antonio brought to the attention of headquarters an item from the *Daily Texan*, the University of Texas student newspaper. With bureau approval, the following letter was mailed to the Editor, the *Daily Texan*, Drawer D, University Station, Austin, Texas 78712.[62] As always, the headquarters instructed that "commercially obtained stationery is used in the preparation of this material so that the Bureau cannot be identified as the source."

> Dear Sir:
>   The January 30, 1969 issue of the *Daily Texan* carried an article entitled "Demonstrations Need Support" which was a reprinted article by Paul Bower from the Minnesota Daily, the student newspaper of the University of Minnesota.
>   There are two sides to every coin. The following editorial appeared in the San Antonio Light on January 22, 1969:
>   "Study in Contrasts
>   "Most of the nation's newspaper readers know the name of Mark

Rudd—the young revolutionary who led last year's student uprising at Columbia University.

"For many violent weeks he defied college and police authority alike while effectively disrupting normal operations at one of the nation's greatest centers of education.

"How many readers ever heard of Karo Modelewski and Jacek Kuren? Probably very few—and that's because they were doing what Mark Rudd was doing last spring, only they were doing it at the University of Warsaw.

"They didn't do it long. At the very start of the Polish student disorders last March they were slung into jail for instigating 'public state unrest.'

"A news dispatch a few days ago reported what subsequently happened to Modelewski and Kuren. After 10 months in jail, they were found guilty and slung back into their cells to serve the balance of 3-1/2 year sentences each.

"By contrast, the last we heard of Mark Rudd he was going around lecturing students at various American colleges on the techniques of campus hellraising.

"It is quite a contract, this example of American permissiveness versus Communist clampdown.

"It should be food for thought for the current crop of our campus disrupters who follow the leftist line and use the leftist rhetoric. It should be—but it won't be."

I agree with the Light, that this should be food for thought.

Very truly Yours,
Dillon J. O'Rourke[63]

On April 9, 1969, San Antonio received authority to send a fictitious letter to University of Texas president Norman Hackerman to keep up the pressure on the SDS at the university. It was noted that Mr. Hackerman had previously denied the SDS use of university facilities by the SDS for a national council meeting. Also enclosed was a clipping from the March 20, 1969 *Christian Science Monitor* which pointed out that the University of Missouri had already expelled the SDS from its campus.

Dear President Hackerman:

I read in the local press that you have denied the National Council of the Students for a Democratic Society the use of University of Texas facilities to hold a meeting.

This is a refreshing stand taken by you since other college administrators have seen fit to give into [sic] this revolutionary group.

I noticed in the local press that Governor Ronald Reagan of California recently gave testimony in Washington before the U.S. House of Representatives Education Sub-Committee in which he was critical of college administrators who he said "have typically been slow to act and quick to concede" in dealing with student unrest. This criticism, obviously, does not apply to you.

I have also read in the news that because of threats of sabotage made by anti-Vietnam War groups, the nation's railroads have instituted the tightest security precautions in history on shipments of munitions and military supplies. FBI Director J. Edgar Hoover is quoted as stating there has been a marked increase in acts of sabotage against government installations. The newspaper article indicates that there have been several instances of sabotage and Mr. Hoover traces the incidents to last June when the SDS held their National Convention at Michigan University. At that time the SDS, according to news accounts, conducted workshops on sabotage and explosives.

The decision was based on charges following a hearing that the SDS was distributing obscene literature.

The UT Officials should now follow the University of Missouri's example.

Very truly yours,
Dillon J. O'Rourke[64]

The decision by the University of Texas to deny the SDS the use of campus facilities was tested in the courts, and the university's position was upheld. The Central Texas ACLU took strong exception to the whole matter in a letter to the *Daily Texan* dated April 30, 1969. Their criticism centered on the alleged denial of First Amendment privilege. The San Antonio field office followed on May 13, 1969 with the follow-up letter below to the *Daily Texan*.

Editor:
The April 30, 1969, issue of the *Daily Texan* carries a letter in "Firing Line" written by Roy M. Mersky, President, Central Texas Chapter, American Civil Liberties Union, critical of the UT administration cancelling the use of campus facilities for the Students for a Democratic Society Convention.

Mr. Mersky's letter fails to mention that the SDS had its day in court, not only in U.S. District Judge Jack Robert's court, but also in the U.S. 5th Circuit Court of Appeals where a three-judge panel unanimously rejected an appeal.

The American Civil Liberties Union should keep the record straight.
Very truly yours,
Dillon J. O'Rourke[65]

Around this time, FBI headquarters prepared a study for the Justice Department which came to be known as "Youth in Rebellion." The report dealt with the possible worldwide ramifications of black and New Left extremist actions, and their possible collective threat to the security of the United States. The Justice Department, operating with no knowledge of the COINTELPRO disruptive actions then taking place, instructed the FBI "to determine whether there is any underlying subversive group" providing illegal guidance to the New Left and campus disorders nationwide.[66] No underlying subversive group conducting demonstrations and disorder was ever found.

The Justice Department was also considering a series of grand jury investigations of campus disorders with possible prosecution "under the anti-riot act, the Smith Act, the Voorhis Act, and Statute on Seditions, conspiracy and insurrection." In line with this, Justice officials asked the FBI to provide names and any other intelligence data regarding individuals and organizations planning disruptions.[67] These special investigations placed an additional work load on the FBI, but the COINTELPRO-New Left operations were not curtailed in any way.

At this same time the FBI also increased its Key Activists program. Reports from field offices were made every ninety days on fifty-five individuals, the "key activists" in the New Left antiwar movement. Photographs and biographies of all of them were prepared and distributed to every FBI field office. There was constant internal pressure to expand this listing and "obtain recordings of our reliable witnesses to inflammatory speeches or statements made which may subsequently become subject to criminal prosecution."[68]

During the spring and early summer, more than four thousand student activists were arrested. New Left dissidents were expelled, suspended, or faced the loss of financial aid at twice the rate as other student groups. The SDS was banned completely from Florida Southern, St. Bonaventure, Colorado State, Kent State, Arizona, and Maryland. The nationwide efforts of the FBI, utilizing its network of special agents and undercover informants, was, to some degree at least, having an inhibiting effect on the demonstrations and the violence. One special agent reported: "Our inside information has caused the SDS to get more conspiratorial in a lot of places. They make their plans at the last minute to fool us." He added, "I think the conspiratorial mood is hurting the SDS a lot."[69]

Undercover informants were used during the life of the New Left COINTELPRO, primarily to disrupt antiwar plans. David Dellinger remembers that SDS and New Mobilization Committee meetings became increasingly secretive and private. Key leaders ultimately refused to discuss antiwar plans openly because it was generally assumed by members that undercover informants were present. In time the bureau's undercover informants were so successful and their penetration was so complete that many of the New Left group leaders all but succumbed to paranoia. Ultimately, any form of democracy within the NMC and the SDS became impossible.[70]

Interestingly, the first half of 1969 also witnessed the extraordinary decline of the Students for a Democratic Society—originally the most powerful New Left organization in the country. Perhaps because of myopia and a seemingly self-imposed isolation, the national SDS organization lost touch with the rank and file, and its loss of influence and power was profound. Incredibly, at the very moment of the greatest explosion of New Left power and influence in a decade, the SDS "was diminishing itself, losing its student constituency, its women, its alumni, failing to connect with the high schools, the soldiers, the workers."[71]

The ninth and final SDS convention, with about fifteen hundred delegates in attendance, took place in Chicago June 18–22, 1969. From almost the opening day, the entire structure of the organization was traumatized by the inevitable confrontation between the Progressive Labor faction and the SDS national office faction under the leadership of Bernadine Dohrn. "In the wake of the convention, SDS was shattered."[72] Various splinter groups, including the extreme Weatherman faction, emerged from the wreckage.

Until the spring of 1969, the SDS was the most vocal and active of all the groups in the New Left movement. But that spring, the Weather Underground broke away from the SDS. The Weather Underground, which probably numbered no more than four hundred members at any time, was the ultraradical, extremely violent wing of the New Left movement. Their original name, the Weathermen, came from a verse in Bob Dylan's 1965 song "Subterranean Homesick Blues": "You don't need a weatherman to know which way the wind blows."[73]

Their rampaging violence horrified much of the nation. Their activities, as Robert D. McFadden has observed, "estranged even many of the leftists who shared their liberationalist, anti-Establishment views." Many feel—even today—that the Weathermen "besmirched civil rights, anti-war and other legitimate causes and organizations from which they sprang."[74]

On October 8, 1969, the Weather Underground launched their "Days of Rage" rampage in Chicago—an orgy of violence and destruction that hit neighborhoods, business firms, and an army induction center. They followed the Chicago action with nineteen bombings across the country. Targets included the U.S. Capitol building, government facilities in Pittsburgh and New York, and recruiting and draft centers. In 1970, the group disappeared into the underground, and several were not apprehended until the 1980s.

Enormous national pressures were at work on the New Left. The American public, together with the news media, continued to direct an enormous hostility toward student protest as if it "was as disturbing as the Vietnam War." *Time* magazine reported that there was, by the spring and early summer, "a growing feeling throughout the nation that the rebels have gone too far."[75]

On the other hand, other elements of the antiwar movement were regrouping and, in effect, waiting for the announcement of the new Nixon administration's policy in Vietnam. Indeed, much of the immediate future of the New Left and the antiwar movement depended in large measure on Richard M. Nixon. Early in May, Nixon announced somewhat ambivalent plans for a gradual withdrawal of "non-Vietnamese combat forces" in Vietnam. At some future date there would be internationally supervised elections for South Vietnam to decide its own political future without intervention. In early June, as part of the new Nixon doctrine, the president announced the withdrawal of the first twenty-five thousand Americans from South Vietnam. Secretary of Defense Melvin Laird defined the new American strategy as changing from maximum pressure to protective reaction.

The policy was met with almost universal disapproval by the antiwar movement. It became apparent that the government really had no plans to end the war in the immediate future. The war could, conceivably, go on for decades. Three antiwar groups—the strengthened Student Mobilization Committee, the New Mobilization Committee to End the War in Vietnam, and the Vietnam Moratorium Committee—would soon challenge the government's war policy with the largest mass demonstrations ever seen in the western hemisphere.

NOTES

1. FBI Memorandum, Cincinnati Field Office to Headquarters, Dec. 13, 1968.

2. FBI Memorandum, Headquarters to Cincinnati Field Office, Dec. 27, 1968.

3. Sidney Lens, *Unrepentant Radical. An American Activist's Account of Five Turbulent Decades* (Boston: Beacon Press, 1980), p. 341.

4. FBI Memorandum, Washington Field Office to Headquarters, Jan. 9, 1969; Headquarters to Washington Field Office, Jan. 10, 1969.

5. FBI Memorandum, Washington Field Office to Headquarters, Jan. 21, 1969.

6. Lens, *Unrepentant Radical*, p. 341.

7. Charles DeBenedetti and Charles Chatfield, *An American Ordeal: The Antiwar Movement of the Vietnam Era* (Syracuse: Syracuse University Press, 1990), p. 244.

8. FBI Memorandum, New York Field Office to Headquarters, Jan. 21, 1969; Headquarters to New York Field Office, Jan. 24, 1969.

9. Ibid., Jan. 21, 1969.

10. Fred Halstead, *Out Now! A Participant's Account of the Movement in the U.S. against the Vietnam War* (New York: Pathfinder Press, 1978), p. 446.

11. Kirkpatrick Sale, *SDS* (New York: Vintage Press, 1974), pp. 512–513.

12. Ibid., p. 543.

13. FBI Memorandum, Los Angeles Field Office to Headquarters, Nov. 7, 1968.

14. FBI Memorandum, Los Angeles Field Office to Headquarters, Dec. 12, 1968.

15. FBI Memorandum, Headquarters to Los Angeles Field Office, July 7, 1969.

16. FBI Memorandum, San Diego Field Office to Headquarters, Jan. 28, 1969; Feb. 3, 1969.

17. FBI Memorandum, San Diego Field Office to Headquarters, Apr. 30, 1969.

18. FBI Memorandum, Chicago Field Office to Headquarters, Jan. 8, 1969.

19. FBI Memorandum, Headquarters to Chicago Field Office, Jan. 13, 1969.

20. Ibid.

21. FBI Memorandum, Chicago Field Office to Headquarters, Feb. 7, 1969; Headquarters to Chicago Field Office, Mar. 17, 1969.

22. FBI Memorandum, Chicago Field Office to Headquarters, May 1, 1969; May 19, 1969.

23. FBI Memorandum, Headquarters to Chicago Field Office, May 21, 1969; Detroit Field Office to Headquarters, Feb. 10, 1970; Headquarters to Detroit Field Office, Mar. 3, 1970.

24. FBI Memorandum, Chicago Field Office to Headquarters, June 6, 1969.

25. FBI Memorandum, Chicago Field Office to Headquarters, June 18, 1969.

26. FBI Memorandum, Chicago Field Office to Headquarters, June 30, 1969.

27. FBI Memorandum, New York Field Office to Headquarters, Jan. 14, 1969; Headquarters to New York Field Office, Jan. 24, 1969.

28. Ibid., Jan. 14, 1969.

29. FBI Memorandum, New York Field Office to Headquarters, June 18, 1969; Headquarters to New York Field Office, June 24, 1969.

30. FBI Memorandum, Detroit Field Office to Headquarters, Feb. 7, 1969.

31. Ibid.

32. FBI Memorandum, Detroit Field Office to Headquarters, Feb. 28, 1969.

33. FBI Memorandum, Headquarters to Detroit Field Office, Mar. 27, 1969.

34. FBI Memorandum, Detroit Field Office to Headquarters, Apr. 18, 1969; Headquarters to Detroit Field Office, May 2, 1969.

35. FBI Memorandum, Headquarters to Atlanta Field Office, Jan. 22, 1969.

36. FBI Memorandum, Atlanta Field Office to Headquarters, May 22, 1969.

37. FBI Memorandum, Albuquerque Field Office to Headquarters, Apr. 2, 1969.

38. Ibid.

39. FBI Memorandum, Baltimore Field Office to Headquarters, Jan. 2, 1969; Headquarters to Baltimore Field Office, Jan. 22, 1969; "Creatures of the Dark," *Newark Delaware Weekly*, Sept. 18, 1968.

40. FBI Memorandum, Headquarters to Baltimore Field Office, Apr. 22, 1969.

41. FBI Memorandum, Cleveland Field Office to Headquarters, Nov. 25, 1968.

42. Eugene Kaza, telephone interview with author, Oct. 23, 1989.

43. FBI Memorandum, Cleveland Field Office to Headquarters, Mar. 24, 1969; Headquarters to Cleveland Field Office, Feb. 27, 1969.

44. FBI Memorandum, Denver Field Office to Headquarters, Nov. 12, 1969; Headquarters to Denver Field Office, Apr. 3, 1969; FBI Memorandum, Denver Field Office to Headquarters, Apr. 29, 1969; Headquarters to Denver Field Office, May 13, 1969.

45. FBI Memorandum, Denver Field Office to Headquarters, May 27, 1969.

46. FBI Memorandum, Richmond Field Office to Headquarters, Jan. 11, 1969.

47. FBI Memorandum, Richmond Field Office to Headquarters, Apr. 22, 1969.

48. FBI Memorandum, Indianapolis Field Office to Headquarters, Dec. 17, 1968.

49. Ibid.

50. FBI Memorandum, Newark Field Office to Headquarters, May 23, 1969; Headquarters to Newark Field Office, June 4, 1969.

51. FBI Memorandum, Houston Field Office to Headquarters, May 16, 1969.

52. FBI Memorandum, Headquarters to Houston Field Office, May 27, 1969; Houston Field Office to Headquarters, June 24, 1969.

53. FBI Memorandum, Philadelphia Field Office to Headquarters, Mar. 28, 1969.

54. FBI Memorandum, Philadelphia Field Office to Headquarters, Jan. 23, 1969.

55. Ibid.

56. FBI Memorandum, Headquarters to Pittsburgh Field Office, Apr. 9, 1969.

57. FBI Memorandum, Pittsburgh Field Office to Headquarters, June 12, 1969; Headquarters to Pittsburgh Field Office, June 19, 1969.

58. FBI Memorandum, Washington Field Office to Headquarters, Jan. 6, 1969; Headquarters to Washington Field Office, Jan. 22, 1969.

59. FBI Memorandum, Washington Field Office to Headquarters, Apr. 18, 1969; Headquarters to Washington Field Office, Apr. 30, 1969.

60. FBI Memorandum, San Antonio Field Office to Headquarters, Jan. 28, 1969.

61. FBI Memorandum, Headquarters to San Antonio Field Office, Feb. 11, 1969.

62. FBI Memorandum, San Antonio Field Office to Headquarters, Jan. 30, 1969; Headquarters to San Antonio Field Office, Feb. 11, 1969.

63. Ibid., Feb. 11, 1969.

64. FBI Memorandum, San Antonio Field Office to Headquarters, Mar. 26, 1969; Headquarters to San Antonio Field Office, Apr. 9, 1969.

65. FBI Memorandum, San Antonio Field Office to Headquarters, May 1, 1969; Headquarters to San Antonio Field Office, May 13, 1969.

66. Memorandum from Assistant Attorney General J. Walter Yeagley to the FBI Director, Feb. 8, 1969.

67. Memorandum from Assistant Attorney General J. Walter Yeagley to the FBI Director, May 3, 1969.

68. FBI Memorandum, Headquarters to Field Offices, Mar. 10, 1969.

69. Sale, *SDS*, p. 592.

70. David Dellinger, *More Power Than We Know, The People's Movement Toward Democracy* (Garden City, NY: Anchor Press, 1975).

71. Sale, *SDS*, p. 528.

72. Halstead, *Out Now!*, p. 467.

73. Lucinda Franks, "U.S. Inquiry Finds 37 in Weather Underground," *New York Times*, Mar. 5, 1975, p. 38.

74. Robert P. McFadden, "Issue of Conspiracy: As Investigators Seek Terrorist Links, Scope of Radical Threat Is Debated," *New York Times*, Oct. 26, 1981, pp. 8–9.

75. Sale, *SDS*, p. 549.

6

The New Mobilization Committee to End the War in Vietnam and the Vietnam Moratorium Committee

"Nixon is not going to end this war . . . and it's clear that we have to resume our efforts to stop the war because these people aren't going to."

—David Hawk

On April 29, 1969, national security advisor Henry A. Kissinger and presidential assistant John Ehrlichman met privately with a group of antiwar protesters in the White House Situation Room. Dr. Kissinger recalls a wide-ranging discussion of the war in Vietnam which lasted over two hours.

The small group of students was led by Cornell graduate David Hawk, 24, a former McCarthy campaign worker and staff member of the National Student Association. They represented 253 campus leaders from 38 states who had signed a declaration of conscience that stated flatly: "We will not serve in the military as long as the war in Vietnam continues." The *Washington Post* considered the students to be from "the conventional leadership sector of the universities."[1]

Hawk remembers that Kissinger said, "I don't disagree with you as to the wisdom of our original involvement, but we cannot leave in a way that would cause dishonor." Kissinger's approach was to seem generally sympathetic to the students' basic antiwar position. Nevertheless, he added that "conscientious objection is destructive of society."[2] Much of the Nixon administration's policy was, of course, an anathema to the students and they strongly expressed their dissatisfaction with it in the meeting. In the end, it was clear that the administration and the student activists were worlds apart on the future course of Vietnam policy. Hawk announced after the meeting that it was obvious that they would have to resume their efforts to stop the war because "these people aren't going to."[3]

It was almost certainly not realized at the time, but the group of students that emerged from the White House on April 29 would ultimately form the central action group for the largest single antiwar demonstration ever held in the United States.

Other antiwar forces were also at work. On April 20, 1969, Mass Pax, a New England peace group, held an executive meeting directed by its chairman, Jerome Grossman. Grossman proposed the unusual idea of a nationwide domestic strike to put an end to the war in Vietnam. His position paper on the subject explained that such an action would tell the Nixon administration "that those who strike are determined to end the war even if it meant shutting down all American institutions."[4] Soon thereafter, David Hawk made contact with Sam Brown, another McCarthy campaign worker, and Jerome Grossman. With funding support promised by Grossman, the Vietnam Moratorium Committee (VMC) was formed with the express purpose of building a national protest of such size that it simply could not be ignored by the White House. The target date was October 15. The VMC intended "to mobilize the broadest combination of antiwar citizens in a legal and traditional protest action which would have a painful impact on all with power and influence."[5] In effect, it would be a moratorium on business as usual in the United States. On June 30, VMC set up national headquarters at 1029 Vermont Avenue N.W. in Washington, D.C.

Another action group, the New Mobilization Committee to End the War In Vietnam (New Mobe), was created by the Cleveland Area Peace Council at a meeting that included David Hawk. This new group pledged full support for the VMC and advocated a policy of nonviolent, but very determined, antiwar protest. It came into being at almost the same moment that the SDS was in stages of disintegration. The New Mobe was organized to tap the enormous—and, some thought, unused—energies of pacifist and New Left groups in almost every state. The goal of the New Mobe was also to organize a national demonstration that would demand immediate withdrawal of all Americans from Vietnam, to be held in Washington November 13–15. New Mobe also set up its national headquarters at 1029 Vermont, just a few floors away from the VMC headquarters.

Events moved very quickly. By the end of July, David Hawk reported to a somewhat astonished New Mobe steering committee that the VMC already had active workers on 225 college campuses, with good progress being made at almost a hundred more schools. Hawk was particularly fortunate to have been a staff member of the National Student Association, which provided him with many college contacts. Hawk's assistants included Marge Sklencar and David Mixner. The VMC call to action was unequivocal: "Ending the War in Vietnam is the most important task facing the American nation." All of their collective energies were now focused on October 15, 1969. The direct invitation from David Hawk to become active in support of the Vietnam Moratorium meant access to millions of moderate American youth who "believed in their country's political processes," yet opposed the war in Vietnam and believed that non-violent protest on an enormous scale might bring an end to American participation.[6]

By late August, VMC had received endorsements from members of Congress, labor and business leaders, much of the academic community, and individuals from virtually every walk of life. Financial contributions were substantial. Twelve regional offices were quickly established with a full-time administrative staff of thirty. Full-page VMC fund-raising display ads ran in the *New York Times* to great effect. By early September, the VMC had student leaders at almost four hundred colleges, large and small, public and private.

Early on, David Hawk and Sam Brown began the practice of holding "briefing sessions" for a growing base of reporters, many of whom had been skeptical of the committee. As media interest began to grow over the summer, the VMC message was consistent: "This is what students are going to do in the fall." Hawk remembers that by mid-September reporters from all across the United States were in constant contact with his office. They wanted to know what was planned, who was in charge, and what was "the moratorium business."[7]

While the VMC and the New Mobe were preparing for the autumn, antiwar demonstrations were continuing to occur at the rate of at least one per day and by the end of 1969 had reached an incredible 65 percent of the nation's higher educational institutions. A new kind of protest, "reading of the war dead," involved recitations of the names of Americans killed in Vietnam. It was a long list by August of 1969—more than thirty-eight thousand.

There were at least eighty firebombings during the first ten months of 1969. Targets included induction centers, Selective Service headquarters, ROTC facilities, and government buildings. The antiwar movement was supported, by the fall of 1969, by 20 percent of the American public. A presidential commission reported, "The crisis has roots in division in American society as deep as any since the Civil War."[8] In the world's oldest republic, where the very authority of the government itself is based on the consent of the governed, such a situation could not continue indefinitely.

On July 10, just a few days after the Cleveland Area Peace Council meeting, eight hundred American servicemen returned home to Seattle to find protesters chanting, "Welcome home, Bring them all home." Some carried signs reading, "WELCOME HOME GIs. JOIN THE ANTIWAR MOVEMENT."[9]

On the same day, the Student Mobilization Committee announced plans for a nationwide strike on November 14, the day before the massive march in Washington, D.C. Committee members predicted that more than a million high school and college students would participate. The following day, members of Women Against the War were arrested at the White House grounds while attempting to deliver a letter to President Nixon. On July 17, several Quaker-led demonstrators were arrested at the Pentagon where they were reading the names of Americans killed in Vietnam. In New York, later in July, the Fifth Avenue Peace Parade Committee marked the twenty-fourth anniversary of the atomic bombing of Hiroshima with a march of twenty-five thousand on Seventh Avenue.

Nixon administration officials, including Nixon himself, were beginning to feel the heat. They were being directly confronted at every opportunity everywhere in the nation. In an action fully supported by New Mobe, about eight thousand protesters converged on the Summer White House in San Clemente, California.

On August 14, about three thousand gathered in front of the Century Plaza Hotel in Los Angeles, the scene of a state dinner honoring the Apollo 11 astronauts. One of the protesters, Peggy Mullett, then a twenty-year-old college student, remembers thinking, "Nixon has been slow at ending the war and I'm not sure he really wants to."[10] Several in the group carried signs which read, "August 13, 1,450 Vietnamese and 200 Americans dead" and "IMPROVE, DON'T DESTROY, MAN'S ENVIRONMENT." The demonstration was organized by the Student Mobilization Committee.

The next week in San Francisco, about ten thousand massed along

Powell and Post Streets and in Union Square opposite the St. Francis Hotel where President Nixon was hosting a state dinner for Park Chung-Hee, the President of South Korea. Arriving guests, including South Korean officials, saw and heard obscenities meant for Nixon. The San Francisco field office later reported that sources had advised them that the New Left had planned to disrupt the diplomatic visit. Information was quickly given to the State Department and Secret Service. As a result, security was so extensive that, according to FBI officials, "the new Left's efforts were a bust."

On June 10, a report issued by the National Commission on the Causes and Prevention of Violence sharply criticized Hoover and the bureau for creating a hostile environment in which police officers believed that "any kind of mass protest is due to a conspiracy promulgated by agitators, often Communists who misdirect otherwise contented people."[11] The report emphasized that the United States cannot have it both ways: America will either commit itself to meaningful social and economic reform or develop into a garrison state where law and order are enforced without any guarantee of due process. The commission could not in any way support Hoover's claim that communist elements had infiltrated the New Left. An FBI spokesman said that the bureau would have no official comment. Hoover's personal response within the confines of the bureau was almost certainly unprintable.

Nevertheless, by the summer of 1969, the FBI had more than two thousand agents investigating the New Left movement. Additionally, it had well over a thousand undercover informants in operation and reporting findings to the FBI. In 1969, according to bureau documents, 271 law enforcement conferences were held by the FBI on the subjects of extremist groups and violence, attended by more than twenty-three thousand representatives of various criminal-justice and law-enforcement agencies across the United States.

As the New Left began to focus on the two momentous events planned for the fall of 1969, the FBI continued its almost daily efforts to disrupt the activists. Within the COINTELPRO-New Left operations, however, there was almost no mention of the fall peace offensive.

Baltimore special agents mailed inflammatory post cards to individual SDS members at their home addresses—where it was hoped their parents would be the first to read them. They warmly congratulated the activist for his or her energetic participation in the Chicago riots during the Democratic convention. The plan, of course, was that the parents would force "their child to leave the SDS."[12]

Baltimore was also authorized to continue efforts to disrupt the somewhat tenuous relationship between the SDS and the Black Panther Party (BPP). BPP undercover sources were told to portray the SDS as "a corps of elite white chauvinistic students who would like to exploit the BPP." The efforts must have succeeded.[13] An August 26, 1969, memo reported, "BPP members have been instructed not to associate with SDS members or attend any SDS affairs." Another memo reported "an officer of the Baltimore BPP [*name deleted*] was expelled from the BPP for his association with an SDS member."[14]

Special agents were encouraged to interview SDS and BPP leaders to get their view of the split between the two organizations. One media question in particular, directed to the SDS, was a bombshell: How did the SDS react to the comments featured in the August 16, 1969, *Guardian*, in which BPP chairman Bobby Seale and BPP chief of staff David Hilliard referred to the SDS as a "fascist organization?"[15] The SDS had no comment.

In a July 31, 1969, memo, the Columbia, South Carolina, field office reported on antiwar activities at the UFO Club, a coffee house in Columbia. This club, a project of New Mobe, was believed to be "an antiwar, antidraft type club catering to the soldiers at Ft. Jackson and other nearby military bases."[16] Two FBI undercover informants from nearby Shaw Air Force Base advised special agents that the club provided draft counseling and was involved in illegal drugs. They suggested that the club might have difficulties with the IRS. On August 7, Hoover authorized the South Carolina office to contact the IRS and "furnish it information concerning alleged tax violations."[17] Acting on information provided by bureau special agents, city police and the Richland County Sheriff's Department made almost two dozen arrests at the club for drug use and possession.

In the prolonged New Left COINTELPRO operations, Hoover left very little doubt about who was in charge and what his feelings were on any situation. The Knoxville field office demonstrated extremely bad judgement in advising headquarters that school officials at the University of Tennessee were doing everything necessary to prevent the formation of active SDS chapters in the state. In Knoxville's opinion, the New Left counterintelligence file could be closed.[18]

In an angry headquarters memo to Knoxville dated July 5, 1969, Hoover stated, "There has been no evidence whatsoever to substantiate the conclusion that the New Left's efforts on the Nation's campuses are abating." Knoxville was told to reopen the New Left counterintelligence file immediately and pay particular attention to SDS plans to replace the

Southern Student Organizing Committee. "You should thoroughly review this problem," the director concluded, "as it relates to your division and advise whether efforts can be taken to frustrate any attempts to organize SDS in your territory."[19] There was little doubt that heads would roll if Knoxville didn't get busy.

In a July 31, 1969, memo, Hoover excoriated the Denver office for an apparent lack of follow-through on possible New Left actions during the summer months. He said, correctly, that the field office had no information at all on a July 28 SDS rally at the University of Colorado and a subsequent disruption of the local Institute for Defense Analysis. Hoover said flatly that the special agents assigned to the New Left were simply not grasping the aims, objectives, and importance of the COINTELPRO operations. He hinted that personnel changes might be made. Special agents were admonished to pursue the New Left aggressively and "with imagination." Opportunities for neutralizing the New Left were not to be missed. In a parting shot, he said that a "lackadaisical attitude toward this program would not be tolerated."[20]

Denver responded on August 26 with an analysis of the SDS/BPP relationship in the area. It reported on a combined SDS/BPP rally at the Denver City County Building, in which demonstrators demanded freedom for BPP leaders Huey Newton, Landon Williams, and others.[21] Thirty days later, Denver reported that the area BPP was experiencing extreme internal problems and that a strong COINTELPRO action would probably be warranted. The plan was to increase tension within the BPP by attempting to aggravate the SDS/BPP relationship at the same time.[22] With these objectives in mind, the following letter, appearing to come from the SDS, was sent to the *Black Panther Newspaper* in Berkeley, California.

Sorry we haven't registered sooner our disgust at the stab in the back you fair weather friends gave us in the August issue of the "Guardian," but we have been occupied with planning and carrying out revolutionary action—which is more than we can say for your group here in Denver. There are a lot of us in SDS in the Denver–Boulder area, especially in the Denver Collective, who take exception to, and outright resent, being called fascists and nazis, especially by representatives of a fellow minority group which is supposed to have the same long-range goals as we do.

The disagreement which brought on the unwarranted attack relates only to tactics and should never have been made public. It was strickly [purposely misspelled] an internal matter to be ironed out by the leadership of the two organizations, and as far as the dispute goes, there is much to be said for our position that control of white communities by white pigs only will end up increasing white supremacy.

If we *are* right, neither you nor we want this. The point is, you should never have made a national issue of, and in doing so, have driven a large wedge between cooperative efforts of both bodies.

If you are sincere in your revolutionary goals as they have been stated to us, make an effort to publicly bridge this chasm you have dug—or else step aside and let some truly dedicated people get the revolutionary job done.

This letter can't be said to be an official statement of SDS either nationally or regionally; therefore, it will not bear our signatures, but you can bet your ass it expresses the private and group feelings on the matter in this part of the country.

All power to the people

SDS
Denver–Boulder Area[23]

The Oklahoma City office was concerned about possible New Left attempts to extend the antiwar movement directly into the military compound of Fort Sill. In fact, the director himself followed the situation at Fort Sill and other military bases quite carefully. In a memo to headquarters dated July 25, Oklahoma City reported that a close liaison was being maintained with the 112th Military Intelligence Group. "Bar Letters" (letters in this situation which prohibit return entry to the base by New Left activists) would be issued on an "as needed" basis. Such reentry meant virtually automatic arrest and prosecution for violation of Title 18, Section 1382, U.S. Code.[24] Members of the New Left evidently understood the seriousness of the matter. By year end, no "bar letters" had been issued at Fort Sill. Hoover congratulated Oklahoma City special agents on the apparent success of this COINTELPRO operation.

The Los Angeles field office received authority on July 1 to use the classic "snitch jacket" technique against a Key Activist in the area who had been "active in developing a close working relationship between the Black Panther Party and New Left organizations."[25] In this situation Los Angeles prepared and anonymously distributed a brochure to BPP and New Left leaders. It implied that this person, who had been working with both groups, was actually an undercover police informant. This was a very serious accusation which, although completely untrue, destroyed his reputation among both groups.

The "snitch jacket" technique was an extremely dangerous procedure that caused violence, although no fatalities, in a number of COINTEL-PRO actions. Years later, New Left supervisor C. Moore was asked about its use. He replied that when falsely labeling somebody as an informant, "you would want to make certain that it served a good purpose before you did it." When asked if the fact that no targets were killed was the result of luck or planning, he answered, "Oh, it just happened that way, I am sure."[26]

Another memo, also dated July 1, stated that a Los Angeles organization [*name deleted*] planned to make incoming freshmen "aware of the danger from Students for a Democratic Society (SDS) and other New Left organizations."[27] All new students at Occidental College, Pasadena City College, and the University of Southern California were provided with J. Edgar Hoover's *Fourteen Points on How to Establish the Real Character of An Organization*; other items included materials "which will help them recognize the danger from the left."[28] At Occidental College, 26 percent of incoming freshmen said that they had taken part in some form of demonstrations in high school. About twenty thousand copies of a news article titled "Rebellion," published by Copley News Service, were mailed to teachers, principals, and other educational officials throughout the greater Los Angeles area.[29]

On August 18, Los Angeles received approval to mail this letter to the parents of identified SDS members. Ostensibly, it came from a fictitious organization named "Concerned Educators and Parents (CEAP), Los Angeles, California."

Dear Concerned Parents:
    Perhaps you have heard of CEAP, which has as its main concern the education of our children as they seek knowledge in many colleges and universities here in California. It is composed not only of parents themselves, but also many educators who can and want to teach the student seeking knowledge in our schools.
    We seek justice for all Americans, just as you do.
    We are concerned with the many injustices that are prevalent in our country today . . . just as you are concerned.
    The young tell us that changes must be made, and they are right. . . . *but how to change, how to change*!!!!
    We are sending you part of an article which appeared in the June 28th issue of "National Guardian," an independent liberal newspaper published in New York City, self-described as an "independent radical newsweekly." This issue of "National Guardian" contains an account of the

recently held Students For a Democratic Society (SDS) Convention held in Chicago, Illinois. Perhaps some good came out of this convention but we of CEAP question many of the tactics of SDS and especially those in SDS who condone the use of "pussy power" in gaining their end. When they allow an individual like Chaka Walls of the Black Panther Party to advocate "pussy power" then we at CEAP question the sincerity and integrity of SDS and whether they are the answer for the needs of our students.

And why this letter to you Mr. and Mrs. _____? We at CEAP are sending you this letter and the article from "National Guardian" because your daughter _____, a student at _____, is a member of SDS.

It is assumed that your daughter is attending _____ because she desires an education and hopes that this education can and will help her to make the necessary changes in our country. But must she be sacrificed on the altar of sex because she wants these changes? Must she lie prone for the revolution as Chaka Walls suggests? *We think not.* . . . and hope that you, as concerned parents, agree.

Sincerely[30]

Another mailing went out to college officials. It included a copy of the letter to the parents, and confirmed in a cover letter that the student was indeed an identified member of the local area SDS chapter.

CONCERNED EDUCATORS AND PARENTS
LOS ANGELES, CALIFORNIA

Dear Sir:

Our organization, composed of concerned teachers and parents, is in the process of mailing the attached letter to the parents of young ladies who are attending your school and who are members of SDS.

As there may be inquiries from concerned parents, we of CEAP are making this letter available to you.

Let it be clearly understood that our organization caused this letter to be sent only after many hours of deliberation and soul searching on the part of the members. But I think you must agree that SDS will do anything, will stoop to any tactic just so long as they can completely infiltrate a school, disrupt the educational process and cause nothing but headaches for the school administrators.

We feel, perhaps the word is HOPE, that many of the parents of student members will take note of the danger from the SDS and act accordingly. CEAP feels that a college or university is for education and not disruption.[31]

The Boston field office, working with established undercover sources, identified an SDS faculty member in the Department of Humanities at the Massachusetts Institute of Technology. This instructor was being considered for reappointment for the 1969–1970 academic year—normally a routine procedure. The bureau, however, took action. In a memo dated August 21, 1969, Boston confirmed that its direct contact with department heads at MIT resulted in the cancellation of the instructor's contract. The memo reported that MIT officials were "very grateful" and confirmed that the bureau's participation would be kept confidential.[32] The same memo said that special agents, working with the Cambridge Police Department, had taken photographs of a group of radical students forcibly ejecting tenants from a Harvard University building. The Cambridge Police Department, working without an intelligence unit, was grateful for the FBI assistance, which led to the identification and arrest of a much-sought-after New Left Key Activist. Hoover congratulated Boston for their fine intelligence work.

In the late summer of 1969, the Cleveland field office reported that the local SDS, almost dismembered by internal conflict, had become perhaps even more radical, entering a new phase almost certainly based on "the concept of revolution and increasing militancy." Beyond that, the memo said, it was impossible to even guess what the SDS would do next in northern Ohio or, in fact, anywhere in the country. Cleveland did assure Hoover that every effort would be made "to diminish, disrupt and bring public condemnation" upon the SDS.

Cleveland also reported on the attempt by the SDS to hold its next national convention at either Case Western Reserve University or Bowling Green State University. Special agents made direct contact with the school's officials, and warned them that other institutions that had hosted an SDS convention were "rewarded with damaged property, rowdy and disruptive activity on the campus," as well as unfavorable publicity, upset alumni, and, in at least one situation, litigation. Both colleges informed the SDS "that their facilities were unavailable."[33]

An August 27 Chicago memo reported that the main protest activity in the city concerned the trial of the eight activists indicted after the 1968 Democratic National Convention. The field office explained that the SDS had scheduled a National Action for Chicago from October 8, 1969 to November 1969, which would include demonstrations protesting the "court action against those indicted for violation of the Anti-Riot Laws."[34] A September 9 memo said that highly placed informants had been instructed to do everything possible to encourage and intensify the dispute between the SDS and the BPP, to "prevent their possible reconciliation." They were instructed to use extreme care "to avoid compromising their position by this activity."[35]

The New Orleans field office reported on August 27 that the Spartacist League had dissolved, the Southern Student Organizing Committee merged its efforts with the SDS, and the Revolutionary Youth Movement (RYM) developed in New Orleans. The same memorandum reported on a summer Radical Youth Forum held at the First Unitarian Church. A New Left Key Activist, whose name has been deleted, spoke on the subject of the "movement." Following his speech, there was considerable excitement as members of the Workers Student Alliance/Progressive Labor faction clashed with RYM members in attendance. Informants reported that there was a good deal of shouting between the groups, then some pushing, which was followed by fist fighting. Special agents, of course, obtained a minute-by-minute account of the whole affair. New Orleans reported that the hostility demonstrated "the factionalism present in the New Orleans area New Left." New Orleans planned a variety of COINTELPRO techniques to "capitalize on the differences" between the groups in hopes of rendering them ineffective.[36]

J. Edgar Hoover received a New York memo dated September 18, which explained that the SDS was in confusion. The expulsion of the Progressive Labor Party (PLP) from the SDS during the June National Convention had been traumatic. Elements of what was left of the SDS included the RYM, the Weathermen, and RYM Two. The Worker Student Alliance, comprised mostly of PLP members, was trying to acquire the national identity of the SDS.[37] To aggravate the situation, New York targeted all factions with anonymous inflammatory mailings pitting one group against the other on July 4, August 4, August 11, September 16, and September 19.[38]

In September, the director received a file from New York that reveals just how far the FBI would go to complete a specific COINTELPRO action. In this case, the New Left target was Jerry Clyde Rubin.[39] The information dated from 1965, when the FBI confirmed Rubin's attendance at the national membership conference of the SDS at the University of Illinois. On June 24, 1966, an FBI source confirmed that Rubin attended, as an observer, the National Convention of the CPUSA. His address was discovered to be apartment #16, 5 St. Mark's Place, New York, New York. His Social Security number was 285–32–7441. Undercover informant NYT-7 advised that as of February 23, 1996,

Rubin was a secret member of the PLP in New York. NYT-4 confirmed that an account under [*name deleted*] was opened in October 1969 with a deposit of $62 under the special checking account number 2138794169 at the University branch of the Wells Fargo Bank, Bancroft Way, Berkeley, California. The account, reported to have been used by Rubin, received a deposit in the amount of $340.29 on October 25, 1968, another in the amount of $6812.14 on October 28, 1968. Checks were written in the amount of $425 on November 8, 1968, $6000 on November 11, 1968, and $500 on November 25, 1968. The account was closed on January 8, 1969, with a bank draft made to Amalgamated Bank of New York, 11–15 Union Square, New York City, in the amount of $346.63. NYT-5 reported that check number 28 was made payable to the New York Telephone Company in the amount of $18.70 in payment of a bill for Rubin's telephone number. The check was dated January 27, 1969.

Informant NYT-9 advised that Rubin was a speaker at the Symposium Group of Northwestern University on January 7, 1969. NYT-10 confirmed that Rubin was paid $300 plus expenses. Rubin stayed with [*name deleted*], a member of the Northwestern University SDS. A few days later, NYT-11 advised that Rubin was paid with check number 6289922 drawn on the account of "Student Affairs of Northwestern University." Jerry Rubin and [*name deleted*] endorsed the check. NYT-16 and NYT-17 confirmed that Rubin spoke on April 10, 1969, in the Rodney Room of the Student Center on the University of Delaware campus at Newark, Delaware. His visit was sponsored by the Seminars Committee of the university student government which paid him $800. On April 22, NYT-5 reported that Rubin's checking account at Amalgamated Bank in New York had a balance of $1078.49. An FBI special agent monitored Rubin's appearance at "A Conference on the New Politics" held at Grinnell College in Iowa on April 18. Rubin was paid $424 by the college and the check was made payable to "NY Review Presentations."

On May 1, NYT-19 reported that Rubin spoke at the Meissner Lounge, Freshman Dormitory, Lafayette College, Easton, Pennsylvania. Rubin's expenses and fees were paid by student contributions. On May 2, NYT-14 confirmed that Rubin was paid by student contributions to appear on March 7 at the campus of San Fernando Valley State College. A few days later, on May 7, NYT-14 reported that Rubin was paid $225 by the Associated Student Body Fund of UCLA for his appearance on March 6. NYT-6 advised on May 9 that a regular checking account, 084–003146, was opened at the Chemical Bank, 756 Broadway in New

York, under the title "Rubin Defense Committee." The address given was Rubin's New York apartment. Officers' names were deleted.

On May 13, the Richard Fulton Lecture Agency, 200 West 57th Street in New York confirmed booking Rubin for a speech at Mankato State College in Minnesota for May 16. Rubin's fee was $400. Following this, NYT-21 advised that Rubin was probably paid by student contributions for a speech at Harvard University on May 14. Rubin spoke at the University of Massachusetts on May 12 at Amherst. NYT-20 confirmed that Rubin was paid $400 by the Reorganized Student Association.

NYT-15 reported that Jerry Rubin had requested $1,000 for an appearance at Beloit College in Wisconsin. Sources confirmed that he was paid $200 for this speech on March 17. Cleveland advised that they were unable to determine any financial information regarding Rubin's speech at Case Western Reserve University. On June 10, NYT-5 reported, for reasons not determined, that the Amalgamated Bank of New York would no longer accept checks made payable to the Jerry Rubin fund.

Rubin spoke at Penn State on February 13, and his fee could not be determined by NYT-12 reporting on June 13. The bureau was unable to determine Rubin's speaking fees for appearances at NYU, State University of New York, Bowling Green, University of Cincinnati, and Rutgers Law School during the summer of 1969. NYT-8 reported that the Rubin Defense fund, account number 084–003146 at the Chemical Bank, had a July 31 balance of $1,114.41. Less than a week later, NYT-5 advised that the name of the Jerry Rubin Defense fund account had been changed to the Social Education Foundation—Jerry Rubin fund.[40]

The Rubin file is one of the largest of all the New Left COINTEL-PRO. New York recommended that it be submitted, after Hoover's review, to the IRS to assist in their investigation of Rubin's failure to file income tax returns.

The bureau continued to concern itself about a possible alliance between the SDS and the BPP long after the SDS was a power in the New Left. The San Francisco field office proposed and received approval on September 5 for a mailing to a Black Panther newspaper in the Bay Area. The letter expresses dissatisfaction with the SDS and asserts that blacks were being used by the white New Left.

EDITOR:
    What's with this bullshit SDS out fit? I'll tell you what they has finally showed there true color WHITE. They are just like the commies and all the other white radical groups that suck up to the blacks and use us. We

voted at our meeting in Oakland for community control over the pigs but SDS says no. Well we can do with out them mothers. We can do it by ourselfs.

OFF THE PIGS   POWER TO THE PEOPLE

—Soul brother Jake[41]

In the August 16, 1969, issue of the *Guardian*, Black Panther leader David Hilliard criticized the SDS in violent terms. The Newark field office proposed quoting the letter in a fictional reply from an SDS leader to the Jersey City BPP headquarters.[42] Newark anonymously mailed this letter on August 25.

To Former Comrade [*name deleted*]

As one of "those little bourgeois, snooty nose"—"little schoolboys"— "little sissies" Dave Hilliard spoke of in the Guardian of 8/16/69, I would like to say that you and the rest of you black racists can go to hell. I stood shoulder to shoulder with Carl Nichols last year in Military Park in Newark and got my a— whipped by a Newark pig all for the cause of the wineheads like you and the rest of the black pussycats that call themselves Panthers. Big deal; you have to have a three hour educational session just to teach those ✲✲✲ (you all know what that means don't you! It's the first word your handkerchief head mamma teaches you) how to spell it.

Who the hell set you and the Panthers up as the vanguard of the revolutionary and disciplinary group. You can tell all those wineheads you associate with that you'll kick no one's "✲✲✲" because you'd have to take a three year course in spelling to know what an a— is and three more years to be taught where it's located.

Julius Lester called the BPP the vanguard (that's leader) organization so international whore Cleaver calls him racist, now when full allegiance is not given to the Panthers, again racist. What the hell do you want? Are you getting this? Are you lost? If you're not digging then you're really hopeless.

Oh yes! We are not concerned about Hilliard's threats.

Brains will win over brawn. The way the Panthers have retaliated against US is another indication. The score:

US   –6
Panthers   –0

Why, I read an article in the Panther paper where a California Panther sat in his car and watched his friend get shot by Karenga's group and what did he do? He run back and write a full page story about how tough the Panthers are and what they're going to do. Ha Ha— B—— S—— .

Goodbye [*name deleted*]—and watch out. Karenga's coming.
                              "Right On" as they say.⁴³
                              No signature will be given.

In a memo written on August 4, the Washington field office advised headquarters that the SDS regional office in Washington, as well as the chapters at American University and Georgetown, were, to all intents and purposes, neutralized. This successful COINTELPRO action, the field office added, was carried out over a period of eight to ten months and utilized the techniques of causing dissension "among the SDS in the WDC area, utilizing sources well versed in the political differences of the New Left."⁴⁴

The FBI, it seems, was curiously out of step with the major developments in the antiwar movement during the summer of 1969. At least forty COINTELPRO documents written in the summer deal with the faltering SDS. Hoover was nearly obsessed with the potential of an SDS/Black Panther partnership.

The New Mobilization Committee to End the War in Vietnam is not even mentioned in the COINTELPRO files until August 21, about six weeks after its formation in Cleveland.⁴⁵ This memo sent to the field offices in Chicago, Cleveland, Detroit, Los Angeles, New York, Philadelphia, San Francisco, and Washington announced that New Mobe was sponsoring "a massive antiwar demonstration in Washington D.C., 11/15/69."⁴⁶ Turnout was estimated to be a hundred thousand. The memo also reported, incorrectly, that the Black United Front (BUF) had sent a letter demanding that New Mobe pay the BUF $1 per demonstrator. If New Mobe did not agree to pay BUF this ransom (or bribe), the Black United Front would disrupt the demonstration in Washington. Shortly thereafter, the memo reported, the black organization had reduced its demands to a flat $25,000, half to be paid immediately, and half prior to November 15.⁴⁷

Additionally, according to the memo, BUF had demanded a position on the policy-making committee of New Mobe, and the entire matter had started a furious debate within New Mobe. The Washington field office recommended, and the bureau agreed, that this was "an ideal situation to exploit through the Counterintelligence Program." The eight recipient field offices were instructed to submit proposals on this matter by "8/29/69 without fail."⁴⁸ Follow-up memos dated August 22 and September 5 advised that the New Mobe would be placed in an impossible situation: either meet the BUF demands, which would weaken the organization, or lose black support. "It is conceivable," the August 22 memo said, "that the resulting situation might force the NWC to cancel its mass rally in Washington D.C., 11/15/69."[49] Incredibly, the BUF was actually a hoax. The FBI wrote the letter. Special agent Robert Wall remembers, "The letter we composed was approved by the bureau's counterintelligence desk, and was signed with the forged signature of a leader of the black group. Later, through informants in the NMC [New Mobe], we learned that the letter had caused a great deal of confusion."[50]

Oddly enough, there is no mention of the Vietnam Moratorium Committee in any of the COINTELPRO documents prior to the target date of October 15. One internal headquarters memo from C. D. Brennan to W. C. Sullivan dated October 9 does discuss the SMC's plan for a national student strike scheduled for November 14—the day before New Mobe's March Against Death in Washington, D.C.[51]

Brennan's memo points out that the three national officers of the SMC, Carol Lipman, Danny Rosenshire, and Don Gurvewitz, were all Security Index subjects. "SMC," the memo asserts, "is completely dominated and controlled by the Young Socialist's Alliance." Brennan recommended that this information be distributed to friendly media at the earliest possible date.[52]

In the meantime, the impending VMC demonstration continued to gain momentum—far more than anyone thought possible. David Mixner remembers, "In June, I was very cynical about our chances for success." However, in the fall, when Mixner began to visit college campuses, "That's all anybody can talk about." Indeed, he recalled, "The period of giving Nixon a choice is over."[53] Activist Sidney Lens remembers that "Ron Young, Sid Peck, Dick Fernandez and myself spoke at universities in sixty cities, coast to coast, mobilizing for both autumn actions."[54]

On September 21, as noted, a series of full-page fund-raising display ads began to appear in the *New York Times*. These powerful statements were prepared by one of the nation's leading advertising agencies. One caption read, "To be against the war in Vietnam and to do nothing about it is indefensible."[55] On September 23, several of the nation's most prominent college professors—including John Kenneth Galbraith, Noam Chomsky, and Hans Morgenthau—issued a statement supporting the VMC student boycott of classes for October 15. "The majority of Americans," it said, "recognize the senselessness of Vietnam and desire to end that war."[56] A *New York Times* editorial of October 7, titled

"Freedom on Campus! October 15," said that the impending Vietnam Moratorium was testimony to "the anguish the war stirs in the intellectual community—and especially among young people."[57]

By October 10, the Vietnam Moratorium Committee had a staff of more than sixty, virtually all of them under twenty-five years of age. Most were in daily contact with field organizers, of whom there were seventy-five hundred. The *New York Times* observed that "in their own cluttered way they are organizing with precision what is expected to be the largest-ever nationwide student protest."[58]

A CIA document prepared in October of 1969 reported that the agency saw the VMC as "shaping up to be the most widely supported public action in American history."[59]

On October 11, a group of Protestant, Roman Catholic, and Jewish theologians and educators released a statement in full support of the VMC. Dr. R. H. Edwin Espy, general secretary of the National Council of Churches, told reporters that "never before has there been an observation in which the religious forces of the United States have been in greater accord."[60] The next day, the *New York Times* reported, "Not since the civil rights march of 1963 has Washington been caught in a maelstrom of popular protest such as now buffets politicians on the Vietnam issue."[61]

Vietnam Moratorium Day, October 15, practically defied comparison. *Life Magazine* called it "a display without parallel, the largest expression of public dissent ever seen in this country."[62] One researcher described the day that had "attained a diversity, persuasiveness, and dignity unprecedented in the history of popular protest."[63] Fully one-third of the institutions of higher learning in America participated in some way with teach-in, vigil, and rally. The marches were immense: a hundred thousand at Boston Common, two hundred and fifty thousand in New York, a hundred thousand in Chicago, fifty thousand in Washington; the national total was in the millions. Many were demonstrating against the war for the first time. One of the leaders, Fred Halstead, said, "The antiwar movement had indeed made some potential changes in America."[64]

Still to come were the Student Strike, the March Against Death, and the Washington protest rally sponsored by the New Mobilization Committee to End the War In Vietnam.

On November 11, SMC ran full-page newspaper ads in major cities appealing to all Americans to support or participate in the great events taking place during the weekend of November 15. The *New York Times* quoted Sidney Peck, a New Mobe official, as saying, "Those who are not willing to be non-violent are not invited."[65] On November 13, the *New York Times* reported on the arrival of nine thousand federal troops in the nation's capital—to support more than thirty-seven hundred metropolitan police officers.[66]

The March Against Death was a sober affair. On the night of November 13, over forty-six thousand people made their way across the Arlington Memorial Bridge in single file, at the rate of twelve hundred per hour. Each carried a lighted candle and the name of a fallen American soldier. They walked for four miles, passing the illuminated White House. The event seemed to many a moving testimony to the nation's outrage and almost overwhelming sense of grief.

On November 15, a crowd estimated at more than half a million paraded down Pennsylvania Avenue and to a rally at the Washington monument—the largest march ever seen in the nation's capital. A reporter at the scene described it as "a solid moving carpet of humanity extended from the foot of the Capitol, ten long blocks up Pennsylvania Avenue to the Treasury Building, four blocks down 15th Street and out across the grassy hill on which the Washington Monument stands."[67]

There were simultaneous events across the nation, which included the more than one hundred moderate and radical New Left organizations which comprised the New Mobe. More than one hundred thousand marched in San Francisco—the largest single gathering ever on the west coast. Judy Droz, then twenty-three, fully captured the moment: "There is no light at the end of the tunnel, only the darkness that overcame my husband."[68] Eileen Garner, then a twenty-year-old student at the University of Maryland, expressed the emotion of the day and her generation: "Nixon is trying to achieve goals in the Vietnam War that this country just can't achieve any more—yet people are still dying."[69]

A review of contemporaneous COINTELPRO documents reveals an astonishing lack of concentration on the two major peace offensives occurring during the second half of 1969. For example, on October 7, Buffalo received permission to anonymously target an area New Left group known as the Buffalo Nine Defense Committee.[70] San Francisco's proposed distribution of twenty thousand brochures describing the friction between New Mobe and the SWP during the November 15 peace rally was denied as being "too risky."[71] On November 6, 1969, San Antonio was permitted to send an anonymous letter to the *Daily Texan* pointing out that National Mobe events generally resulted in violence.[72] A recommended San Antonio anonymous letter to Texas Attorney General Waggoner Carr to advise that the Vietnam Moratorium was planned in Cuba by Bernadine Dohrn, of the SDS, was turned down on December 18.[73] New York received permission to conduct small anonymous mailings on October 8, October 15, and December 1—none dealt directly with National Mobe or the VMC.[74] Cleveland submitted memos on October 3, October 13, and December 31.[75] New Mobe was mentioned in only one sentence. These particular COINTELPRO memos are noteworthy, however, because the violent Weatherman faction of the SDS is mentioned for the first time. Boston also mentioned the Weathermen several times, but did not bring up VMC or New Mobe even once in five memos from October 29 through the end of the year. Detroit, in six memos, mentioned the Weathermen several times, but not the two fall peace offensives. While FBI special agents were certainly out in force during the October 15 and November 13–15 demonstrations, there are almost no COINTELPRO documents confirming their activity.

Interestingly, a memo of November 7 from C. D. Brennan to W. C. Sullivan reveals how bureau headquarters ineptly handled an attempt to influence the world of the antiwar movement in the United States. Brennan advised Sullivan that the "Communist Party U.S.A. sent a clandestine message to the Government of North Vietnam giving grossly exaggerated figures of participants in 10/15/69 demonstrations protesting war in Vietnam."[76] Three days later the director submitted "a draft of an article which presents the true picture" to legal attachés in London and Tokyo.[77] The lengthy draft said that the Vietnam Moratorium Day attracted only small crowds—only 1/4000 of the general population and one-sixth of college-age youth in the United States. The demonstration, the draft said, did not reflect "a mass cry for immediate withdrawal from Vietnam," but one from those next in line for military service in a war "they cannot understand."[78]

London advised headquarters on November 18 that the October moratorium was "no longer newsworthy because of the pending November one." If the FBI material had reached London on October 17, it would have been usable, but at this point, London press contacts "would not be in the least bit interested." London told the FBI to submit future material of this type immediately to the United States Information Agency and request submission "to pertinent Embassies for the wireless file."[79] Tokyo told the FBI that "to present the facts now, so long after the actual demonstration, would have no impact."[80]

By the end of 1969, it appeared as if the war in Vietnam would go on forever. Indeed, it had been twenty-three years—the span of an entire generation—since the first American soldier had been killed there.

NOTES

1. Nancy Zaroulis and Gerald Sullivan, *Who Spoke Up? American Protest against the War in Vietnam 1963–1975* (Garden City, NY: Doubleday, 1984), p. 243.

2. Ibid., pp. 244–245.

3. Ibid., p. 245.

4. Ibid., p. 246.

5. Ibid.

6. Ibid., p. 258.

7. Ibid., p. 267.

8. Kirkpatrick Sale, *SDS* (New York: Random House, 1973), p. 640.

9. Fred Halstead, *Out Now! A Participant's Account of the Movement in the U.S. against the Vietnam War* (New York: Pathfinder Press, 1978), p. 475.

10. "State Dinner in Los Angeles," *New York Times*, Aug. 14, 1969, p. 22.

11. "To Establish Justice, to Insure Domestic Tranquility; Final Report," National Commission on the Causes and Prevention of Violence (Washington, D.C.: Government Printing Office, 1969).

12. FBI Memorandum, Headquarters to Baltimore Field Office, June 16, 1969.

13. FBI Memorandum, Baltimore Field Office to Headquarters, Aug. 26, 1969.

14. Ibid.

15. Ibid.

16. FBI Memorandum, Columbia Field Office to Headquarters, July 31, 1969.

17. FBI Memorandum, Headquarters to Columbia Field Office, Aug. 7, 1969.

18. FBI Memorandum, Knoxville Field Office to Headquarters, June 24, 1969.

19. FBI Memorandum, Headquarters to Knoxville Field Office, July 4, 1969.

20. FBI Memorandum, Headquarters to Denver Field Office, July 31, 1969.

21. FBI Memorandum, Denver Field Office to Headquarters, Aug. 26, 1969.

22. FBI Memorandum, Denver Field Office to Headquarters, Sept. 26, 1969.

23. Ibid.

24. FBI Memorandum, Oklahoma City Field Office to Headquarters, July 25, 1969.

25. FBI Memorandum, Headquarters to Los Angeles Field Office, July 1, 1969.

26. Senate Select Committee to Study Governmental Operations with Respect to Intelligence Investigations, "COINTELPRO: The FBI's Covert Action Programs Against American Citizens," Book III, 94th Cong. 2d Sess., Nov. 3, 1975, p. 9.

27. FBI Memorandum, Los Angeles Field Office to Headquarters, July 1, 1969.

28. Ibid.

29. Ibid.

30. FBI Memorandum, Headquarters to Los Angeles Field Office, Aug. 18, 1969.

31. Ibid.

32. FBI Memorandum, Boston Field Office to Headquarters, Aug. 21, 1969.

33. FBI Memorandum, Cleveland Field Office to Headquarters, Aug. 29, 1969.

34. FBI Memorandum, Chicago Field Office to Headquarters, Aug. 27, 1969.

35. FBI Memorandum, Chicago Field Office to Headquarters, Sept. 9, 1969.

36. FBI Memorandum, New Orleans Field Office to Headquarters, Aug. 27, 1969.

37. FBI Memorandum, New York Field Office to Headquarters, Sept. 18, 1969.

38. Ibid.

39. FBI Memorandum, New York Field Office to Headquarters, Sept. 22, 1969.

40. FBI Memorandum, New York Field Office to Headquarters, Sept. 9, 1969.

41. FBI Memorandum, San Francisco Field Office to Headquarters, Aug. 27, 1969; Headquarters to San Francisco Field Office, Sept. 5, 1969.

42. FBI Memorandum, Newark Field Office to Headquarters, Aug. 25, 1969.

43. FBI Memorandum, FBI Headquarters to Newark Field Office, Sept. 16, 1969.

44. FBI Memorandum, Washington Field Office to Headquarters, Aug. 4, 1969.

45. FBI Memorandum, Headquarters to Field Offices, Aug. 21, 1969.

46. Ibid.

47. Ibid.

48. Ibid.

49. FBI Memorandum, Washington Field Office to Headquarters, Aug. 22, 1969; C. D. Brennan to W. C. Sullivan, Sept. 5, 1969.

50. *New York Review of Books*, Jan. 27, 1972.

51. FBI Memorandum, C. D. Brennan to W. C. Sullivan, Oct. 9, 1969.

52. Ibid.

53. John Kifner, "Protest Leaders Hope to Renew Students' Opposition to the War," *New York Times*, Sept. 16, 1969, p. 32.

54. Sidney Lens, *Unrepentant Radical. An American Activist's Account of Five Turbulent Decades* (Boston: Beacon Press, 1980), p. 350.

55. Steven V. Roberts, "Students Trial Seen as Vital," *New York Times*, Sept. 21, 1969, p. 46.

56. "Professors Back Student Boycott," *New York Times*, Sept. 23, 1969, p. 7.

57. "Freedom on Campus: Oct. 15," *New York Times*, Oct. 7, 1969, p. 46.

58. David E. Rosenbaum, "The Moratorium Organizers: Cluttered Precision," *New York Times*, Oct. 10, 1969, p. 12.

59. Special Information Report (Special): 15 October 1969 Activities," Oct. 10, 1969.

60. George Dugan, "Religious Leaders Endorse Vietnam Moratorium," *New York Times*, Oct. 11, 1969, p. 25.

61. "Congress Reacts to the Rising Chorus of Vietnam Dissent," *New York Times*, Oct. 12, 1969, p. 1.

62. Halstead, *Out Now!*, p. 488.

63. Charles DeBenedetti and Charles Chatfield, *An American Ordeal: The Antiwar Movement of the Vietnam Era* (Syracuse: Syracuse University Press, 1990), p. 255.

64. Halstead, *Out Now!*, p. 489.

65. David E. Rosenbaum, "2 Antiwar Groups Strive for Unity," *New York Times*, Oct. 22, 1969, pp. 1, 16.

66. Paul Delaney, "9,000 Troops Due in Capital Area," *New York Times*, Nov. 13, 1969, pp. 1, 32.

67. John Herber, "250,000 War Protesters Stage Peaceful Rally in Washington; Militants Stir Clashes Later," *New York Times*, Nov. 16, 1969, p. 60.

68. David E. Rosenbaum, "March Against Death Begun by Thousands in Washington," *New York Times*, Nov. 14, 1969, pp. 1, 20.

69. Peter Grose, "Marchers Give Reasons Why," *New York Times*, Nov. 15, 1969, pp. 1, 20.

70. FBI Memorandum, Headquarters to Buffalo Field Office, Oct. 7, 1969.

71. FBI Memorandum, Headquarters to San Francisco Field Office, Nov. 13, 1969.

72. FBI Memorandum, Headquarters to San Antonio Field Office, Nov. 6, 1969.

73. FBI Memorandum, Headquarters to San Antonio Field Office, Dec. 18, 1969.

74. FBI Memorandum, Headquarters to New York Field Office, Oct. 8, 1969; Oct. 15, 1969; Dec. 1, 1969.

75. FBI Memorandum, Cleveland Field Office to Headquarters, Oct. 3, 1969; Oct. 13, 1969; Dec. 31, 1969.

76. FBI Memorandum, C. D. Brennan to W. C. Sullivan, Nov. 7, 1969.

77. FBI Memorandum, Headquarters to Legats London and Tokyo, Nov. 10, 1969.

78. Ibid.

79. FBI Memorandum, Legat, London to Headquarters, Nov. 10, 1969.

80. FBI Memorandum, Legat, Tokyo to Headquarters, Dec. 12, 1969.

7

Cambodia, Kent State, Etc.

"Dear FBI: 'Let your foot be seldom in your neighbor's house, lest he become weary of you and despise you.' " Proverbs 25:17

— *William Sloan Coffin, Jr.*

By January 1, 1970, there were 472,000 American troops in Vietnam. This was down from the total of more than 525,000 reached during the Johnson administration, but still a considerable force. Richard Nixon, almost certainly pondering the matter every day in the Oval Office, later wrote that "as 1970 began, our intelligence indicated that Communist infiltration from North into South Vietnam was increasing substantially."[1] With this consideration in Nixon's mind, there was little doubt that the killing of Americans and Vietnamese troops, at a greater level than in 1967, would continue into the foreseeable future. In addition, the Nixon administration had been conducting secret bombing raids into Cambodia since March of 1969.

The antiwar movement was, in early 1970, in a state of fatigue. The two great peace offensives of late 1969 had exhausted the New Left financially, physically, and emotionally. The SDS still maintained a mailing list of more than seventy thousand, but much of its power and influence was gone. The Vietnam Moratorium Committee ceased to exist on April 19, 1970. New Mobe was in a state of philosophical transition.

It seemed to many across the extraordinary New Left political spectrum that, in spite of their gargantuan efforts, nothing had really changed. At this juncture, thirty-eight percent of Americans approved of the Nixon administration's policy in Vietnam. Seven percent felt that the war should be expanded. Many activists felt, as one researcher wrote, that the goal of the antiwar movement in early 1970 had shifted slightly: "not to transform America in a revolt over Vietnam, but rather to save the society from the effects of a further war."[2] Nevertheless, in spite of the troop level reductions, a "further war" in Vietnam was continuing with stupendous expenditures in firepower, manpower, and casualties.

Protest activities were, of course, still occurring. For example, on January 6 at the University of Wisconsin, two campus ROTC facilities were firebombed and an army reserve training center was destroyed.

In February 3,308 members of the Student Mobilization Committee met in Cleveland to plan antiwar strategy. Interestingly, this was the "largest working conference in the history of the antiwar movement."[3] Thus, even though the SDS, the VMC, and the New Mobe were catching their breath or disbanding, the Cleveland SMC Conference gave every indication that the war was by no means forgotten. The *Cleveland Press* said of the SMC conference that "despite the emotional fever with which most students embraced their ideas an almost overwhelming democracy prevailed."[4]

In an event no way connected to the SMC, an explosive being assembled at the New York bomb factory of the Weathermen, the violent SDS splinter group, accidentally exploded and killed Ted Gold, Terry Robbins, and Diana Oughton. The Greenwich Village townhouse was completely destroyed, but the aftershocks were tremendous. The blast ended the possibility that the New Left and the antiwar movement would ever be seen by the public as anything but "mindlessly violent."[5]

On April 11, the White House announced a dramatic increase in the level of surveillance and undercover operations to be conducted by the nation's intelligence agencies—principally the FBI—in an effort to combat the rising violence created by militant antiwar groups. What the White House did not say, because the FBI New Left COINTELPRO was top secret within the bureau, was that the nation's largest investigative agency had been making enormous and fully disruptive counterintelligence efforts against the New Left for at least two years. Further, as we have seen, other intelligence programs conducted by the government had also been in place for two decades with full White House knowledge.

Nevertheless, following the Cleveland conference, the SMC moved aggressively and, demonstrating considerable managerial skills, orchestrated an impressive nationwide student strike against the war on April 15—the largest such action since Vietnam Moratorium Day. The numbers, assisted to some degree by support from New Mobe and the Parade Committee, were considerable: Chicago had twenty-five thousand, San Francisco twenty thousand, Boston sixty-five thousand, New York thirty-five thousand, Houston six thousand, Seattle eight thousand, Detroit eight thousand, and so forth. Some schools shut down completely. Half of all New York City high school students went out on strike. A number of ROTC facilities were hit hard by strikers as the event moved across the republic—in large measure as a harbinger of things to come in May.

The FBI New Left COINTELPRO continued, of course, with no interruption. In Boston, special agents discovered an area Weathermen enclave on the top floor of an apartment house at 509 Franklin Street in Cambridge. A March 6, 1970, memo stated: "The bureau should note the eviction procedures and eventual movement of the Weathermen from this address are the result of investigative activity over the past six weeks by agents of this office." Sources had indicated that as many as twenty radicals "were observed in this residence at any given time living in a communal fashion."[6]

As soon as the eviction was completed, the FBI men, at the invitation of the landlord, moved in to photograph the physical condition of the collective, which was "in shambles with lewd, obscene and revolutionary slogans displayed on the walls."[7] The publicity potential was obvious. On February 25, Boston furnished all twenty-eight graphic photographs, together with suggestive commentary, to [*name deleted*], a free-lance lecturer and writer on extremist activities. At least one prominent New England paper ran feature articles with photographs that were, as Hoover noted, "derogatory in nature and might serve to neutralize Weathermen." Headquarters considered using the photographs "in training conferences, etc., concerning the Weathermen faction of the SDS."[8]

The Atlanta field office reported to headquarters that the area's two major New Left factions—Socialist Workers Party/Young Socialists Alliance and Atlanta Revolutionary Youth Movement/Students for a Democratic Society—had evidently put aside their acrimony and joined forces in a new spirit of cooperation. Sources reported that the groups planned to make the February 21 visit of Spiro Agnew to Atlanta as unpleasant as possible. Atlanta had advised, on January 21, that efforts should be made "not to let these two major factions in the Atlanta antiwar movement become overly friendly and cooperative."[9] Thus, the following anonymous letter was mailed on February 11 to a member of the Revolutionary Youth Movement.

Dear [*name deleted*],

How can you RYM people be so naive and gullible as to continue to let the Trots run the whole show their way as they did again at the antiwar conference at Emory. It looks like you could see that they have the whole thing figured out, and have all the answers before these so-called "conferences" even start.

As a communist, which they say you are, you sure don't show any knowledge of communist tactics. Why don't you check out your Trot friends on the night before your "conference," and you might find that they are together, busy with plans as to how they will manipulate the coalition to their own specifications—being gracious enough to throw you a few scraps to keep you happy.

Our revolution is a long way off if we have to wait for them to do it their way—they've been carrying the ball for years, now it should be someone else's turn.

—A Friend[10]

A follow-up Atlanta memo could only report that "no indication that receipt of same [the anonymous letter] by addressee has resulted in any change of relationship or policy."[11]

The Buffalo field office also attempted to disrupt the local antiwar movement with an anonymous letter. Buffalo reported that tension had been developing locally between the area chapter of Youth Against War and Fascism (YAWF) and the SDS chapter of the State University of New York at Buffalo. Of prime importance was an SDS key activist named Stanton, an individual prone to violence. Buffalo recommended a letter, on YAWF letterhead, designed to ridicule Stanton and infer that he was really a police informant—an explosive accusation. Incredibly, Buffalo suggested that the letter should be "distributed surreptitiously by Special Agent personnel on campus."[12] The director probably couldn't believe what he was reading. His March 3 reply memo left little doubt about his opinion of the proposal: "Such a procedure is extremely dangerous and this procedure is not being approved."[13]

In early January, the director learned through Los Angeles undercover sources that a female SDS activist had been "found to be suffering from gonorrhea and possibly tuberculosis."[14] Since what was left of the SDS was headquartered in Chicago, Hoover contacted that field office on January 2, 1970, and instructed them to "determine whether carriers of infectious diseases are required to report their infection to local agencies." He further instructed Chicago to determine how this information might be used to neutralize the SDS by making it public. He suggested that Chicago should consider furnishing this information to "a cooperative and reliable news service representative who could possibly use it as the basis for an investigation for news value."[15]

Chicago evidently didn't think too highly of the director's idea. On January 27, the field office advised Hoover that "there are no local or state ordinances requiring infected persons" to report to local health authorities. Further, Chicago felt that providing information regarding the infection of an SDS leader to friendly media "could endanger [*name deleted*] as this information has been discussed in highly confidential conversations with their doctors or close associates and is not freely discussed by these individuals."[16] The matter was dropped.

On March 31, Chicago advised Hoover that as many as twelve Weathermen would almost certainly be federally indicted by April 2 for violation of Anti-Riot Laws. Nine were FBI Key Activists. This action "will effectively remove the national leadership of Weathermen." Further, six female members of the organization were now "Bureau fugitives since they failed to appear in a local court on March 16."[17]

In a report to headquarters dated April 8, the Cincinnati field office reported that the Weathermen were the only New Left activists in the area, and that they were limited to two small communes. The one in Columbus was staffed by about "seven hard core Weathermen." The other, in Cincinnati, was staffed by as many as ten. Neither group had been able to mount any significant activity in the area. Cincinnati did add that the "underground tactics"[18] of the group, and rapid movement from one commune to another, made the obtaining of reliable information from undercover informants far more difficult.

In the same memo, Cincinnati informed the director of efforts to monitor two underground newspapers in the area, the *Independent Eye* and the *Queen City Express*. Special agents had little difficulty in obtaining complete bank records for each—as well as payroll, advertising, circulation, earnings, and tax information. The FBI also obtained the closely guarded names of the newspaper's financial backers—who would, of course, themselves become COINTELPRO targets.

The Detroit field office wrote to the director on February 24, 1970, advising him of developments at the University of Michigan. A previous

COINTELPRO action involved the notification of Michigan's Board of Regents of the faculty leadership for area New Left groups. The memo noted that several young faculty activists were not given tenure. Additionally, "confidential sources close to the U of M Administration" had advised that a tougher disciplinary line had recently been taken against New Left elements by the university. The president's action "was brought on by the fact that he was contacted personally by every member of the Board of Regents at the U of M who reportedly counseled him to react vigorously to this current round of New Left disruption."[19]

It was about at this same time—spring of 1970—that the document shown below was drafted. This particular document, evidently prepared by the Detroit field office, was issued nationwide under the title "FBI COINTELPRO 1968–1970 Ann Arbor, Memoranda on Master Plan for Disruption of New Left Etc." It demonstrates, in chronological order, the extraordinary efforts undertaken by the Detroit field office to disrupt and hopefully neutralize the New Left in Ann Arbor, Michigan. It seems almost certain that Hoover ordered the preparation of this master plan to show other FBI field offices how a successful COINTELPRO operation should be handled.

FBI COINTEL PRO 1968–1970 ANN ARBOR
As Sent Nationwide

Memoranda on Master Plan for Disruption of New Left Etc.

a) 4/9/68: Outline theory "expose disrupt neutralize New Left." 2 pps. Theory

b) 5/10/68 Asks for suggestions how "disrupt organized activity." 3 pps

c) May 22, 1968 request info discredit New Left re Police Brutality Friendly Media

d) May 23, 1968 letter attached to above re Police Brute, Left Immorality, college Administrator attitudes, possible embarrassment of New Left, "a realistic imaginative approach is solicited" 2 pps.

e) Request Identity members ringleaders New Left college campus, increased coverage, anonymous letters State Senator, Tangible results disrupting Radical Education Project location. 4/28/68 SDS disrupt 3 pps

f) 5/29/68—Campus newspaper items "radical profanity . . . repulsive" clips for dissemination legislators. News Media 1 p

g) 7/3/68 (July) Cover letter summary Disruption tactics

h) 7/5/68 MASTER PLAN COINTEL 12 point program disrupt new left 3 pps: Leaflet obnoxious pix, instigating personal animosities, informant paranoia, depravity press clip Marijuana arrests, anonymous letters parents employers anonymous letters faculty & grad assistants to legislators regents press "A concerned Alumni . . . Taxpayer," cooperative press contacts, SDS-YSA-SWP-PLP

i) hostility exploited, coffee house marijuana media law enforcement, cartoon photo anonymous ridicule,misinformation. 3 pps Wash. to All Bureaus.

i) 10/7/68 Obscene inscription placard persons notify students parents school officials Cover letter 1 p.

j) 10/9/68—Disrupt New Left Moral Depravity . . . Field Offices "urged to be particularly alert" . . . obscene display . . . parents local press . . . insidious movement 2 pps

k) 10/26/68—Fictitious name letter communist to Regents mass media on Al Haber University activist YUCDFP 3 pps.

l) 2/7/69—Investigate REP's Al Haber for disaffection

m) 5/27/69—Disrupt Radical Education Projection location 1 page

n) 8/6/69—Disrupt REP 7 SDS vehicles' Detroit trips for films Disrupt SDS conference facilities 2 pps

o) 8/25/69—Disrupt SDS/Black Panthers Detroit forged anonymous letter 2 pps

p) 8/28/69—Disrupt New Mobe Committee thru provocateur's demands $25,000 anonymous letter D.C.to White Panther party from BPP pressure MOBE for money publish in Michigan Daily 2 pps

q) Review Haber Backsliding 10/25/68[20]

On February 18, the Indianapolis field office committed the cardinal sin of telling Hoover that the area COINTELPRO operations should be terminated since the only functioning New Left groups in the area consisted of the Young Socialists Alliance and the Student Mobilization Committee.[21] That was not something the director wanted to hear. He shot back that "every evidence points to the fact that militant Leftists are continuing their efforts to disrupt higher education."[22] Even the most naive special agent knew it was time to reactivate the program—immediately. Questioning the director's judgment was not healthy.

Confidential informants advised the Washington, D.C., field office that animosity was developing within the SM Committee membership over the issue of the group's control by the Young Socialists Alliance. Special agents saw this as an opportunity for a COINTELPRO disruptive action. Informants obtained SMC letterhead, envelopes, and an SMC mailing list. Hoover approved an anonymous mailing designed to

attack "the SMC national and regional leadership for the way it domi-
nates college students within its membership."[23] On March 3, the field
office hand-addressed each envelope. Every precaution was "taken to
avoid any future embarrassment to the Bureau."[24] By coincidence, on
the day the mailing was completed, "[*name deleted*] ha[d] led a group
of dissident students into a new regional office" and this new organization would "be called Students Against the System (SAS)."[25]

In memos dated January 7 and April 8, the Seattle field office advised
that the departure of an SDS key activist [*name deleted*] led to the
creation of three smaller New Left groups. The Weathermen faction,
while weak, did "exercise control of the duplicating machines and office
equipment which was formerly available to SDS members when it was
operating as a campus group." The memos added, however, that 60
percent of the known Seattle SDS Weathermen, a group of about twenty,
were "either in jail or out on bond in connection with local charges."
The second group, based at the University of Washington, became part
of the Revolutionary Youth Movement. A third group, the Seattle Liberation Front, had succeeded "in attracting a large number of 'street'
people and high school age youth to participate in rallies, demonstrations, and other activities." Seattle anticipated a future COINTELPRO
action that would "capitalize on the differences" between these groups.[26]

Headquarters received information from the San Francisco field office
on February 18 regarding a New Left activist, [*name deleted*], who had
been placed on two years' probation in November of 1968 on charges of
resisting arrest and interfering with a law officer. One of the conditions
of his parole was that "he not engage in any further unlawful disturbance
or any unlawful activity." Area special agents reviewed a copy of the February–March issue of *The Movement* and discovered that [*name deleted*
] was a participant "as the people's prosecutor in a people's trial of the
American Army held at the University of Washington at Seattle on January 21, 1970, at which time the Army was sentenced to death."[27]

San Francisco received authority on March 3 to furnish the Adult
Probation Office of the County of San Francisco with information "relating to [*name deleted*]'s participation in New Left activities at the University of Washington on January 21 and with material he has written
while on probation."[28] San Francisco also hoped to bring this information to the judge who had originally sentenced [*name deleted*].

San Francisco also reported to headquarters that special agents had
been in contact with the IRS's Exempt Organizations Section, Field
Audit Division, which was evidently quite interested in information on

New Left groups that had applied for or received tax-exempt status. These included the Glide Memorial Church, the American Friends Service Committee, the San Francisco Mime Troupe, and the Bay Area Peace Action Council. San Francisco strongly suggested that New Left intelligence information in bureau files would be of great value to the IRS "in their effort to deny or expel organizations from their tax exempt status." This would also deny deductions for contributors to New Left organizations.[29] On April 3, San Francisco reported that a liaison had been established with the "Tax Exempt Squad of the IRS," and that it was "anticipated we will work with them on individual organizations and individuals involved in the New Left movement."[30]

In a very unusual memo dated April 30, 1970, San Diego reported that an extremist or an extremist group, apparently right wing, had decided to take action against the New Left. On the night of April 29, a "person or persons unknown drove by the Movement For a Democratic Military (MDM) office at 519 Freeman Street in Oceanside" and fired eleven rounds from what was believed to be a .45 caliber machine gun. The shooting almost certainly came from a moving vehicle, and injured a man who turned out to be a U.S. Marine deserter. San Diego added that they did not plan to proceed with any counterintelligence actions "while violent harassment of these groups continues by unidentified persons." In the same memo, it was reported that the violence or threat of violence against New Left groups had made it quite difficult to "maintain membership at high level and in carrying out proposed activities."[31]

A Philadelphia memo dated February 9, 1970, reported that a group of nine activists, led by two SDS Weathermen from New York, raided the CBS affiliate station in Philadelphia on January 10. They caused about $1,500 in damages but were unable to gain access to the broadcast area of the facility. The group evidently opposed a program on WCAU-TV which criticized the Black Panther Party. All were arrested.

Area special agents wanted to determine if the action was somehow involved with the local SDS Labor Committee's underground newspaper, *The Philadelphia Free Press*. To determine if the paper was involved, undercover informants attended *Philadelphia Free Press* meetings on January 21 and February 4. What they found was a "violent factional dispute" over the financial status of the operation, which was reported to be $7,000 in the red. Some members had been collecting money from advertisers and keeping the funds for personal use. One individual, [*name deleted*], was accused of handling *Philadelphia Free Press* finances so badly that "the newspaper would get into serious trouble if the IRS should check the paper's finances." Both informants were instructed to "learn as much as possible concerning PFP [*Philadelphia Free Press*] financial troubles during future PFP meetings."[32] The information would be given to the IRS; the paper's advertisers and contributors would almost certainly become COINTELPRO targets themselves.

Another Philadelphia memo to the director, this one dated March 31, was accompanied by two newspaper articles written by Bayard Bruut and Albert Gaudiosi, investigative reporters for *The Sunday Bulletin*. The first was headlined "Two Suspects in Raid on WCAU Visit Cuba to Harvest Sugar Cane," the second "Parents Grieve for 2 Sons Lost to Student Revolution." They dealt at length with what special agents called "the interlocking nature of the New Left conspiracy and the unhappiness it creates in understandable human terms." The articles reported on the relationship between the Weathermen, the Communist Party of Eastern Pennsylvania and Delaware, and the Venceremos Brigade. According to the memo, they were "stimulated by a reliable relationship which has developed with these reporters."[33]

Still another Philadelphia memo, this one dated September 23, 1970, provides additional insight into FBI thinking at the time. Written after the shootings at Kent State and much of the violence of the Weather Underground, the memo—from Special Agent William D. Anderson, Jr.—assigned eighteen special agents to monitor antiwar protests at sixty-nine colleges and universities in the greater Philadelphia area. These institutions had a combined enrollment of more than 150,000 students. The memo listed more than seventy categories of protest activity to be monitored. Major headings included such categories as "Student Agitator" or "Students for a Democratic Society." Under the heading "New Left Movement," subcategories included violence, religion, communist influence, student disorder, race relations, publications, mass media, and factionalism.[34] Careful attention was paid to expanding the coverage of campuses by informants. A steady flow of memos stressed that special agents were to exercise extraordinary care in recruiting new student informants.

The bureau worked with the *Philadelphia Bulletin* in the summer of 1970 to produce a series of lengthy articles on "the new revolutionaries." The first installment explained to the public what the bureau could and could not do in countering the New Left. Another discussed in considerable detail the New Left fugitives that the FBI was then pursuing. Court cases that authorized the bureau's antiradical campaign were cited.[35]

J. Edgar Hoover received a memo from Los Angeles on March 16 which gave him the information that Angela Davis, a Security Index subject, had caused a "furor among both members of the Communist Party (CP) and young members of the New Left." She made a number of appearances at California schools and, on the University of California Santa Barbara campus, she stated, "The only thing to do is overthrow this government. I'm not supposed to say that, but I'll say it anyway . . . overthrow this government."[36] Angela Davis, an instructor at UCLA, was widely known for her extraordinarily radical views. She was scheduled to speak at Mt. San Antonio College, Walnut, California, on March 10, 1970. In anticipation of her visit, area special agents put together what they called Angela Davis "kits"—a package of newspaper articles about her career and political philosophies and her adherence to the Communist Party. Bureau agents knew beforehand that a number of area people, both on and off the campus, were flatly opposed to her scheduled appearance. Copies of these "kits" were mailed anonymously to known anticommunists and school officials prior to March 10. It was believed that this mailing helped school officials decide to cancel the entire program. Davis was not to be denied and made an appearance, but the crowd was very small. The fact that she appeared at all caused much confusion, and there were some who wanted to prosecute her for trespassing. Los Angeles requested authority "for the future use of these news articles" in order to arouse public sentiment against her. On March 30, Hoover said no. "The Davis incident," he wrote, "has already received sufficient publicity in the California area to arouse public sentiment."[37]

In another Los Angeles situation, special agents sought to neutralize a Key Activist named Klonsky, in a "snitch jacket" approved by Hoover on March 31: it was to "discredit Klonsky and break up his following in the Revolutionary Youth Movement (RYM) by showing that he is some type of informant." Special agents prepared a fake informant report of an actual RYM meeting at which a bureau undercover informant was in attendance—thus making the report appear entirely authentic. Photocopies of the spurious report were mailed, accompanied by a note explaining that the material was found in a white car (Klonsky owned a white car) near the Haymarket—the meeting place for the RYM. The obvious conclusion, of course, was that Klonsky had written the report for his police contact and simply left it in his car. This package of explosive information was mailed anonymously to SDS college chapters and BPP headquarters. As always, in order to ensure absolute secrecy, the paper was purchased from nongovernment sources. Only a small number of copies were mailed because, as Hoover noted, this will "imply that limited funds are available and that the letters are being mailed as an individual undertaking."[38]

It is difficult, if not impossible, to follow Hoover's sometimes abrupt and evidently capricious thinking in his dealings with individual field offices. On the one hand, there was constant pressure to develop COINTELPRO proposals that would "infiltrate, disrupt, and otherwise neutralize" the New Left. On the other, it appears that the director was quite arbitrary in the COINTELPRO approval process, if for no other reason than to demonstrate who was in charge. For example, on December 8, 1969, San Antonio requested bureau authority to send an anonymous letter to Texas Attorney General Waggoner Carr regarding a speech he made about the SDS and the Vietnam Moratorium Committee. On December 18, 1969, headquarters denied authority for this mailing.[39] On January 15, 1970, San Antonio provided information on events at the University of Texas and also made reference to unanswered memos to the director dated October 29, November 5, November 7, and November 13, 1969.[40]

On February 12, 1970, San Antonio requested bureau authority to make up a series of printed cards, ominously featuring a crosshair sight superimposed over a message to the effect that there were individuals in San Antonio with the training to destroy traitors, that is, elements of the New Left. It would be signed "The Minutemen," a right-wing strike force known to be led by an officer of the San Antonio police department, and would be sent anonymously to the San Antonio Committee for Peace and Freedom.[41] On February 27, the proposal was denied by advising that such a mailing would not produce an "appreciative benefit" in the effort against the New Left.[42]

On March 2, 1970, San Antonio requested bureau authority to anonymously mail the letter shown below to American Bar Association president Leon Jaworski, asking why the association had not disciplined radical lawyers William Kunstler and Leonard Weinglass. Copies would also go to the *San Antonio Light* and the *San Antonio Express & News*.

Mr. Leon Jaworski, Esq.
President
American Bar Association
Bank of the Southwest Building
Houston, Texas 77002

Dear Mr. Jaworski:

Has the American Bar Association a means of disciplining such members as William Kunstler and Leonard Weinglass for their conduct in and out of the courtroom at Chicago?

I am thinking particularly of the aftermath of Mr. Kunstler's inflammatory speech at Santa Barbara, California, in the recent past. He appears to be a liability to the ABA and the ethical conduct for which its membership is known.

> Very truly yours,
> Dillon J. O'Rourke[43]

Hoover replied on March 20 that Kunstler and Weinglass were already the subject of contempt citations for their courtroom antics and it was not deemed appropriate that letters "be sent out at this time."[44]

On March 19, San Antonio submitted still another COINTELPRO proposal that focused on the Chicago trial. It included a copy of an article from the University of Texas student paper that concerned a speech by prominent attorney Louis Nizer, and a request to mail the letter below to Editor—Firing Line, *The Daily Texan*, Drawer D, University Station, Austin, Texas.

Editor:

Since the verdict was handed down in the conspiracy trial in Chicago, we have been deluged with rhetoric from many sources about the poor defendants.

It was therefore very refreshing to read in *The Daily Texan* the article regarding the remarks made by noted Attorney Louis Nizer who spoke at the 48th Annual Texas Law Review banquet and the proposals he made to thwart future spectacles of this type.

In addition, *The Daily Texan* is to be congratulated for giving Mr. Nizer front-page coverage and not having this article buried in the Classified Ads section as some other papers have done.

> Very truly yours,
> Dillon J. O'Rourke[45]

Hoover replied on March 26 that "it is not felt that appreciable benefit can be expected from such a letter."[46]

San Antonio tried again. In a March 31 memo, the field office reminded the director that "the major portion of San Antonio's security work in the academic field is centered at the University of Texas." They requested authority to prepare a newsletter to be named *The Longhorn*

Tale. It would be mailed to students on a periodic basis "to neutralize anti-war anti-draft sentiment contained in the legitimate campus newspaper."[47] Hoover apparently pondered the matter and then replied on April 9 that he did not feel "that any appreciable benefit would accrue from such a publication."[48]

On February 19, 1970, Hoover received a memo from the New York field office reporting on the financial affairs of prominent activist Abbot Howard Hoffman. A total of fifteen undercover informants were used in this COINTELPRO action, which again demonstrates the extraordinary efforts put forth by the FBI to complete a COINTELPRO-New Left assignment. Hoffman, a New Left Key Activist, was the subject of field office memos to headquarters dated May 7, May 13, July 18, August 25, September 4, September 26, and November 5, 1969.

It was confirmed that Abbot Howard Hoffman, also known as Abbie Hoffman, lived with his wife, Anita, at a roof apartment located at 114–116 East 13th Street, New York City. Informant NYT-3 reported that the April–May–June issue of *Rights*, a self-described publication of the Emergency Civil Liberties Committee, seemed to confirm that Hoffman was a new member of the organization's national council. COINTELPRO documents refer to this particular committee, ECLC, as an organization whose main purpose was to abolish the House Committee on Un-American Activities. It stated the ECLC was established in 1951, and "although representing itself as a non-communist group, actually operates as a front for the Communist Party."

On April 30, a source in Spokane, Washington, advised that Hoffman spoke in the Student Union Building of Gonzaga University on April 29 under the auspices of the Associated Students of Gonzaga University, which paid him $600. Informant NYT-9 advised on May 13, 1969, that Hoffman was paid $400 for his lecture at St. Joseph's College, Rensselaer, Indiana, on April 15, 1969, by Richard Fulton, Incorporated, Lecture and Artist Bureau, 200 West 57th Street, New York City. In addition, the source stated that all of Hoffman's expenses for this speaking appearance were paid by Richard Fulton, Incorporated, which money was reimbursed by the Student Association of St. Joseph's College, the sponsoring organization for Hoffman's appearance at the college. NYT-10 advised on July 23, 1969, that the University of Denver, Denver, Colorado, paid Hoffman $500 from the "student funds" by check dated April 28, 1969, for a speaking appearance at the university on April 28, 1969. The National Speakers Bureau, 3020 Hanover Street, Los Angeles, California, which was the booking agent for Hoffman's appearance, was also paid $350 by check from the university. Hoffman was also paid for an airline ticket in the amount of $210 for his speaking appearance. The source stated that there were no known expenses that Hoffman had to pay out since the university furnished the auditorium and the cleaning services after its use.

NYT-6 advised on July 28, 1969, that Wright State University, Fairborn, Ohio, gave Hoffman a check in the amount of $200 dated March 19, 1969, for a speaking appearance at that university on March 17, 1969, as part of the school's "Artists and Lecturers" series. The amount was agreed upon between Hoffman and his agent and the Artists and Lecturers Series Committee of Wright State University. On July 31, NYT-5 confirmed that Hoffman gave a speech to students at Antioch College, Yellow Springs, Ohio, on March 16. He was paid by student donations and the amount could not be confirmed. NYT-2 advised on August 4, 1969, that Hoffman was paid the sum of $70 for an appearance as a guest speaker at Richmond College, Staten Island, New York, on February 20, 1969, as part of an experimental class called a "commune." This money was from funds of the student government at Richmond College. NYT-7 advised on August 27, 1969, that the Bug House Square Group, an official student activity group at Northern Illinois State College, Chicago, Illinois, with funds from student activity fees at the college, paid Hoffman $300 for a speaking appearance at the college on April 10, 1969, and that Hoffman donated his check to the BPP of Chicago, Illinois. NYT-11 advised on September 3, 1969, that Hoffman received $750 for a public appearance at the North Dakota State University, Fargo, North Dakota, on April 30, 1969. NYT-4 advised on September 12, 1969, that Hoffman received $500 for speaking at the New York State University College at Potsdam, New York, on March 4, 1969. A Hartford, Connecticut, source reported on October 2 that Hoffman received $750 for an appearance as a speaker at the University of Hartford, Hartford, Connecticut, on September 17, 1969. NYT-13 advised on October 3, 1969, that the Cultural Committee at the University of Maryland, Baltimore County, Catonsville, Maryland, had booked Hoffman for speaking appearances at the university on September 19, 1969, and had allotted $600 for his appearance. Sources advised on October 14 that Hoffman was paid $1,000 for a speaking appearance at Western Michigan University in Kalamazoo, Michigan. The sum was paid out of the University Student Association fund.

Hoffman spoke to an audience of about 125 at Atwood Hall, Clark University, in Worcester, Massachusetts, on October 26. Sources said that those in attendance were requested to pay $1. The source was unable to provide any information concerning any money paid to Hoffman. NYT-14 advised during October 1969 that Hoffman spoke at Lowell Lecture Hall, Harvard University, Cambridge, Massachusetts, on October 26, 1969. A source reported that an admission charge of $1.50 was made and 1,200 persons attended the speech. The source said a collection was taken up to aid Hoffman's defense fund and that approximately $200 was collected. Hoffman, as the main speaker, was also given a part of the admission charge. NYT-15 advised on December 8, 1969, that Hoffman was paid $265 plus transportation for an appearance at Wisconsin State University, Superior, Wisconsin, on December 5, 1969, by the business office of the university drawn on the Program Board account.

The accompanying February 19, 1970, New York cover memo to Hoover noted that the entire Hoffman report was "confidential" because it included information from NYT-5 and NYT-15. The public identification of the informants would "impair their future effectiveness" and "could have an adverse effect on the national defense interests of the country." New York concluded, "It is recommended that copies of this LHM [letterhead memorandum] be furnished to the Internal Revenue Service for their assistance concerning any investigation being conducted by that agency."[49]

On January 19, 1970, the Minneapolis field office reported that the University of Minnesota had permitted "the use of public facilities to hold a recent Young Socialists Alliance (YSA) National Conference" at the college. It was also learned that students had invited one of the defendants in the Chicago conspiracy trial to the campus as a speaker. Minneapolis noted that [name deleted] had publicly challenged the decision by the college, and recommended the mailing of the anonymous letter shown below in the hope of bringing pressure on the New Left students within the Union Board of Governors—those largely responsible for inviting the controversial organizations and speakers to the campus.[50] Hoover approved, on February 3, the mailing to [name deleted] in support of his position.

Dear Mr. [name deleted]:

It is high time someone like you came along to challenge these Left Wingers at this university about bringing in revolutionaries to show us how to destroy this country. This type of thing, I presume you know, is nothing new. The recent YSA convention just happened to be more highly publicized.

For your information, during last November, a group of Left Wing students on the Union Board of Governors at this school decided to use tax money to bring in [*name deleted*] as a future speaker. By the way, at the time he was under trial, being one of the "Chicago Eight." This can be verified through the November 19 issue of *The Minnesota Daily*. I suspect a good hunk of the taxpayers' dough was used to get him here. Maybe if the students here were really interested in these clowns, you could justify spending the taxpayers' money. The truth of the matter is that less than 30 students showed up to hear [*name deleted*]. Just another example of how the radicals are manipulating behind the scene at the taxpayers' expense.

From One Who Knows[51]

Dr. K. Ross Toble, a professor of history at the University of Montana, wrote a newspaper article that was sharply critical of the current generation of college students. He suggested that it was time for the older generation to "deal with the antics of the younger generation in a forceful manner." Dr. Toble pointed out that "the older generation should be proud of its achievements, not cringe guiltily before the accusations of the younger generation."[52] Such an article could well have been written by J. Edgar Hoover himself.

Minneapolis requested, on April 11, authority to send the article anonymously to the president of the University of Minnesota.[53] Hoover responded on April 23 by granting authority to reproduce and anonymously mail copies of the article to the university president "and other key administrators and the Board of Regents of that University." The director also added that "copies of this may also be mailed to other college administrators as circumstances may dictate."[54]

Friction had been developing between the Socialist Workers Party, the Young Socialists Alliance, and New Mobe since the fall of 1969. Informants reported that YSA and SWP elements were infiltrating New Mobe on a regular basis and were creating tremendous internal difficulties. The New York field office prepared a brochure designed to cause further disruption in the ranks of the New Left by a "direct attack on the influence in NMC by the Socialist Workers Party (SWP)" and also to "cause confusion in the SWP itself."[55] Authority for the mailing came on January 20, 1970. Targets included individuals within the New Mobe, SWP, and the Student Mobilization Committee. A portion of the text is shown below:

Dig it. It's time to pull the chain, brothers and sisters. If the peace movement in Amerika is to survive, the crap influence of the Socialist Workers Party and its bastard youth group—Young Socialist Alliance— must be flushed from the New Mobe once and for all. Stagnant zeros like [*name deleted*] and [*name deleted*], both members of the SWP Nat'l Committee, must be dumped. Let's get rid of the [*name deleted*], [*name deleted*], and the [*name deleted*], along with other SWP shits. DEMAND AN END TO SWP BALLING! Write New Mobe today at Suite 900, 1029 Vermont Ave., N.W., Washington, D.C.[56]

Three hundred and seven copies were mailed to New Left activists. New York later reported that recipients believed the memo had "been prepared by dissident elements within the NMC itself." It was further noted that "some persons active in NMC and SWC are very much opposed to the continued influence of the SWP in those organizations."[57]

The director received another proposal from New York on February 3 suggesting another anonymous mailing. In this instance, the field office suggested the mailing of a "memorandum" concerning the National Steering Committee of the New Mobilization Committee To End the War in Vietnam (NMC), which would be designed to aggravate internal leadership tensions by "pitting the non-Trotskyites against radicals who are members of the Socialist Workers Party (SWP)." The memo would criticize the steering committee for a perceived lack of support of black members.[58] On February 17, Hoover authorized the anonymous mailing shown below to members of the NMC Steering Committee and other officials within the organization, and to selected members of the Vietnam Moratorium Committee. Seventy-five copies were sent out.

NEW MOBILIZATION COMMITTEE TO END THE WAR IN VIETNAM
1029 Vermont Avenue, N.W., Washington, D.C. 20005
Area Code 202 737-8600

MEMO TO: National Steering Committee
RE: The Absolute Radial Imbalance of The NSC

Having for a short time served as a member of the NSC, and currently active in the Moratorium Committee—both in Washington and New York, I find it necessary to call attention to certain facts overlooked or shovelled under the rug by NMC leadership.

My understanding at the time I joined NMC was that it was to be run as a non-exclusionary organization—devoted to one primary cause: the immediate end of the frightful war in Vietnam. We were not to be side-tracked into supporting the aims of the militant left. We were not to be sucked into protests against the government's trial of the Conspiracy 8 in Chicago and the like. Our sights were to be adjusted at some later time when the war terminated. Or, so I thought.

Over the past several years the Trotskyites have literally taken control of the body proper and have repeatedly resisted efforts to recruit black brothers into NMC leadership. In addition, they have seen fit to use the good offices of the NMC to further their own political aspirations, nebulous as they are.

I have been sickened—on more than one occasion—by the promises made to the Black United Front, promises not kept, promises made with the mouth and not the heart. The attitude of the Steering Committee towards the BUF was and is a matter of disgrace. In the main, NMC leadership has been no better than the racist politicians and phony liberals who give lip service to the black community and turn their backs on any positive action.

The NMC leadership has demonstrated an appalling lack of sensitivity towards the largest minority in the country. If NMC is to survive the coming months, the situation must be rectified immediately. Our leadership—including the omni-present Trotskyites and other radicals—had better take positive steps before those who disagree with current policy, *and there are many,* either withhold future support or take decisive action to remove NMC leadership. It is my belief the NMC would greatly benefit under a leader like Sam Brown of MC.

To avoid senseless imbroglio, I choose to remain anonymous until the proper time. Just for the record—I am not Black. . . .⁵⁹

The Newark field office, acting on information obtained from undercover sources within the local BPP, planned to exploit tensions with the local SDS. On January 9, the letter below was mailed to Black Panther Party, 384 Pacific Avenue, Jersey City, New Jersey. As was customary, it was typed on 5" × 10" nongovernment paper, with a nonbureau typewriter. Hoover said the action was approved because it "may serve to drive a wedge between the SDS and the Black Panthers."

Sirs:

In view of the difficulties between the Panthers and my organization, the SDS, I find I can no longer furnish money to [*name deleted*] for use in the breakfast program. We need the money ourselves just as much now. She'll know who I am. I'm not putting my name down because I'm afraid the federal police power structure has a way of knowing who is in contact with you.[60]

On April 17, Hoover ordered all COINTELPRO-approved field offices to "make every effort" to obtain "informant coverage of every New Left commune."[61] Later in the year, the director approved recruiting in the eighteen-to-twenty-year-old age group to expand coverage of New Left communes, collectives, and underground newspaper writers and editors.

On April 29, 1970, activist Sidney Lens attended a meeting of the coordinating committee of New Mobe in the living room of Cora Weiss's home in the Riverdale section of New York. The matters under discussion included an anticipated winter–spring antiwar offensive that would focus on smaller monthly demonstrations in various parts of the country. "Cora excused herself," he remembers, "to take a call from someone on the *New York Times*." When she returned, she said that her newspaper source had told her that Nixon "would announce an invasion of Cambodia by American and South Vietnamese forces the next day." The group was stunned. "We voted," Lens said, "to conduct a protest rally at the White House on May 9, ten days away."[62]

Within hours of President Nixon's speech, college students from coast to coast came out in protest. The National Student Association immediately called for Nixon's impeachment and for a national student strike. Eighty percent of the nation's institutions of higher learning experienced some kind of protest action. Student newspapers from eleven colleges called for an immediate nationwide strike. The Senate voted to repeal the Gulf of Tonkin Resolution the day after Nixon's Cambodia speech.

Dr. Clark Kerr, former president of the University of California at Berkeley, said the Cambodian protests were without equal, unmatched by any other crisis "in the history of American education."[63] Interestingly, on the day before the speech, Nixon told his secretary, Rosemary Woods, "It's possible that the campuses are really going to blow up after this speech."[64] Fred Halstead, writing many years later, observed that the response to the speech "simply exploded with unprecedented force across the country, organized on each campus by whatever local activists there were."[65]

On May 4, at 12:25 P.M., a detachment of National Guardsmen standing on Blanket Hill at Kent State University fired sixty-one rounds at a group of demonstrators. They killed four and wounded nine others. The aftershocks were unprecedented: 536 colleges closed completely. Half of all the colleges and universities in the United States experienced protest of some form. More than eighteen hundred were arrested across the country. A state of emergency was declared on campuses in four states. The National Guard was activated twenty-four times. One government report concluded that "in May 1970, entire universities were, in effect, mobilized against the policies of the present national administration."[66] Max Frankel, writing in the *New York Times*, observed: "America was a nation in anguish last week, her population divided, her campuses closed, her capital shaken, her government confused, her President perplexed."[67]

In a rally organized by New Mobe, 130,000 gathered to demonstrate near the White House on May 9. Although the event was covered by every major television network, it was largely disorganized and ineffective. Antiwar leader Norma Becker remembered, "What happened in Washington on May 9 was not commensurate either to the invasion of Cambodia or Kent State."[68] Incredibly, at what was perhaps the very apex of the nation's sense of outrage against the war, the antiwar movement itself seemed to become almost quixotic. Students went to Washington with a total sense of outrage and returned to their colleges in a state of disillusionment. New Mobe had dropped the ball.

The last meeting of the Steering Committee of New Mobe took place in Atlanta just two weeks after the massive May 9 White House demonstration. New Mobe, acting with several different names over the past four years, had given a sense of overall uniformity to the antiwar movement. In similar fashion to the demise of the SDS, New Mobe's time was simply past. In June, the SWP and the YSA seemed to break away altogether and formed the National Peace Action Council which had the support of the SMC and Cleveland Area Peace Action Council. Another group—with the ambitious name National Coalition Against War, Racism and Repression—formed with the support of the Fifth Avenue Peace Committee. Still another, the Committee of Liaison with Families of Servicemen Detained in North Vietnam, had previously developed from direct contacts between members of Women Strike for Peace and a women's delegation from Vietnam. Astonishingly, with no assistance from or even acknowledgment by Washington, the Committee, by summer 1970, had established a regular flow of correspondence between American prisoners and their families.

While these new organizations were coming into focus, the antiwar efforts continued. Protest actions against Selective Service centers occurred at the rate of about one per day. Federal facilities and recruiting centers were firebombed. One firebombing at the Army Mathematics Research facility at the University of Wisconsin killed a researcher. Father Daniel Berrigan, a leader of the Catholic left, was captured by FBI agents in August.

On September 25, *The Report of the President's Commission on Campus Unrest* was released to the public. It again warned that "in May 1970, students did not strike against their universities; they succeeded in making their universities strike against national policy."[69] Nixon, although authorizing the study, reportedly paid little attention to it.

On September 20, Hoover issued an "Open letter to College Students." He expressed "concern about the extremism which led to violence, lawlessness, and disrespect for the rights of others on many college campuses during the past year."[70]

On October 31, the National Peace Action Council coordinated antiwar protest demonstrations in about twenty cities nationwide. About a hundred thousand were involved—down drastically from the dramatic peace offensives in 1969. The National Coalition Against War, Racism and Repression led a demonstration of about fifteen hundred at the United Nations on November 15.

On November 27, Hoover appeared before the Subcommittee of the Senate Appropriations Committee and requested additional funding for the FBI budget to add one thousand new special agents.[71] It was also at this hearing that Hoover made his sensational accusation that elements of the New Left, more specifically the Catholic Left, were planning to dynamite selected government buildings and kidnap national security advisor Henry Kissinger. In spite of such accusations, the general thrust of the antiwar movement was changing. There was evidence, perhaps hard to see at first, that struggle over the war had indeed shifted. The basic political elements comprising the antiwar movement were shifting more to the center of the American political spectrum. These observations notwithstanding, the bureau's COINTELPRO-New Left operations continued as if nothing had changed.

Within forty-eight hours of the Cambodian invasion, it was business as usual for the bureau's COINTELPRO-New Left operations. On May 1, 1970, Hoover responded to a Cleveland request that the FBI cooperate with a group of speakers and business leaders organized by private industry to speak on behalf of "the American economic system and against attacks by New Leftists." Cleveland further suggested that FBI data on various New Left organizations should be provided to these speakers as background material. Hoover replied that the bureau must know "the identities of the speakers who would be chosen for this program as well as those individuals who would be in control of such a program." In closing this memo, Hoover added: "You are reminded that recommendations for counterintelligence action should not be made in quarterly progress letters under this program."[72] Cleveland evidently had a change of heart, because the proposal was never mentioned again.

On July 31, Hoover approved a Cleveland proposal to provide selected New Left intelligence data to area "high school principals and school superintendents which will enable these officials to resist the encroachments of the Student Mobilization Committee (SMC) and the Young Socialists Alliance (YSA)." The package of materials included miscellaneous copies of *New Left Notes*, referring to the Weathermen, a YSA document entitled "The New Stage In The Anti-War Movement; A Strategy For Young Socialists," a second YSA document entitled "The Deepening Radicalization: Revolutionary Perspectives for the 1970s,"[73] together with copies of *The Militant* and *The Guardian* that had articles aimed at high school students. Hoover admonished special agents that school officials must not divulge the fact that the material in question came from the FBI.

As noted previously, the FBI made several very concerted efforts to utilize the investigative machinery of the Internal Revenue Service to disrupt selected New Left activists. In Cleveland, one target was Sidney Morris Peck (Key Activist). In a memo dated July 31, 1970, Cleveland advised the bureau that the IRS reported that the investigation had been completed with the result that "all the 'contributions' to SDS and other questionable groups, which Peck had claimed as deductible items, had been thrown out and Peck had been required to pay an additional tax approximating $500, the exact amount being unknown to [*informant's name deleted*]."[74]

On May 1, 1970, the Pittsburgh field office requested permission to target an economics professor at the University of Pittsburgh, who, according to FBI documents, had a very long record of disruption. He had been involved in a number of demonstrations prior to 1967 when he publicly surrendered his draft card. He was arrested on October 15, 1969, on charges of assaulting a law officer and resisting arrest. He was arrested on May 23, 1969, at a sit-in at Pittsburgh's Duquesne Club. The professor had written newspaper articles about a planned disruption of the Gulf stockholders' meeting. In one article, he stated: "Gulf should be state-owned as in communism."[75]

On May 15, 1970, Hoover authorized the local FBI office to contact an individual [*name deleted*] known to be influential at the university.[76] On May 21, contact was made and information was provided on the professor's arrest record.[77] On July 16, the contact person advised that "he had been in contact with the UP Administration and had questioned the desirability of [*name deleted*] continuing as a Professor of Economics at the UP." The FBI contact soon advised special agents that "he had been informed by the UP Administration that [*name deleted*]'s contract with the UP would not be renewed upon its termination this fall."[78]

The Los Angeles field office reported to the bureau on June 26 that a confidential source had provided to special agents the personal diary of [*name deleted*], a local Security Index subject and member of the executive committee of the Los Angeles Progressive Labor Party (PLP). The field office saw the opportunity for a COINTELPRO action and suggested a snitch jacket.[79] Los Angeles requested that selected additions and revisions be made to the diary text by the Documents Section of the FBI Laboratory Division. In a very careful process, laboratory technicians would add listings to the diary which would contain the telephone numbers and names for local Secret Service and Army Intelligence contacts. Notations would be added to suggest that the diary's owner had been supplying information on the PLP to government agencies on a regular basis. In his approval memo dated August 12, 1970, Hoover noted that "since these alterations will possibly be subject to close scrutiny, the Document Section advises that painstaking practice is involved." This was necessary "since the alterations have to be done perfectly on the first attempt."[80] In any event, the diary was mailed anonymously with a cover letter "written in the vernacular of the New Left," which, of course, pointed out that the owner was quite obviously a government informant and had, in fact, been one for some time. The intention was to seriously impugn the reputation of the PLP official and, by doing so, neutralize him.

Several months later, in the November 1 issue of the PLP publication *Challenge*, the police were accused of forgeries which involved "an old memo book of one of our leading members."[81] Los Angeles, however, was undaunted. A December 28 memo to Hoover advised, "This office is now composing another letter to [*name deleted*] and this will accuse him of naiveness in not realizing [*name deleted*] is a police tool."[82] A second letter "indicated that an unofficial committee had been organized in Los Angeles to investigate traitors in the PLP ranks" and that the committee had discovered the diary.[83]

The Boston field office demonstrated just how complete their undercover operations were—even within the national headquarters of the SDS. Special agents were searching for four SDS activists wanted on criminal trespass charges, for their part in a highly disruptive picket line at Harvard on May 8, 1970. On October 21, informants within the headquarters reported that the suspects were in the headquarters facility at 173-A Massachusetts Avenue in Boston. They immediately advised the Intelligence Unit, Boston Police Department. The Boston Police, accompanied by Cambridge detectives, entered the facility and made the arrest of all four. In a report to Hoover on November 17, the Boston field office said that "this caused a great deal of disruption at the NH [SDS national headquarters] and consternation within the membership within the days to follow. The NH suspects an informant within their ranks and paranoia is running high." As late as November 16, there was still a great deal "of suspicion on the part of the NH staff as to who the informant is within their ranks."[84]

FBI special agents monitored a tense situation at the University of South Carolina. In a June 26 memo, the Columbia field office reported that New Left activists had called a student strike and refused to leave Russell House, the student center. Forty-one were arrested, including members of the Student Mobilization Committee to End the War in Vietnam, the group Aware, and a women's-liberation group. Nine were permanently dismissed from the university and nineteen were placed on probation. Four days later, the activists struck again. They entered the administration building and destroyed all records and furniture in the building's south wing. Thirty-six were arrested and most were dismissed from the university. The Columbia field office reported that those permanently dismissed included the most active members of the New Left movement at USC.[85] A year-end memo to Hoover from Columbia reported that the SMC, the main New Left group at USC, was largely ineffective. Sources reported to special agents that SMC members "are of the opinion that the FBI and local authorities have numerous informants in the dissident groups and for this reason they are afraid to take any action which would possibly result in their arrest."[86]

In an unusual situation in Iowa City, a few students at Central High School wanted to form an SDS chapter. The school's administrators were horrified and contacted the Omaha field office requesting any information they "might use to influence the faculty to vote against permission for this group to organize at Central High."[87] Omaha responded immediately with a package of literature including "The SDS and the High School," "An Open Letter to College Students," "A Study in

Marxist Revolutionary Violence: Students for a Democratic Society 1967–69," and more. This was probably more than anyone at Central High ever wanted to know about the SDS, but the result was favorable to the FBI. The faculty voted 41–10 against permitting a chapter to be formed. Omaha advised that the school expressed "deepest appreciation to the FBI."[88]

On July 1, 1970, headquarters received a Houston memorandum that reported that the field office recently came in contact with a well-placed informant within the area YSA group. This person, evidently quite enterprising, planned to invite YSA leaders to his house for a barbecue and beer party on July 5. He advised special agents of his intention to provide the YSA people with "substantial alcoholic beverages" in order to obtain inside information relevant to the investigation of the YSA and its membership in Houston.[89]

On June 26, the Washington, D.C., field office reported to the bureau regarding a continuing liaison with local university administrations "in an attempt to convince them of the potential danger New Left radicals pose to their institutions." Bureau New Left literature, together with copies of Hoover's public messages on the New Left, had "been used to the fullest extent."

It also reported on surveillance of the headquarters of *Voice from the Mother Country*, an underground newspaper reportedly connected with the Weathermen. A search warrant was obtained and officials moved in to the facility at 1932 17th Street N.W. in Washington. The raid caused the occupants of this area to become unnerved and several attempted to escape with their weapons. Two were arrested and others "proclaimed themselves to be out of the revolutionary movement."[90] The facility was closed on June 14, 1970.

Less than a month later, the Washington field office advised that responsibility for Weathermen SDS fugitives was reassigned from a Criminal Fugitive Squad to a Security New Left Squad. The field office soon reported that the *Quicksilver Times*, another underground newspaper, ran an article to make activists aware of "their legal rights during contact with the FBI."[91]

By August 27, the field office had assigned as many as half a dozen special agents to work evening shifts "in areas heavily traveled by the New Left Community" to identify and make contact with potential undercover informants. This effort was being made in addition to "the regular informant program" to provide the "additional coverage which will be needed during the coming months."[92]

In what appeared to be a very imaginative proposal, the field office suggested obtaining the names of prominent alumni of area universities. Anonymous letters would suggest that they exert whatever pressure they could on the officials of their respective alma maters to take strong action against New Left elements. On September 15, Hoover indicated that he liked the idea, but "if it ever became public knowledge that the Bureau was connected with such a letter" it was entirely possible that "cries might erupt that the Bureau was infringing upon academic freedom."[93]

The Washington field office was a seemingly inexhaustible source of counterintelligence ideas. It reported on December 15 that special agents had developed close relationships with several real estate firms, which had resulted in "good coverage of commune type dwellings in the WDC area." The same communication advised that special agents "had developed a close confidential relationship with one of the administrators of the District of Columbia welfare office." With this new source of information, the FBI was able to determine if New Left individuals were illegally receiving food stamps and welfare payments. They were right on target. By the time this memo to Hoover was written, subjects had already been "removed from the welfare roles." Washington also stepped up its physical surveillance and direct target interview programs to "play upon the seemingly inherent paranoia of the New Left community." Informant coverage was also increased through a program of contacting "returning servicemen and more mature college students."[94]

From a July 1, 1970, memorandum, Hoover learned that the Chicago office had "obtained Federal warrants for numerous Weathermen who have failed to appear in local court cases."[95] Some were sentenced under the Work Release Program in which they would work during the day and be confined only at night.

The Revolutionary Union was another faction of the New Left that came under scrutiny by Chicago. A December 3, 1970, memo said that a Chicago informant attended a RU meeting chaired by a New York City delegation held in a park in Washington, D.C. It was, reported the source, negative and chaotic; delegates tried to make it "both an open and closed meeting." Some in attendance complained that "too many of the RU delegates were student types who had a blatantly sycophantic attitude toward the BPP." Another mentioned that the Detroit RU chapter was making "Mao Tsetung shirts and selling them." "Chairman Mao is depicted on the front and the slogan 'political power grows out of the barrel of a gun' appears on the back." One delegate reported that he was "up tight" about the "attempt to interview him and other RU members by FBI agents." Another said he was not "totally surprised by the interview as Bay Area RU had warned Collectives to expect such harassment." Still another said the FBI made him "edgy" and claimed "that all his friends, political as well as nonpolitical types, will now be subjected to interview and this bothers him."[96] Delegates said that security would have to be improved as a result of FBI interviews.

Two university professors were targeted by the Mobile, Alabama, field office in late 1970. These two professors were involved in support of an underground newspaper that was described as "left of center." Special agents believed that, if the professors were forced to withdraw their support, the newspaper would quickly fail and the local voice of the New Left would be silenced. An anonymous letter was sent to the university administration warning that the instructors' support of the left-of-center newspaper would be made public if they did not halt their activities. Both professors were placed on probation by the university president in early 1971.[97]

The Minneapolis field office reported that the University of Minnesota SDS chapter was being reorganized because members feared "that the group is completely infiltrated by FBI informants." The memo went on to say that "during the interview of a local SDS leader relative to local bombings, the Agents were advised that the local SDS chapter would 'kick out' any Weathermen types who tried to join the organization."[98]

The San Francisco field office was concerned about the Bay Area Institute, referred to by Hoover as "a New Left-type organization located in San Francisco, and an affiliate of the Institute for Policy Studies." With this in mind, the field office requested authority to contact someone at *The San Francisco Examiner*, known by special agents as an "established source." The information listed below was meant to persuade this person to write an article concerning the activities of the Bay Area Institute. Hoover approved the project on July 2, 1970, with the admonition, "Under no circumstances is he to divulge the Bureau's interest in this matter."[99]

(1) A copy of an article in *Barron's* weekly magazine captioned "Radical Think Tank" from the 10/6/69 issue

(2) A copy of an article in *Barron's* captioned "Ivory Tower Activists," from the 10/13/69 issue

(3) A pamphlet concerning a meeting of the Committee of Concerned Asian

Scholars of Stanford University, to be held 4/3/70 at Glide Memorial Church in San Francisco

(4) A newspaper article from *The Oregon Daily Emerald* issue of 4/10/70 captioned "Weisberg—Possible Ecology Not Effective"

(5) An article from *The Daily Californian* issue of 10/19/65 captioned "Katzenbach Protests SDS"

(6) Article from *The Daily Californian* issue of 11/4/65 captioned "VDC May Hold Legal March"

(7) An article from *The Daily Californian* issue of 2/4/66 captioned "Cohelan's Office Locked"

(8) A blank page containing two typed notices of articles in *The Ann Arbor News*, Ann Arbor, Michigan, dated 3/24 and 25/65, concerning ALLAN HABER[100]

The San Francisco friendly media source told special agents that the material was of interest although not necessarily timely. The newsman evidently planned to retain the material for future use when the SDS was engaged in a newsworthy matter. "It would make it easier for them," the September 28 bureau memo explained, "to ask more direct and embarrassing questions."[101]

J. Edgar Hoover received a memorandum from the Philadelphia field office dated June 3, 1970, which reported that primary New Left targets in the area consisted of the SDS-Weathermen forces, along with supporters "such as the *Philadelphia Free Press*, an underground newspaper, self-described as an 'independent and radical newspaper.' " Special efforts were being made to create dissension between "the Weathermen and other New Left groups."

Sources had also advised that IRS intelligence was concerned that the War Resister's League and the Weathermen might join their energies to withhold payment of income taxes—or at least that amount used to finance military operations in Vietnam. The FBI observed that it would be quite easy for these two radical groups to invade the local IRS office and "destroy IRS records" relating to their taxes.[102]

The Indianapolis field office received permission, on December 16, 1970, to prepare this anonymous letter critical of Keith Parker, president of the student body at Indiana University. The director noted in his approval memo that Parker, "a field lieutenant of the Black Panther Party, has traveled to North Vietnam with others to 'negotiate a separate peace treaty.' " He was a prime COINTELPRO-New Left target.

THE PARKER "COP OUT" OR MORE
APTLY, "NO MORE BULLSHIT"

Keith Parker, liberated I.U. Student Body President, has made his trip to North Viet Nam, via Moscow. Parker, representing all I.U. students (all 8%) and his associates have indicated that they will solve the problems trained negotiators cannot. Parker will no doubt provide us all with the answers to the elusive search for peace. Thoughtful, indeed. More thoughtful are some of the questions which may go unanswered by our traveling liberator:

While acknowledging* that Parker's travel to Hanoi was not paid for by student funds, (50¢ a semester) who will repay the loan made to Parker by a local communal leader for the trip? Who will pay the expenses for Parker on projected speaking tours away from the I.U. while he represents us?

*Jot Kendall (alias Jot who?) leader of the SMC, said in our newspaper recently, "Not a dime of student government money is being used." Jot should know . . . he should be knowledgeable, having free access to student government offices and affairs while *not being a student at I.U.*

Who approved Parker's Trip? The student body who he supposedly represents? Or Huey Newton of the Black Panthers of which Parker is a self-admitted field lieutenant?

Where is our 50¢ a semester going? For us at I.U. or for auditorium rental (Rennie Davis, 11/27/69); setting up of platforms and PA systems (BPAC, 10/31/70); or for the support and rental of films "The Battle of Algiers" ET AL (Bobby Seale weekend, 10/9–10/70) and II World Conference (12/11–13/70)? Or maybe to support the aims of the Panthers or USM or SMC.

What type of liberated curriculum does IU have that permits a student to travel extensively, unsponsored, with no apparent academic worry?

Working within the system, how can a student body president be impeached by his own senate (the core of our 8%)?

Who does Parker really represent? Is he using IU for his own gain?

Why can't the student body find the answers to these questions even though they are quite evident?

—CONCERNED STUDENTS AT IU[103]

The New York field office wanted to target the Venceremos Brigade, a group of New Left individuals who reportedly went to Cuba to cut sugar cane. Special agents determined that the Gay Liberation Front wanted to form their own separate brigade which would also go to Cuba for the same purpose. Cuban authorities evidently felt that gays "do not make good communists," a fact which the FBI would make clear.[104] On June 17, 1970, New York was authorized to prepare a leaflet in the format of a teletype addressed to an individual who had previously been arrested for homosexual behavior and other selected members of the New Left movement. The message below was mailed anonymously.

WE OF THE HOMOSEXUAL COMMUNITY WELCOME YOUR SUPPORT IN OUR FIGHT FOR EQUAL RIGHTS IN THE NEXT VENCEREMOS BRIGADE THIS SUMMER. STOP. IT IS GRATI-FYING THAT A WORKER FOR PEACE OF YOUR STATURE SHOULD RECOGNIZE THE IMPORTANT CONTRIBUTION TO WORLD REVOLUTION THAT CAN AND WILL BE MADE BY GAY LIBERATION. DESPITE COMMENTS BY CUBAN OFFI-CIALS THAT QUOTE FAGS UNQUOTE DO NOT MAKE GOOD COMMUNISTS, WE INTEND TO SHOW THEM OUR REAL PO-SITION THIS SUMMER.

—PEACE[105]

New York and a number of other field offices explored the rather extraordinary idea of checking U.S. Post Office box applications "in an effort to identify Weathermen mail drops." Special agents quickly dis-covered that New York alone had 159 post office stations in which boxes were located. This represented a total of 68,172 boxes.[106] The whole idea was dropped.

As it demonstrated many times before, the FBI did have the ability to become quite myopic at certain times. The Newark field office became quite concerned about a very small demonstration at the Stevens Insti-tute of Technology in Hoboken, New Jersey. This was a sit-in staged by ten students, out of a total class of thirteen hundred, which was an "agitation for a pass-fail examination system and a full time SIT-paid draft counselor on campus."[107] On June 5, 1970, Newark received ap-proval to anonymously mail five copies of *Barron's* article called "Cam-pus Battleground? Columbia Is a Warning to all American Universities" to Jesse H. Davis, president of the Stevens Institute. Across the top of each copy, handwritten in red ink, was the message "It begins with 10 like a deadly spore and soon the whole campus is infected with an in-curable affliction. Don't give in to a vocal minority that wants agitation for agitation's sake."[108]

As 1970 was coming to an end, J. Edgar Hoover was entering the forty-sixth year of his FBI stewardship—a record for longevity almost certainly unmatched in American governmental history. Although nei-ther he nor anyone else within the bureau could predict it, the CO-

INTELPRO operations would come to a sudden, abrupt end before midsummer 1971.

NOTES

1. Richard Nixon, *The Memoirs of Richard Nixon* (New York: Grosset and Dunlap, 1978), p. 445.

2. Charles DeBenedetti and Charles Chatfield, *The American Ordeal: The Antiwar Movement of the Vietnam Era* (Syracuse: Syracuse University Press, 1990), p. 272.

3. Fred Halstead, *Out Now! A Participant's Account of the Movement in the U.S. Against the Vietnam War* (New York: Pathfinder Press, 1978), p. 527.

4. Ibid.

5. Nancy Zaroulis and Gerald Sullivan, *Who Spoke Up? American Protest against the War in Vietnam, 1963–1975* (Garden City, NY: Doubleday, 1984), p. 113.

6. FBI Memorandum, Boston Field Office to Headquarters, Feb. 26, 1970, Mar. 6, 1970.

7. FBI Memorandum, Headquarters to Boston Field Office, Feb. 25, 1970.

8. Ibid.

9. FBI Memorandum, Atlanta Field Office to Headquarters, Jan. 21, 1970.

10. Ibid.

11. FBI Memorandum, Atlanta Field Office to Headquarters, Apr. 23, 1970.

12. FBI Memorandum, Headquarters to Buffalo Field Office, Mar. 3, 1970.

13. Ibid.

14. FBI Memorandum, Los Angeles Field Office to Headquarters, Jan. 2, 1970.

15. FBI Memorandum, Headquarters to Chicago Field Office, Jan. 20, 1970.

16. FBI Memorandum, Chicago Field Office to Headquarters, Jan. 27, 1970.

17. FBI Memorandum, Chicago Field Office to Headquarters, Mar. 31, 1970.

18. FBI Memorandum, Cincinnati Field Office to Headquarters, Apr. 8, 1970.

19. FBI Memorandum, Detroit Field Office to Headquarters, Feb. 24, 1970.

20. "FBI COINTELPRO 1968–1970 Ann Arbor as Sent Nationwide." Freedom of Information Act, Selected Files, Ann Arbor, Mich. Detroit, Master Plan COINTELPRO.

21. FBI Memorandum, Indianapolis Field Office to Headquarters, Feb. 18, 1970.

22. FBI Memorandum, Headquarters to Indianapolis Field Office, Mar. 16, 1970.

23. FBI Memorandum, Headquarters to Washington Field Office, Mar. 26, 1970.

24. FBI Memorandum, Washington Field Office to Headquarters, Mar. 31, 1970.

25. Ibid.

26. FBI Memorandum, Seattle Field Office to Headquarters, Jan. 7, 1970; Apr. 8, 1970.

27. FBI Memorandum, San Francisco Field Office to Headquarters, Feb. 18, 1970.

28. FBI Memorandum, Headquarters to San Francisco Field Office, Mar. 3, 1970.

29. FBI Memorandum, San Francisco Field Office to Headquarters, Mar. 31, 1970.

30. FBI Memorandum, San Francisco Field Office to Headquarters, Apr. 3, 1970.

31. FBI Memorandum, San Diego Field Office to Headquarters, Apr. 30, 1970.

32. FBI Memorandum, Philadelphia Field Office to Headquarters, Feb. 9, 1970.

33. FBI Memorandum, Philadelphia Field Office to Headquarters, Mar. 31, 1970.

34. FBI Memorandum, Special Agent William B. Anderson, Jr. to Philadelphia Special Agent-in-Charge, Sept. 23, 1970.

35. FBI Memorandum, Philadelphia Field Office to Headquarters, Aug. 6, 1970.

36. FBI Memorandum, Los Angeles Field Office to Headquarters, Mar. 16, 1970.

37. FBI Memorandum, Los Angeles Field Office to Headquarters, Mar. 16, 1970; Headquarters to Los Angeles Field Office, Mar. 30, 1970.

38. FBI Memorandum, Los Angeles Field Office to Headquarters, Mar. 31, 1970.

39. FBI Memorandum, San Antonio Field Office to Headquarters, Mar. 5, 1970.

40. FBI Memorandum, San Antonio Field Office to Headquarters, Jan. 15, 1970.

41. FBI Memorandum, San Antonio Field Office to Headquarters, Feb. 12, 1970.

42. FBI Memorandum, Headquarters to San Antonio Field Office, Feb. 27, 1970.

43. FBI Memorandum, San Antonio Field Office to Headquarters, Mar. 2, 1970.

44. FBI Memorandum, Headquarters to San Antonio Field Office, Mar. 20, 1970.

45. FBI Memorandum, San Antonio Field Office to Headquarters, Mar. 19, 1970.

46. FBI Memorandum, Headquarters to San Antonio Field Office, Mar. 26, 1970.

47. FBI Memorandum, San Antonio Field Office to Headquarters, Mar. 31, 1970.

48. FBI Memorandum, Headquarters to San Antonio Field Office, Apr. 9, 1970.

49. FBI Memorandum, New York Field Office to Headquarters, Feb. 19, 1970.

50. FBI Memorandum, Minneapolis Field Office to Headquarters, Jan. 19, 1970.

51. FBI Memorandum, Headquarters to Minneapolis Field Office, Feb. 3, 1970.

52. FBI Memorandum, Headquarters to Minneapolis Field Office, Apr. 23, 1970.

53. FBI Memorandum, Minneapolis Field Office to Headquarters, Apr. 11, 1970.

54. FBI Memorandum, Headquarters to Minneapolis Field Office, Apr. 23, 1970.

55. FBI Memorandum, New York Field Office to Headquarters, Jan. 14, 1970.

56. FBI Memorandum, Headquarters to New York Field Office, Jan. 20, 1970.

57. FBI Memorandum, New York Field Office to Headquarters, Nov. 31, 1970.

58. FBI Memorandum, New York Field Office to Headquarters, Feb. 3, 1970; Headquarters to New York Field Office, Feb. 17, 1970.

59. Ibid., Feb. 3, 1970.

60. FBI Memorandum, Newark Field Office to Headquarters, Dec. 22, 1969.

61. FBI Memorandum, Headquarters to Field Offices, Apr. 17, 1970.

62. Sidney Lens, *Unrepentant Radical. An American Activist's Account of Five Turbulent Decades* (Boston: Beacon Press, 1980), pp. 353–364.

63. Zaroulis and Sullivan, *Who Spoke Up?*, p. 320.

64. Nixon, *Memoirs of Richard Nixon*, p. 451.

65. Halstead, *Out Now!*, p. 537.

66. Presidential Commission, *The Report of the President's Commission on Campus Unrest* (New York: Arno Press, 1970), p. 46.

67. Lens, *Unrepentant Radical*, p. 364.

68. Zaroulis and Sullivan, *Who Spoke Up?*, p. 328.

69. *Report of the President's Commission on Campus Unrest*, p. 46.

70. *Congressional Record* (House of Representatives), Sept. 21, 1970.

71. Frank J. Donner, *The Age of Surveillance* (New York: Alfred A. Knopf, 1980), p. 159.

72. FBI Memorandum, Headquarters to Cleveland Field Office, May 1, 1970.

73. FBI Memorandum, Headquarters to Cleveland Field Office, July 31, 1970.

74. FBI Memorandum, Cleveland Field Office to Headquarters, July 31, 1970.

75. FBI Memorandum, Pittsburgh Field Office to Headquarters, May 1, 1970.

76. FBI Memorandum, Headquarters to Pittsburgh Field Office, May 15, 1970.

77. FBI Memorandum, Pittsburgh Field Office to Headquarters, July 28, 1970.

78. Ibid.

79. FBI Memorandum, Los Angeles Field Office to Headquarters, June 26, 1970.

80. FBI Memorandum, Headquarters to Los Angeles Field Office, Aug. 12, 1970.

81. FBI Memorandum, Los Angeles Field Office to Headquarters, Dec. 28, 1970.

82. Ibid.

83. Ibid.

84. FBI Memorandum, Boston Field Office to Headquarters, Nov. 17, 1970.

85. FBI Memorandum, Columbia Field Office to Headquarters, June 26, 1970.

86. FBI Memorandum, Columbia Field Office to Headquarters, Dec. 29, 1970.

87. FBI Memorandum, Omaha Field Office to Headquarters, Dec. 31, 1970.

88. Ibid.

89. FBI Memorandum, Houston Field Office to Headquarters, July 1, 1970.

90. FBI Memorandum, Washington Field Office to Headquarters, June 26, 1970.

91. FBI Memorandum, Washington Field Office to Headquarters, July 17, 1970.

92. FBI Memorandum, Washington Field Office to Headquarters, Aug. 27, 1970.

93. FBI Memorandum, Headquarters to Washington Field Office, Sept. 15, 1970.

94. FBI Memorandum, Washington Field Office to Headquarters, Dec. 15, 1970.

95. FBI Memorandum, Chicago Field Office to Headquarters, July 1, 1970.

96. FBI Memorandum, Chicago Field Office to Headquarters, Dec. 3, 1970.

97. FBI Memorandum, Mobile Field Office to Headquarters, Dec. 9, 1970; Headquarters to Mobile Field Office, Dec. 31, 1970.

98. FBI Memorandum, Minneapolis Field Office to Headquarters, Oct. 1, 1970.

99. FBI Memorandum, Headquarters to San Francisco Field Office, July 2, 1970.

100. FBI Memorandum, San Francisco Field Office to Headquarters, June 15, 1970.

101. FBI Memorandum, San Francisco Field Office to Headquarters, Sept. 28, 1970.

102. FBI Memorandum, Philadelphia Field Office to Headquarters, June 3, 1970.

103. FBI Memorandum, Headquarters to Indianapolis Field Office, Dec. 16, 1970; Indianapolis Field Office to Headquarters, Dec. 8, 1970.

104. FBI Memorandum, New York Field Office to Headquarters, May 18, 1970.

105. FBI Memorandum, Headquarters to New York Field Office, June 17, 1970.

106. FBI Memorandum, New York Field Office to Headquarters, Oct. 21, 1970.

107. FBI Memorandum, Newark Field Office to Headquarters, May 26, 1970.

108. FBI Memorandum, Headquarters to Newark Field Office, June 5, 1970; Newark Field Office to Headquarters, May 26, 1970.

8

The End of the
New Left COINTELPRO

"Neither a million people in the streets nor several hundred schools and colleges on strike altered Washington's determination to escalate its war of aggression in Indochina."
—David Dellinger

In an analysis of the war in Southeast Asia, Theodore H. White wrote: "In Vietnam there was no phrase to which one could pin emotion; Americans were required to fight a war without hate. The real culprit—ignorance—could never be made clear."[1] By 1971, in spite of overwhelming military firepower, over forty thousand Americans had died in the most ferocious kind of jungle warfare; military expenditures had reached billions per month.

Richard Nixon, undoubtedly sensing the national mood, recalled, "The first months of 1971 were the lowest point of my first term as president." The problems facing the administration, primarily Vietnam, were "so overwhelming and so apparently impervious"[2] that Nixon had very real doubts about his reelection chances. "By late January," Henry Kissinger remembers, "I was approaching battle fatigue."[3]

The antiwar movement, always in a state of transition and tension, was at a low ebb. The New Left had been unable to orchestrate demonstrations anywhere near the size of the two great peace offensives of the fall of 1969 or the post-Cambodia/Kent State national uproar: it was losing momentum. Indeed, David Dellinger later reflected that neither millions of protesters in the streets [November 1969] nor hundreds of striking colleges and universities [May 1970] altered the government's decision to "escalate its war of aggression in Indochina."[4]

On January 8, 1971, the National Coalition Against War, Racism and Repression met in Chicago, amid severe philosophical disputes, in an attempt to pull a faltering movement together. In February, the name was changed to the People's Coalition for Peace and Justice (PCPJ). This new group, with headquarters in Washington, D.C., would attempt to merge their efforts with the Washington Area Peace Action Coalition, the National Peace Action Council, the Vietnam Veterans Against the War, the Student Mobilization Committee, and the May Day Coalition.

This new patchwork, nominally under the auspices of the SMC, immediately responded to the expanding American bombing operations in Laos which began in January of 1971. In very cold weather, about fifty thousand demonstrators protested at MIT, Harvard, Boston University Boston Common, Cleveland, and Madison, Wisconsin. SMC spokesman Mike Arnall told reporters, "I would characterize the reaction now as a slow burn which will, without question, grow."[5]

A privately organized Citizens' Commission of Inquiry into U.S. War Crimes in Vietnam, with the support of lawyers, clergy, veterans, and Quaker groups, was founded in 1970. In February 1971 the commission completed its hearings into possible atrocities committed by American soldiers in Vietnam. The report ran to more than three hundred pages. Several asked the Pentagon to conduct a formal inquiry into possible war crimes.[6]

Also in February, the Student Mobilization Committee met at Catholic University to plan a strategy. The event was "attended by 2,500 young antiwar activists." Elton Golden of New York University recalled, "What impressed me most about the national meeting of SMC in Washington last weekend was the political maturity of the left."[7]

Hy L. Dubowsky covered the event for the York College newspaper and concluded, "We walk along and shrug our shoulders, there is nothing else we can possibly do to end the war." He added: "Come April 24 Nixon and company will not get much sleep, amidst the shouting voices of a concerned people."[8]

On March 26, in an action fully supported by the American Friends Service Committee and groups called Clergy and Laity Concerned and The Fellowship of Reconciliation, more than a hundred and fifty church leaders issued an appeal for the government to establish a fixed date for total withdrawal from Vietnam. The entire group had "flown to Paris where they had consulted with all the parties represented in the negotiations."[9] Throughout Holy Week, protests came in the form of fast, vigil, and sermon. On Good Friday, seven seminarians chained themselves together at the Justice Department. A number of clergy were arrested when they attempted to plant a charred cross on the White House grounds.

A teach-in was held at New York University in an attempt to create enthusiasm and support for planned April and May antiwar demonstrations. New York City Councilman Theodore S. Weiss, reflecting obvious despair, said, "I can't help bringing a sense of futility to yet another teach-in."[10] David Dellinger said that the protest must continue if "we are going to live with ourselves."[11] David McReynolds believed firmly that it was time to "break off relations" with the government.[12]

On April 23, more than a thousand Vietnam veterans filed slowly past the heavily guarded United States Capitol and literally threw their military medals—Vietnam Crosses of Gallantry, Silver Stars, and Purple Hearts—to the Capitol steps. One said, "This was the final act of contempt." Another veteran reported, "We never took one prisoner alive." Another said his service in Vietnam was "a disservice to my country."[13]

The next day, April 24, approximately three hundred thousand gathered on the Ellipse near the White House and slowly marched—over a period of five hours—to the Capitol steps. In San Francisco about one hundred twenty-five thousand gathered for a rally that was shown live to a nationwide television audience. Some groups also demonstrated near the Justice Department and at the Department of Health, Education, and Welfare as well as the Selective Service headquarters. The mood of the day was perhaps best captured by David Livingston, president of District 65 of the Retail, Wholesale and Department Store Workers, who said to the House of Representatives and the Senate, "Under the Constitution, you can end the war."[14]

Attempts were made by smaller antiwar groups to bring Washington, D.C., traffic to a standstill and, as a result, force the government to stop functioning. The activists didn't have a chance. They were met by National Guardsmen, regular Army troops, National Park Service, and Washington, D.C., police officers at every point of planned protest, resulting in more than twelve thousand arrests—the largest number for any demonstration in American history.

The San Antonio field office, in a memo to headquarters dated January

26, 1971, made reference to an earlier Washington field office memo to Hoover advising that a student peace conference was planned for February 19–21 at Catholic University in Washington, D.C.[15] The San Antonio memo reported on "strong resentment in some Catholic circles in the Archdiocese of San Antonio concerning the use of archdiocese money to support the Catholic University of America."[16] San Antonio also asked the New York and Washington field offices to provide any additional information on the conference.

New York responded on February 1 with a report of an article in *The Militant* headlined "National Student Antiwar Conference Called." The New York office cautioned that any type of program involving a religious institution such as Catholic University must be handled very carefully, "especially when the identity of the FBI is or will be known to individuals and/or officials connected to such institutions."[17]

A headquarters memo, also dated February 1, 1971, from C. D. Brennan, advised that the purpose of the conference was to develop and finalize plans for the massive antiwar demonstration scheduled for Washington in mid-April. Brennan added that many Catholics were evidently offended by the sensational charge that members of the Catholic Left had been involved in a plot to sabotage federal buildings and kidnap Henry A. Kissinger. "It would seem," the memo added, "completely in the public interest to disseminate as widely as possible in the U.S." the fact that the university is hosting the SMC, an organization dominated by the SWP. Brennan's suggested media release is shown below. The intention was to bring "voluminous and vehement criticism of CU decision . . . which might result in cancellation of the SMC conference."[18]

TROTSKYISTS WELCOMED AT CATHOLIC UNIVERSITY!

Following in the wake of bombshell indictments of Catholic priests and nuns in connection with the alleged plot to kidnap a Government official and sabotage Federal buildings in Washington, D.C., it is now reported that Catholic University (CU) will host a national conference of the Student Mobilization Committee to End the War in Vietnam (SMC) in Washington, D.C., during February. Has the Catholic church been duped again? It is almost inconceivable that responsible CU officials or high level officials of the Roman Catholic church would allow themselves to be thrust into the position of providing a sanctuary and planning base for a group of students whose sole purpose in meeting is undoubtedly to draw up battle lines and strategy for massive antiwar demonstrations to be held in Washington, D.C., and San Francisco, California, during April.

The invitation by CU is more puzzling, even appalling, when you consider the established fact that the SMC is communist controlled at every national office level by members of the Trotskyist Socialist Workers Party or its youth affiliate, the Young Socialist Alliance. J. Edgar Hoover, Director of the FBI, made this point perfectly clear in testimony before the House of Representatives Subcommittee on Appropriations during March, 1970. Could it be that CU has not kept abreast of disclosures involving subversive elements in certain activities of the antiwar movement, or does the University merely choose to ignore the facts? Both possibilities should receive serious concern![19]

Edited New Left COINTELPRO memos from February 1971 suggest that the Brennan CU–SMC media release was anonymously mailed to a number of selected newspapers with good results. Catholic University officials evidently received considerable pressure to cancel the SMC conference altogether. CU advised the SMC that they must "take out a million dollar insurance policy against possible damage caused by 'riots.' " John Studer, then on the SMC staff, remembers, "It was crystal clear they [the university administration] had changed their minds and wanted us out. But they didn't want it to appear as a political move. They didn't think we would do it, but we got the policy—from Lloyds of London."[20]

The FBI efforts were to no avail. The SMC conference, attended by twenty-five hundred activists, took place as originally planned.

The Houston field office reported on an unusual situation involving a firebombing of the SWP headquarters in Houston. According to a March 31, 1971, memo, elements of the extreme right were blamed at first, but on closer examination it appeared that, for whatever reason, the SWP had actually bombed their own headquarters! Houston special agents, working with the Intelligence Division of the Houston Police Department, contacted SWP members for interviews. All refused lie detector tests. This investigation, according to the memo, "has shaken the group to the point that two of them have made a trip to New York for guidance from SWP headquarters." Informants reported that SWP officials made a trip to Houston and hired a local ACLU attorney, whom they could not pay, "as all of their efforts are being directed towards obtaining money to rent buses to go to Washington, D.C., on April 24, 1971, for the demonstration there."

After the incident, fund raising was apparently going very badly. Houston advised that they would continue to monitor the SWP situation and indicated that "all efforts are being made to disrupt this activity."[21]

Hoover was informed by a January 28 San Diego memo that the national office of the SWP had changed its membership policy to allow "homosexuals to be considered for membership." The memo also advised that [*name deleted*], a member of the San Diego YSA, "was recently arrested on a felony charge for committing an abnormal act with a negro male in a public place." San Diego requested and received authority to anonymously mail leaflets publicizing this information, with "the desired effect of dissuading would-be new recruits from membership in YSA." These leaflets, inviting the "gay set, to membership in YSA," were also posted on various bulletin boards on the San Diego State College campus.[22]

In the fall of 1970, the New York field office began a campaign of anonymous mailings of inflammatory letters and comic strips designed to cause disruption within the Progressive Labor Party, namely by accusing the PLP National Steering Committee of racism. In September, 160 copies of the PLP comic strip were sent to PLP members, supporters, and allied organizations. In October, thirty-five additional copies were mailed to members and officers of Students for a Democratic Society—Worker Student Alliance (SDS-WSA) across the country.[23]

The mailings obviously hit the target. The November 1, 1970, issue of *Challenge-Desafío*, the PLP newspaper, responded furiously. The November 1 issue contained an article headlined "Police Forgeries Won't Stop PLP," and subheaded "Cops Spend Thousands to Misprint PLP's Program • Mail Out Racist Cartoons and Egg on Nationalist Attacks • Those Using These Police Lies Ought to Think Where That Action Leads." The article reported that various items had been received by many PLP members, friends, and others during the past several weeks, including a racist comic strip cartoon "showing the worst kind of stereotype of a black person." New York suggested that PLP officials obviously blamed "police agencies for the distribution of such disruptive material" in an attempt to refute charges of racism.[24] In an attempt "to add a little more fuel to the fire," Hoover approved, on November 9, 1970, the anonymous letter below sent to the editors of *Challenge-Desafío* on December 13, 1970:

Comrades:
   I read with interest your article on page 2 of the Nov. 1st "Challenge-Desafío" which pointed out that attempts of the pig establishment to disrupt PL through obvious forgeries and whatever.
   A word of caution, however. I am convinced that it is a mistake to make

the basic assumption that all such filthy devices can be laid at the dishonored door of the pigs. Unfortunately, there are today in PL disruptive elements who are not above such tactics. I also feel that many of these leaflets or comic strips (I have one before me) attacking and distorting the report of the Nat'l Steering Comm. are *not* police in origin!

I would suggest a little internal investigation is in order—in fact, absolutely necessary. I would further suggest that PL take a good look at the current activities of people like Epton and others of his ilk. They are out to destroy the party in every respect.

I am, of course, concerned that the bosses and their flunkies will continue to attack our party and the working class but they are the least of our worries. My biggest concern is the traitors in our midst. And, brothers, I for one am going to help ferret them out.

For that reason, you may know me only as . . .

—A Harlem comrade of many years[25]

On February 8, 1971, the New York office submitted to headquarters a proposal for an anonymous mailing designed to aggravate a serious philosophical division between the Students for a Democratic Society and the Progressive Labor Party—or what was perceived as a serious division by informants at "the recent SDS National Convention held in Chicago, Illinois." The enclosed letter, New York said, was "written in the jargon of the New Left necessitating the use of a certain amount of profanity."[26] Hoover approved it, in hopes of encouraging "greater factionalism within the SDS/WSA." "It is noted," Hoover responded, "that the letter contains vulgarisms which would be used by the SDS/WSA activists who, ostensibly prepared the leaflet." During two days in March, 101 copies were mailed to "selected individuals and organizations in the New Left."

SDS—A REMEMBRANCE OF THINGS PAST

In late December a shitty debacle—laughingly described as the SDS National Convention—was held in the windy city of Chicago, with most of the wind (Noxious fumes, if you like) confined to the cavernous interior of the coliseum. It was a mind boggling experience from any standpoint. A thousand red balloons could have been inflated with the crappy helium spouted by Pipers like Alan Spector and Jeff Singleton who carefully restructured SDS into a new organizational image—a 100% puppet of the PLP.

Opposition was nil. Oh, there was some bitching from the floor, mainly centered around the Midnight Special group from New Orleans, and to a slight extent, from the Columbia university delegation, but Alan, Marty Riefe and sweetie Singleton simply rammed the PL shit down our collective throats. In doing so, they paved the way for the inevitable factional splits which, in the last analysis, buried yesteryear's SDS in a deep, deep grave.

The new NIC assures PL domination of any future course taken under the name of SDS. And any course taken under PLP leadership leads straight to oblivion. The election of Riefe as Nat'l Secretary and Singleton as Org. Secretary cemented PL into national control for keeps. A few of us threw up and shuffled our feet but otherwise—nothing!

It was all so sad. And the ultimate in fairy tales appeared in the convention run-down in the January 15th issue of New Left Notes. Wow! According to these dreamers, hundreds of workers joined the December 30th "climatic" demonstration and parade on Washington and State Streets. Bullshit! The parade was just short of pitiful. We marched the whole route and didn't see one worker—not one—do anything but spit at us. One jolly group took up the deathless shout of "Jew-Commie-Punks!" Even the pigs were smirking with joy for what had they to fear from that pathetic rabble of wet-nosed, pimple-faced, middle klass kids!

SDS died in Chicago . . . was eaten and finally defecated by one of the most narrow, stoical, semi-political groups of all time. Compared to PL's leadership in action, a dead man moves with blinding speed. At least, the whole thing left some of us free to contemplate our navels in the sunshine while the PLers bullshit, bullshit and bullshit. . . .

—Mao[27]

In April, New York sent Hoover a proposal for a mailing designed to disrupt the National Peace and Action Coalition and Peoples Coalition for Peace and Justice.[28] Both groups, Hoover noted in his approval memo, were "Trotskyist or communist-infiltrated or dominated" and were known as sponsors of antiwar demonstrations scheduled for Washington, D.C., and San Francisco on April 24.

**SCREW UP   SCREW UP   SCREW UP   SCREW UP
SCREW UP   SCREW UP   SCREW UP   SCREW UP**

THE THIRD . . . WHAT?
According to Chief White Fag Dave McReynolds of the lily-white War Resisters League and the sickening pale Nat'l Peace Action Coalition, the "massive" demonstrations in Washington on April 24th, will change the course of Amerikkan history and—laughingly—force the establishment

to recognize *ALL THE POWER OF THE PEOPLE!* Bullshit, Dave, baby. . . .

The flood of crappy position papers and senseless pronouncements vomited from the headquarters of NPAG and the People's Coalition For Peace and Justice, in recent weeks reveals the usual Queer Cats—like Sweet Dave Dellinger, Fruity Rennie Davis, Old Faggot Stewart Meacham, Nutty Sid Peck and Old Folks Abernathy, have once again combined to give the kiss of death to what could have been a meaningful demonstration of the people's rage against Amerikka. Together, with the stone-heads from the racist Socialist Workers Party and their dead abortion, the Young Socialist Alliance, they will skillfully produce what they produce best: *COMPLETE AND UTTER FAILURE!*

We note with a high degree of nausea that every white Fag group in the country has been urged to mince their way to the capital. Every Jew landlord in . . . Harlem and Bed-Sty have been told to take their hands out of BLACK pockets for just one day. Every white, female Lib group, every lesbian collection of cuckoos, every ranting pervert, every liberal maniac . . . will be in D.C. on the 24th. They forget two small items: *TWENTY-FOUR MILLION BLACKS* and thousands of *NORMAL PEOPLE!*

The outrageous rejection of BLACK participation by the chauvinistic TROTS and their homo friends was bad enough, but sticking Uncle Tom Abernathy up front for all the world to see was a smack in the face of BLACK Liberation everywhere. The good Reverend has stepped in too much mule shit to be of any value to anybody. . . .

The PEACE MOVEMENT has been torn asunder by the ding-dongs who grabbed command years ago. Dellinger and Company are the cancer in the Movement's bloodstream. They must be removed and *NOW!*

DEMAND BLACK PARTICIPATION! DEMAND REMOVAL OF THE FAGGOTS!

Write: Vietnam Peace Parade Committee
         17 East 17th Street, NY 10003[29]

A March 2 Indianapolis memo to the director again concerned Keith Steven Parker, student-body president at Indiana University.[30] Parker had become a COINTELPRO-New Left target because of his suspicious on-campus activities and his controversial and well-publicized trip to North Vietnam. As noted in the previous chapter, the Indianapolis office, with bureau approval, created a leaflet meant to diminish Parker's stature on campus and lessen "any of the effects of the Student Mobilization Committee (SMC) on the campus and to discredit the United Student Movement," which it said had evidently taken control of the IU student government.[31] The student government had direct access to student funds and had used those funds to support campus activities of the New Left and the Black Panther Party. The leaflets were distributed on campus and mailed to the IU newspaper and to every member of the board of trustees. The board quickly voted to abolish the mandatory semester fees paid by all enrolling students to support the student government at Indiana University. This move deprived the United Student Movement of access to funding, which, of course, eliminated their ability to support New Left and Black Panther Party activities at IU.

An article in the Bloomington *Daily Herald Telephone* reported that "some trustees indicated displeasure with student government being used to help finance controversial activities such as the San Francisco Mime Troupe, Bobby Seale Weekend, and the Liberation Movement Weekend."[32] Parker himself was obviously shaken by the mailing. He said that "copies of the leaflet had been mailed to his parents and some acquaintances which had a derogatory effect on his character."[33] The FBI leaflet was signed by the Concerned Students at IU. In a speech, Parker asked any students associated with Concerned Students to please stand. This being a fictitious group, there was, of course, no response. The field office memo reported that Parker's status as a student leader had been reduced to the point "where he is in no real position to organize or lead."[34]

On January 11, 1971, Hoover sent memos to the Boston, New York, New Orleans, Chicago, and Los Angeles field offices instructing special agents to contact informants who had attended the Chicago SDS/WSA national convention and to "obtain details that would make suitable counterintelligence information available against the PLP." More specifically, Hoover wanted any information concerning "the expenditures of funds for travel and lodging, immoral or unusual activities by convention participants." The director also asked for information on "WSA/SDS individuals handling funds and methods of distributing them." Results from field offices were expected within two weeks.[35]

New York, in response to the Hoover memo, conducted an anonymous mailing on February 17 targeting the SDS/WSA group.[36] There is no record, however, that New Orleans, Boston, or Los Angeles responded to the Hoover memo at all. Chicago responded on January 22 to say that informants who had attended the convention found the whole affair to have been badly managed. The PLP held most of the key positions at the convention, the memo reported, and thus "controlled who was allowed on the floor to debate issues." When views contrary to PLP thinking were presented on the convention floor for discussion, PLP members would simply "shout the speaker down." Anti-PLP factions were disorganized and unable to present ideas "over the harassment of PLP members." Those in attendance, including PLP members, complained of poor press coverage. Others complained "WSA was poorly prepared to effectively function as a national organization during the ensuing year."[37]

The Pittsburgh field office was surprised to learn that a controversial economics professor at the University of Pittsburgh, originally targeted a year before, was still employed by the university. It was the bureau's understanding that the professor would be terminated in the summer of 1970.

On March 12, 1971, Pittsburgh special agents again contacted an official [name deleted] at the university with information on the professor's arrest and conviction record. Pittsburgh advised Hoover on April 1, 1971, that this time the target had truly "reached a dead end" at Pittsburgh. The university was "most appreciative of receiving the information." The contact "would in no way divulge the Bureau's interest in this matter."[38]

New Left COINTELPRO activity was reduced all across the nation in early 1971, and this may be taken as evidence that the antiwar movement was losing momentum. As we have seen, FBI field offices in Washington, San Francisco, San Antonio, Houston, San Diego, Pittsburgh, New York, Indianapolis, and Chicago received headquarters' approval for COINTELPRO actions during the first quarter of 1971. But most of the other COINTELPRO-approved field offices had very little antiwar activity to report.

On the night of March 8, 1971, the wall of secrecy surrounding the FBI COINTELPRO operations was destroyed by the burglary of the bureau's resident office in Media, Pennsylvania. On April 8, Hoover issued a memo to all COINTELPRO-approved field offices which advised that the program's "90-day status letters will no longer be required and should be discontinued." Special agents, however, must "continue aggressive and imaginative participation in the program."[39]

On April 27, 1971, C. D. Brennan suggested that to "afford additional security to our sensitive techniques and operations, it is recommended that COINTELPROs operated by the Domestic Intelligence Division be discontinued." The next day, in a memo to all COINTELPRO-approved field offices, Hoover advised that "effective immediately, all COINTEL-PROs operated by this Bureau are discontinued." Future counter-intelligence operations would be considered on a case-by-case basis only.[40]

Through the years of the program, bureau headquarters had received 381 New Left proposals from approved field offices. Of this total, 285 actions were implemented, with confirmed results obtained in 77 actions. Anonymous or fictitious mailings were used in 40 percent of the New Left actions. In twenty-five cases, special agents released public-record information to media sources. Employers and credit bureaus were advised of New Left member status in twenty situations. In eight cases, the bureau contacted businesses and individuals who had financial dealings with New Left members. In twelve actions, the bureau contacted family members and friends of New Left activists.

The use of paid undercover informants in the New Left COINTEL-PRO operations was particularly widespread, and these informants came from a wide range of backgrounds. The FBI traditionally had two types of informants: "criminal informants"—used in connection with investigation of certain types of criminal activity, and "intelligence informants" used, as in the New Left COINTELPRO, to report on associations, groups, and individuals in the course of intelligence investigations of political activity.

The bureau had to walk a careful line between developing productive undercover informants and creating agents provocateur. As a CO-INTELPRO memo dated September 16, 1970, advised, "While our informants should be privy to everything going on and should rise to the maximum level of their ability in the New Left movement, they should not become the person who carries the gun, throws the bomb, does the robbery or by some specific violative, overt act becomes a deeply involved participant."[41]

New Left informants were often in precarious situations. David Sannes, a special agent, worked as an undercover informant in the Seattle area. He later testified that he was instructed by bureau counterintelligence officials to actually develop a terrorist bombing operation, and to develop the explosives in such a way that they would misfire and kill those who were doing the bombing. In May 1971, after he left the bureau, Sannes said that he had "decided to make what I have done public so that the people of the United States could be informed of what was going on."[42]

Larry D. Grantwohl became one of the most militant members of the Weather Underground in Cincinnati. He participated in violent demonstrations while living in underground collectives in Cincinnati and elsewhere. He was in regular contact with the FBI and Guy L. Goodwill, the chief Justice Department official in charge of prosecution against the Underground. Grantwohl supplied information that led to the arrests of many Weathermen.

Grantwohl was known for his particular skill in handling explosives. As former Weatherman Robert Burlington remembers, "Larry was absolutely a provocateur. I can remember one meeting in Cincinnati where there was a discussion going on about the question of armed political resistance and the various bombings that had occurred. Grantwohl took the initiative as was his wont and began castigating people for talking about the destruction of property; he said it wasn't enough to carry on these kinds of bombings. 'True revolutionaries,' he said, 'had to be ready and anxious to kill people.'"[43]

The issue of wiretaps in the New Left COINTELPRO is curious. The wiretap of a "New Left Campus Group" began in 1969 and lasted through 1970. In 1970, the headquarters of the Workers Student Alliance was wiretapped, together with the name of an activist known to be in contact with the Weathermen. A "New Left Activist," a "domestic protest group," and a "violence prone faction of a domestic protest group" were all tapped. Three separate antiwar groups planning the March on Washington in November 1969, including the New Mobilization Committee to End the War in Vietnam and the Vietnam Moratorium, were all wiretapped. Additional wiretap categories included the Weather Underground Support Apparatus, Weathermen organization publications, and the Investigation of Clandestine Underground Groups Dedicated to Strategic Sabotage.[44]

The 1970 tap on a "New Left campus" enabled the bureau "to develop strong ties with the cafeteria, maintenance, and other workers on campus." This particular tap, also according to the FBI, provided the bureau with the identities of 1,428 individuals in contact with the "national headquarters or associated with it"—the unnamed "New Left Campus Group."[45] This type of information was evidently obtained by the FBI in programs outside of the New Left COINTELPRO operations. In fact, there is almost no mention of wiretaps in all of the more than six thousand COINTELPRO New Left documents.

The war itself continued for almost four more years beyond the end of the New Left COINTELPRO. By late spring of 1971, fully 60 percent of the American public favored a complete withdrawal of American troops even if it meant the collapse of the South Vietnamese government.

By the fall of 1971, American troop levels had declined to 220,000. By the fall of 1972, "the mass of the American people considered U.S. involvement in the war virtually over."[46] Henry Kissinger began serious negotiations with the North Vietnamese in January of 1973. American troops left South Vietnam on March 29, 1973. The American embassy in Saigon was evacuated on April 29, 1975. For the United States, the war was over. The cost to the United States was beyond any rational human comprehension: 58,000 Americans killed, 300,000 wounded, at a cost exceeding 150 billion dollars.

Opposition to the war, on a much smaller scale, continued for some time after the COINTELPRO operations were discontinued; but antiwar protest, in large measure, declined in proportion to the declining numbers of American troops in combat.

Several small rallies took place at a number of military bases in May of 1971. The Pentagon Papers, a secret history of America's involvement in South Vietnam, were made public on June 13, 1971, and caused a national uproar. Max Frankel of the *New York Times* read the Pentagon Papers and wrote that the United States had not sought a victory but only the "avoidance of defeat and humiliation."[47]

As late as January 1973, there were smaller, multicity demonstrations, directed primarily at American bombing campaigns in Vietnam. Vietnam Veterans Against the War occupied the Statue of Liberty on December 28, 1971. There were protests at Harvard on April 8, 1972, known as "Peace Action Day." Thousands gathered in protest at the second Nixon inaugural, and in May 1974 many demonstrated to mark the fourth anniversary of the Kent State shootings. By this time, however, the New Left as a protest movement had largely dissolved.

Without the war in Vietnam, the New Left would not have grown to such dimensions as a social and political protest movement. While the New Left alienated significant portions of mainstream America, this largely generational revolt paradoxically played a very great role in helping to mold public opinion against a war that seemed to have no possibility of ending.

The New Left and the antiwar movement provided the largest and most sustained campaign of political protest seen in the United States in the twentieth century. The commensurate efforts of the FBI, together with other government agencies, conducted the most extensive operations against political dissidence ever seen against citizens of the United States. The New Left COINTELPRO, by its nature, went far beyond the actual collection of intelligence information to secret counterintelligence actions designed to disrupt and neutralize the antiwar movement—methods adapted from the bureau's counterintelligence techniques used during World War II. In a constitutional context, the FBI circumvented First and Fourth Amendment guarantees and thus exceeded its authority.

In its broadest context, Hoover's perceived authority was to protect the social order—what he evidently saw as the American way of life. The New Left resisted authority and thereby threatened the status quo. The COINTELPRO-New Left documents betray the belief that any person involved in any way with antiwar protest was, by definition, part of the New Left—regardless of political affiliation or philosophy. This very questionable line of thinking provided the foundation for a long campaign of secret infiltration of and attack on the youth movement of an entire generation—particularly the antiwar part of that movement. Clearly, as the comptroller general's report to the House Committee on the Judiciary stated, "Neither the Justice Department nor Congress exercised adequate control and oversight over FBI domestic intelligence operations."[48]

Edward S. Levi became attorney general in early 1975. Levi, working closely with FBI director Clarence M. Kelley, determined that there had been a total of twelve COINTELPRO operations instead of just the original five, which had included the New Left COINTELPRO. One was directed toward radical Puerto Rican independence groups and comprised thirty-seven actions between August 1960 and April 1971. Two concerned organized crime and the Communist Party, known as "Operation Hoodwink."

On April 5, 1976, Attorney General Levi's guidelines for domestic intelligence investigations became the FBI's approved operating procedure. The Levi guidelines were created to prevent a recurrence of New Left and other COINTELPRO-type operations. According to the comptroller general, "They clearly distinguished between the different phases of investigation—preliminary, limited, and full field—in terms of the duration and scope of investigation, and the investigative techniques permitted."[49]

In addition, the attorney general created the Investigations Review Unit "to monitor and review the FBI's domestic intelligence and counterintelligence operations."[50] Under the new Levi guidelines, the FBI could begin a domestic intelligence investigation "of groups or individuals whose activities are directed toward the overthrow or serious impairment of Government operations or the obstruction of citizens' civil rights with slightly less substantive information than is required to initiate a criminal investigation." However, Levi specified that "government monitoring of individuals or groups because they hold unpopular or controversial political views is intolerable in our society." The guidelines provided for domestic intelligence investigations and the legal use of informants for the purpose of conducting criminal investigations and to anticipate violence, but "no one is subject to full domestic security investigation unless he or she is directly involved in violence or engaging in activities which indicate he or she is likely to use force or violence in violation of a federal law."[51] On April 1,1976, Levi also announced the creation of a special review committee within the Department of Justice to contact individuals who might have been victimized by improper COINTELPRO actions.

On August 11, 1976, Clarence Kelley, after an exhaustive study, transferred domestic intelligence investigations to the FBI General Investigative Division, where they would be administered like other bureau domestic-security investigations such as the New Left. The enormous scope of FBI intelligence investigations before the Kelley and Levi reforms was so broad-based that the General Accounting Office found them to be unproductive. Kelley's main concern was to use the bureau's intelligence resources to meet two basic needs: to prevent terrorist crimes, and to "assist future investigations of specific criminal acts."[52]

FBI domestic security operations were, to use political scholar John T. Elliff's phrase, brought "down to manageable dimensions."[53] Indeed, "the domestic security guidelines brought an end to forty years of FBI investigations of unlawful political activities, conducted in the name of protecting the government from remote, speculative threats of revolutionary overthrow."[54]

By 1976, many congressional investigations had exposed the New Left and other COINTELPRO operations in detail. In a study completed on June 30, 1977, the comptroller general reported that pending FBI domestic-intelligence investigative cases decreased from 9,814 to 642. The number of domestic-intelligence cases initiated decreased from 1,454 to 95. In 1974, the FBI investigated 157 organizations in the name of domestic intelligence; by mid-1977, the number had declined to seventeen organizations. In March 1975, the FBI had 788 special agents involved in domestic intelligence investigations; by midyear of 1977, the total was down to 143. In November 1975, the bureau was utilizing about 1,100 undercover informants in domestic intelligence; by midyear 1977, it was using only about 100.[55]

A 1982 study by the Senate Committee on the Judiciary revealed that, as a direct result of the domestic intelligence reforms, only thirty-eight current domestic security investigations were in progress.[56]

William Webster, who became FBI director in 1978, confirmed that the Levi guidelines and Kelley reforms had a substantial effect in reducing FBI domestic case loads. Webster said that he preferred to "retain the character of domestic security investigations as essentially criminal investigations—as established by the criminal standards of the Levi guidelines—rather than as intelligence investigations."[57]

Although the New Left and other COINTELPRO operations ceased in 1971, the news media have maintained interest in the programs until the present day. On November 22, 1977, the *New York Times* reported on the more than five hundred newly released COINTELPRO documents that outlined the ten-year campaign against Puerto Rican separatist parties. This COINTELPRO, which targeted party members in New York and Puerto Rico, was created to disrupt "parties which seek independence for Puerto Rico through other than lawful means."[58]

In March 1981, the U.S. Justice Department agreed to pay $10,000 to each of five persons whose Constitutional rights had been violated by the FBI. The illegal bureau actions included "wiretaps, burglaries, or mail openings in the early 1970s." One individual, Sara Blackburn, had her telephone tapped and her residence broken into, chiefly because she had once contributed to the Black Panthers. Another target, Lewis Cole, was a leader of the SDS disorders at Columbia University in 1968 and 1969.[59]

Also in 1981, Isaiah J. Poole wrote an article which expressed black feelings about COINTELPRO ten years after its end. "Some blacks perceived," Poole wrote, "shades of COINTELPRO when Attorney General William French Smith told a breakfast meeting of reporters that there was an 'early warning system' that would alert the administration to outbreaks of racial disorders that would occur as a fallout of cuts in special programs."[60]

On March 30, 1983, an intelligence memorandum from FBI headquarters instructed eleven FBI field offices to investigate "the involvement of individuals and the CISPES [Committee in Solidarity with the People of El Salvador] organization in international terrorism as it affects the El Salvadoran government and [authorizes] the collection of foreign intelligence and counterintelligence information as it relates to the international terrorism aspects of this investigation."[61] The bureau focused its attention on more than 160 organizations perceived by FBI officials as supporting international terrorism in Central America—that is, "organizations sympathetic to leftist guerrillas in El Salvador."[62] The investigation was closed after a Justice Department review in 1985, and it came to national attention when twelve hundred pages of FBI intelligence documents were provided to the Center for Constitutional Rights through the Freedom of Information Act in 1988. "Now, as in earlier incidents," Gary M. Stern, a political scholar, wrote in 1988, "purely political activity became the subject of an extensive investigation by the FBI."[63] In September 1988, FBI Director William S. Sessions "imposed disciplinary sanctions against six FBI employees involved in a controversial investigation of a political group that opposed United States policies in Central America."[64]

After a lengthy investigation, the Senate Select Committee on Intelligence concluded that "the CISPES case was a serious failure in FBI management, resulting in the investigation of domestic political activities that should not have come under governmental scrutiny. It raised issues that go to the heart of this country's commitment to the protection of constitutional rights. Unjustified investigations of political expression and dissent can have a debilitating effect upon our political system."[65]

The most important judicial decision regarding the FBI's COINTELPRO practices came on August 25, 1985. U.S. District Court Judge Thomas Griesa released a 210-page decision upholding the right of the Socialist Workers Party and the Young Socialist Alliance to publicize their political views and to participate in political activity "free from interference and monitoring by the FBI or other agencies of the government."[66]

Richard E. Morgan, an expert in American constitutional law, has written: "Domestic intelligence activity is a legitimate law enforcement activity, and, as such, it must be conducted within the parameters of Constitutional law. Activities like the FBI's COINTELPRO operations and harassment of dissenters should end, and warrant requirements for electronic or physical searches should be observed."[67]

The United States, as the oldest republic in the world, should perhaps know more than any nation on earth about individual liberties. However, the matter of actively defending "order"—utilizing the machinery of government to protect liberties without damaging them in the process—remains difficult.

Surely many of those who directed and conducted the COINTELPRO-New Left operations did so with good intentions. However, as we have seen, COINTELPRO-New Left took on a life of its own without any kind of accountability to anyone, in or out of the government, except the bureau. In a most extraordinary paradox, the only act that stopped the New Left and other COINTELPROs was an illegal act: the Media office burglary.

NOTES

1. Theodore H. White, *The Making of the President 1968* (New York: Atheneum, 1969), p. 15.

2. Richard M. Nixon, *The Memoirs of Richard Nixon* (New York: Grosset and Dunlap, 1978), p. 497.

3. Henry Kissinger, *White House Years* (Boston: Little, Brown, 1979), p. 994.

4. Nancy Zaroulis and Gerald Sullivan, *Who Spoke Up? American Protest against the War in Vietnam 1963–1975* (Garden City, NY: Doubleday, 1984), p. 343.

5. *Christian Science Monitor*, Feb. 12, 1971.

6. Zaroulis and Sullivan, *Who Spoke Up?*, pp. 346–355.

7. Fred Halstead, *Out Now! A Participant's Account of the Movement in the U.S. against the Vietnam War* (New York: Pathfinder Press, 1978), p. 296.

8. Ibid.

9. Charles DeBenedetti and Charles Chatfield, *An American Ordeal: The Antiwar Movement of the Vietnam Era* (Syracuse: Syracuse University Press, 1990), p. 303.

10. Zaroulis and Sullivan, *Who Spoke Up?*, p. 349.

11. Ibid.

12. Ibid., p. 340.

13. Ibid., p. 358.

14. Ibid., p. 359.

15. FBI Memorandum, San Antonio Field Office to Headquarters, Jan. 26, 1971.

16. Ibid.

17. FBI Memorandum, New York Field Office to Headquarters, Feb. 1, 1971.

18. FBI Memorandum, C. D. Brennan to A. W. Gray, Feb. 1, 1971.

19. Ibid.

20. Halstead, *Out Now!*, pp. 592–593.

21. FBI Memorandum, Houston Field Office to Headquarters, Mar. 31, 1971.

22. FBI Memorandum, San Diego Field Office to Headquarters, Jan. 28, 1971; Headquarters to San Diego Field Office, Feb. 8, 1971.

23. FBI Memorandum, New York Field Office to Headquarters, Oct. 28, 1970.

24. Ibid.

25. Ibid.

26. FBI Memorandum, New York Field Office to Headquarters, Feb. 8, 1971.

27. Ibid.

28. FBI Memorandum, New York Field Office to Headquarters, Apr. 2, 1971.

29. Ibid.

30. FBI Memorandum, Indianapolis Field Office to Headquarters, Mar. 2, 1971.

31. Ibid.

32. John Faucher, "Parker Going To Vietnam," *Bloomington Daily Herald Telephone*, Nov. 25, 1970, p. 2; John Faucher, "Trustees Abolish IU Student Fee," *Bloomington Daily Herald Telephone,* Jan. 23, 1971, p. 1; Vicki Carter, "FBI COINTEL in Action," *Bloomington Daily Herald Telephone,* Dec. 5, 1975, p. 1.

33. FBI Memorandum, Indianapolis Field Office to Headquarters, Mar. 2, 1971.

34. Ibid.

35. FBI Memorandum, Headquarters to Field Offices, Jan. 11, 1971.

36. FBI Memorandum, New York Field Office to Headquarters, Feb. 17, 1971.

37. Ibid.

38. FBI Memorandum, Pittsburgh Field Office to Headquarters, Feb. 25, 1971; Headquarters to Pittsburgh Field Office, Mar. 11, 1971; Pittsburgh Field Office to FBI Headquarters, Apr. 1, 1971.

39. FBI Memorandum, Headquarters to Field Offices, Apr. 8, 1971.

40. FBI Memorandum, C. D. Brennan to W. C. Sullivan, Apr. 27, 1971; Headquarters to Field Offices, Apr. 28, 1971.

41. FBI Memorandum, "The New Left Notes—Philadelphia," Philadelphia Special Agent-in-Charge, Sept. 9, 1970; Headquarters to Field Offices, Sept. 16, 1974.

42. David Dellinger, *More Power Than We Know: The People's Movement Toward Democracy* (Garden City, NY: Anchor Press, 1975), p. 78.

43. Seymour M. Hersh, "FBI Informer Is Linked to Bombing and Protest by Weatherman Group," *New York Times*, May 20, 1973, p. 52.

44. FBI Memorandum, J. Edgar Hoover to the Attorney General, May 11, 1969; Nov. 4, 1969; Mar. 16, 1970. Letter to Senate Select Committee, Oct. 22, 1975; Oct. 23, 1975.

45. FBI Memorandum, J. Edgar Hoover to the Attorney General, Sept. 16, 1970.

46. Halstead, *Out Now!*, p. 692.

47. Zaroulis and Sullivan, *Who Spoke Up?*, p. 368.

48. Report to the House Committee on the Judiciary by the Comptroller General of the United States, *FBI Domestic Intelligence Operations—Their Purposes and Scope: Issues That Need to Be Resolved*, Feb. 24, 1977, p. 1.

49. Report of the Comptroller General of the United States, *FBI Domestic Operations: An Uncertain Future*, Nov. 9, 1977, pp. 11–14; John T. Elliff, *The Reform of FBI Intelligence Activities* (Princeton, NJ: Princeton University Press, 1979), pp. 55–64.

50. Ibid.

51. Ibid.

52. Elliff, *Reform of FBI Intelligence Activities*, p. 190.

53. Ibid., p. 170.

54. Ibid., p. 190.

55. U.S. General Accounting Office, *Comprehensive Statement on the Federal Bureau of Investigation's Conduct of Domestic Intelligence Operations under the Attorney General's Guidelines*, Nov. 9, 1977, pp. 16–19.

56. Senate Select Committee on the Judiciary, Subcommittee on Security and Terrorism, *Impact of Attorney General's Guideline for Domestic Security Investigations*, 98th Cong., 1st Sess., Nov. 1983, p. 5.

57. Ibid.

58. Jo Thomas, "Documents Show FBI Harassed Puerto Rican Separatist Parties," *New York Times*, Nov. 22, 1977, p. 26.

59. Peter Kihss, "5 Gain Settlements for FBI Acts in the 70's," *New York Times*, Mar. 16, 1981, p. 1.

60. Isaiah J. Poole, "Harking Back to COINTELPRO," *Black Enterprise* (Sept. 1981): 25.

61. Gary M. Stern, *The FBI's Misguided Probe of CISPES*, Center for National Security Studies, CNSS Report No. III, Washington, D.C., June 1988, p. 1.

62. "Bad Habits Die Hard," *Time*, Feb. 8, 1988, p. 33.

63. Stern, *The FBI's Misguided Probe of CISPES*, p. 2.

64. Barbara Bradley, "FBI Chief Disciplines Agents for Misconduct," *Christian Science Monitor*, Sept. 15, 1988, p. 3.

65. Senate Select Committee on Intelligence, *The FBI and CISPES*, 101st Cong., 1st Sess., July 1989, Committee Print, p. 1.

66. "A Fight for Political Rights," Political Rights Defense Fund, New York, 1986, p. 54.

67. Richard E. Morgan, *Domestic Intelligence: Monitoring Dissent in America* (Austin: University of Texas Press, 1980), p. 124.

Selected Bibliography

Albert, Judith Clavir, and Stewart Edward Albert. *The Sixties Papers: Documents of a Rebellious Decade*. New York: Praeger, 1984.

Auron, Jerry L., with Andrew Crane. *Up Against the Ivy Wall*. New York: Atheneum, 1969.

Blackstock, Nelson. *COINTELPRO: The FBI's Secret War on Political Freedom*. New York: Pathfinder, 1988.

Churchill, Ward, and Jim Varder Wall. *The COINTELPRO Papers: Documents from the FBI's Secret Wars against Domestic Dissent*. Boston: South End Press, 1990.

Coffin, William Sloane, Jr. *Once to Every Man: A Memoir*. New York: Atheneum, 1978.

Cowan, Paul, Nick Egleson, and Nat Hentoff. *State Secrets: Police Surveillance in America*. New York: Holt, Rinehart and Winston, 1974.

Davis, James Kirkpatrick. *Spying on America*. Westport, CT: Praeger, 1992.

DeBenedetti, Charles, and Charles Chatfield. *An American Ordeal: The Antiwar Movement of the Vietnam Era*. Syracuse: Syracuse University Press, 1990.

Dellinger, David. *More Power Than We Know*. Garden City, NY: Anchor Press, 1975.

Demaris, Ovid. *The Director: An Oral Biography of J. Edgar Hoover*. New York: Harper's Magazine Press, 1975.

Divale, William Tulio, with James Joseph. *I Lived Inside the Campus Revolution*. New York: Coles, 1972.

Donner, Frank J. *The Age of Surveillance*. New York: Alfred A. Knopf, 1980.

Dorman, Michael. *Witch Hunt: The Underside of American Democracy*. New York: Delacorte Press, 1976.

Drury, Allen, and Fred Maroon. *Courage and Hesitation*. Garden City, NY: Doubleday, 1971.

Ehrlichman, John. *Witness to Power*. New York: Simon and Schuster, 1982.

Elliff, John T. *The Reform of FBI Intelligence Activities*. Princeton, NJ: Princeton University Press, 1979.

Epstein, Jason. *The Great Conspiracy Trial*. New York: Random House, 1970.

Fain, Tyrus G., Katharine C. Plant, and Ross Millay. *The Intelligence Community*. New York: R. R. Bowker, 1977.

Felt, W. Mark. *The FBI Pyramid*. New York: G. P. Putnam's Sons, 1979.

Ferber, Michael, and Straughton Lynd. *The Resistance*. Boston: Beacon Press, 1971.

Gitlin, Todd. *The Whole World Is Watching: Mass Media in the Making and Unmaking of the New Left*. Berkeley; Los Angeles; London: University of California Press, 1980.

Haines, Gerald K., and David A. Langbort. *Unlocking the Files of the FBI: A Guide to Its Records and Classification System*. Wilmington: Scholarly Resources, 1993.

Halberstam, David. *The Best and the Brightest*. New York: Random House, 1972.

Halperin, Morton H., Jerry J. Erman, Robert L. Borosage, and Christine M. Marwick. *The Lawless State: The Crimes of U.S. Intelligence Agencies*. New York: Penguin, 1976.

Halstead, Fred. *Out Now! A Participant's Account of the Movement in the U.S. against the Vietnam War*. New York: Pathfinder Press, 1978.

Hampton, Henry, Steve Fayer, and Sarah Flynn. *Voices of Freedom: An Oral History of the Civil Rights Movement from the 1950s through the 1980s*. New York: Bantam, 1990.

Isseman, Maurice. *If I Had a Hammer: The Death of the Old Left and the Birth of the New Left*. New York: Basic Books, 1987.

Jayko, Margaret, ed. *FBI on Trial*. New York: Pathfinder, 1988.

Johnson, Lyndon B. *The Vantage Point: Prospectives of the Presidency, 1963–1969*. New York: Holt, Rinehart and Winston, 1971.

Kahn, Roger. *The Battle for Morningside Heights: Why Students Rebel*. New York: William Morrow, 1970.

Karnow, Stanley. *Vietnam: A History, the First Complete Account of Vietnam at War*. New York: Viking Press, 1983.

Kearns, Doris. *Lyndon Johnson and the American Dream*. New York: Harper and Row, 1976.

Kelley, Clarence M., and James Kirkpatrick Davis. *Kelley: The Story of an FBI Director*. Kansas City, MO: Andrews, McMeel, and Parker, 1987.

Kelner, Joseph, and James Muuves. *The Kent State Cover Up*. New York: Harper and Row, 1968.

Kissinger, Henry. *White House Years*. Boston: Little, Brown, 1979.

———. *Years of Upheaval*. Boston: Little, Brown, 1982.

Lens, Sidney. *Unrepentant Radical: An American Activist's Account of Five Turbulent Decades*. Boston: Beacon Press, 1980.

Mailer, Norman. *Miami and the Siege of Chicago: An Informal History of the Republican and Democratic Conventions in 1968*. New York: World Publishing, 1968.

———. *The Armies of the Night: History as a Novel, the Novel as History*. New York: The New American Library, 1968.

Massimo, Teodori. *The New Left: A Documentary History*. New York: Bobbs-Merrill, 1969.

Matusow, Allen J. *The Unraveling of America: A History of Liberalism in the 1960s*. New York: Harper and Row, 1986.

McCarthy, Eugene J. *The Year of the People*. Garden City, NY: Doubleday, 1969.

McQuaid, Kim. *The Anxious Years: America in the Vietnam–Watergate Era*. New York: Basic Books, 1989.

Menashe, Louis, and Ronald Radosh. *Teach-Ins: U.S.A. Reports, Opinions, Documents*. New York: Frederick A. Praeger, 1967.

Morgan, Richard E. *Domestic Intelligence: Monitoring Dissent in America*. Austin: University of Texas Press, 1980.

Morison, Samuel Eliot. *The Oxford History of the American People*. New York: Oxford University Press, 1965.

Navasky, Victor S. *Kennedy Justice*. New York: Atheneum, 1977.

Nelson, Jack, and Ronald J. Ostrow. *The FBI and the Berrigans: The Making of a Conspiracy*. New York: Coward, McCann and Geoghegan, 1972.

Nixon, Richard. *The Memoirs of Richard Nixon*. New York: Grosset and Dunlap, 1978.

O'Reilly, Kenneth. *Racial Matters: The FBI's Secret War on Black America, 1966–1972*. New York: Free Press, 1989.

Perkus, Cathy, and Noam Chomsky. *COINTELPRO: The FBI's Secret War on Political Freedom*. New York: Monad Press, 1975.

Powers, Richard Gid. *Secrecy and Power, The Life of J. Edgar Hoover*. New York: Macmillan, 1986.

Powers, Thomas. *The War At Home: Vietnam and the American People: 1964–1968*. New York: Grossman, 1973.

Presidential Commission. *The Report of the President's Commission on Campus Unrest*. New York: Arno Press, 1970.

Reeves, Richard. *President Kennedy: Profile of Power*. New York: Touchstone Books, 1993.

Rorabaugh, W. J. *Berkeley at War: The 1960s.* New York: Oxford University Press, 1989.

Rothman, Stanley, and S. Robert Lighter. *Roots of Radicalism: Jews, Christians, and the New Left.* New York: Oxford University Press, 1982.

Sale, Kirkpatrick. *SDS.* New York: Random House, 1973 (paperback ed. Vintage, 1974).

Schell, Jonathan. *The Time of Illusion.* New York: Alfred A. Knopf, 1976.

Schlesinger, Arthur M., Jr. *The Crisis of the Old Order.* Boston: Houghton Mifflin, 1957.

———. *The Imperial Presidency.* Boston: Hougton Mifflin, 1973.

Schultz, John. *No One Was Killed: Documentation and Mediation: Convention Week, Chicago, August 1968.* Chicago: Big Table, 1969.

Shannon, David A. *The Decline of American Communism.* Chatham, NJ: Chatham Bookseller, 1959.

Sidey, Hugh. *John F. Kennedy, President.* New York: Atheneum, 1964.

———. *A Very Personal Presidency: Lyndon Johnson in the White House.* New York: Atheneum.

Sorensen, Theodore G. *Kennedy.* New York: Harper and Row, 1965.

Sullivan, William C., with Bill Brown. *The Bureau: My Thirty Years in Hoover's FBI.* New York: W. W. Norton, 1979.

Theohoris, Athan. *Spying on Americans: Political Surveillance from Hoover to the Huston Plan.* Philadelphia: Temple University Press, 1978.

Unger, Sanford J. *FBI: An Uncensored Look Behind the Walls.* Boston: Little, Brown, 1975.

U.S. News & World Report. *Communism and The New Left: What They're Up To Now.* New York: Macmillan, 1969.

Walker, Daniel. *Rights in Conflict: Chicago's 7 Brutal Days.* New York: Grosset and Dunlap, 1968.

Welch, Neil J., and David W. Marston. *Inside Hoover's FBI.* Garden City, NY: Doubleday, 1984.

White, Theodore H. *America in Search of Itself.* New York: Harper and Row, 1982.

———. *Breach of Faith: The Fall of Richard Nixon.* New York: Atheneum, 1975.

———. *The Making of the President 1960.* New York: Atheneum, 1961.

———. *The Making of the President 1964.* New York: Atheneum, 1966.

———. *The Making of the President 1968.* New York: Atheneum, 1969.

———. *The Making of the President 1972.* New York: Atheneum, 1973.

Whitehead, Don. *Attack on Terror: The FBI against the Ku Klux Klan in Mississippi.* New York: Funk and Wagnalls, 1970.

Wise, David. *The American Police State.* New York: Random House, 1976.

———. *The Politics of Lying.* New York: Vintage, 1973.

Zaroulis, Nancy, and Gerald Sullivan. *Who Spoke Up? American Protest against the War in Vietnam 1963–1975.* Garden City, NY: Doubleday, 1984.

Index

American Civil Liberties Union (ACLU), 15, 125
Antiwar movement, birth of, 27
Armageddon News, 121–23

Black Hate, 8, 51
Black Liberators, 96
Black Panther Party, 11, 80, 142, 187, 206; *Black Panther Newspaper*, 143; forming an alliance with SDS, 113, 119; Hilliard, David (leader), 151; letter to, 179–80
Black United Front (BUF), 152
Boston Five, 43
Brownell, Herbert, 5
Buffalo Nine Defense Committee, 155

Catholic University, 200–201
Chicago confrontation between activists and police, 82–85; cost of, 85–86
Citizens' Commission to Investigate the FBI, 9–12
Clark, Ramsey, 35
Clark, Tom C., 3
Cleveland Area Peace Council, 140
COINTELPRO. *See* Counterintelligence Programs

Columbia University, 36, 39–42
Committee in Solidarity with the People of El Salvador (CISPES), 213–14
Communist Index, 3
Communist Party USA (CPUSA), 3; membership, 6; Youth, 51; *New York Times* article, 71
Concerned Educators and Parents (CEAP), letter, 145–46
Congress of Racial Equality, 8, 65
Counterintelligence Programs (COIN-TELPRO): Black Hate, 8; discontinuance of, 208; establishment of, 5; informants, 208; master plan, 166–67; methods, 5; New Left, 36, 43–44, 46, 56, 96, 141; purposes of, 2–4; scope of actions, 210–15; "snitch jacket," 145, 171, 184; techniques, 7; wall of secrecy, 207; White Hate, 26; wiretaps, 209
CPUSA. *See* Communist Party USA

Davidon, William C., 9–10, 69
Davis, Angela, 171
Davis, Rennie, 64–65, 74–75, 108; indictment, 111
Deacons of Defense and Justice, 8

Dellinger, David, 26–27, 64–65, 75, 86, 198; anonymous letter about, 115; on the Chicago convention, 100; on demonstrating in Chicago, 74–75; indictment, 111; *Liberation*, 73; report on checking account, 73
Democratic National Convention, 58, 75, 80, 85
Democratic Party, 63

East Side Service Organization (ESSO), 81
Ehrlichman, John, 137
Eisenhower, Dwight D., 1
Emergency Civil Liberties Committee, 174
Emergency Detention Act, 3

FBI. *See* Federal Bureau of Investigation
Federal Bureau of Investigation (FBI): budget, 2; Chicago surveillance, 87–90; Key Activists program, 130; photographs of Chicago surveillance, 87–90
Fifth Avenue Peace Parade Committee, 140, 163
Free love, 72
Free Speech Movement, birth of, 26

Gray, L. Patrick, III, 16

Hawk, David, 137–39
Hayden, Tom, 21, 23, 64–65, 75, 79; indictment, 111
Hoffman, Abbie (Abbot Howard), 71, 111, 174–76
Hoover, J. Edgar, 23, 25, 43; criticism by National Commission on the Causes and Prevention of Violence, 141; memo expressing frustration, 77; NCS meeting, 2
House Committee on Un-American Activities, 23

Internal Revenue Service (IRS), 45, 76–78, 80

Jaworski, Leon, 172
Johnson, Lyndon B., 27, 29, 35, 63, 66

Kelley, Clarence M., 16–17, 211–13
Kennedy, John F., 23
Kent State, 170, 180–81
King, Martin Luther, Jr., 66
Kissinger, Henry, 137, 182, 197, 200, 210
Kleindiest, Richard, 15
Ku Klux Klan (KKK), 7, 28

Law Enforcement Bulletin, 86, 91, 95
League for Industrial Democracy, 21
Levi, Edward S., 211–13
Liberation (magazine), 73
Loyalty and Security Program, 3

Mass Pax, 138
McCarthy, Eugene J., 63–64, 137
McGovern, George S., 10
Media, PA, 8–14, 207, 215
"Minutemen, The," 172

Nation of Islam, 8
National Association of Black Students Convention, 12
National Black Economic Development Conference (BEDC), 12
National Coalition Against War, Racism, and Repression, 198
National Committee for a Sane Nuclear Policy (SANE), 27, 30
National Lawyers Guild, 81
National Mobilization Committee to End the War in Vietnam (National Mobilization), 74–75, 77, 90; anonymous letter about, 115; Nixon inauguration, 108–9; problems facing, 81–82; steering committee, 110; as targets, 76
National Peace Action Council, 182
National Security Council (NSC), 1, 2; March 8, 1965 meeting, 4
National Student Association, 139
New Left (The), 21, 24, 35, 43, 51, 66; accelerated action against, 67–68, 209; advancing antiwar cause, 86; COINTELPRO, 46, 96; establishment of, 46;

first targets, 107; informants, 208; Movement, 170; *New Left Notes*, 8, 11, 183

New Mobilization Committee to End the War in Vietnam (New Mobe), 132, 138–39, 142, 152, 155; in transition, 161–62; wiretaps, 209

Nixon, Richard M., 107, 132, 140, 153, 155, 161, 197; *The Report of the President's Commission on Campus Unrest*, 182

Operation Rolling Thunder, 28

Peace Action Now Committee (PANC), 57

Pentagon Papers, 210

People's Coalition for Peace and Justice (PCPJ), 198, 204

Philadelphia Black United Liberation Front, 13

Port Huron Statement of the Students for a Democratic Society, 21–22, 25

"Present Menace of Communist Espionage and Subversion, The," 4

Progressive Labor Party (PLP), 26, 111–12, 202–3

Progressive Labor Worker Student Alliance (WSA), 114

Radical Circus, 11

Resist, 12

Revolutionary Union, 187

Revolutionary Youth Movement (RYM), 148, 171

Roosevelt, Franklin D., FBI secret directive, 2

Rubin, Jerry, 64, 70, 148–50; checking account, 149; indictment of, 111

Rusk, Dean, 30

Saxbe, William B., 17

Seale, Bobby, 111, 142; Weekend, 206

Security Index, 3

Senate Foreign Relations Committee, 32

Smith Act, 4–5

Socialist Worker's Party (SWP), 71, 177–78, 214; COINTELPRO, 7, 48; Young Socialists Alliance, 53

Southern Christian Leadership Conference, 8

Southern Student Organization Committee (SSOC), 121, 143, 148

Spartacist League, 148

Spock, Dr. Benjamin, 30, 43

Stern, Carl, 14–18

"Stop the Draft Week," 36

Students Against the System (SAS), 168

Students for a Democratic Society (SDS), 21–23, 29, 49, 51–53, 55–57, 95–100; Cleveland Draft Resistance, 53; denial of University of Texas campus facilities, 129; IRS activity against, 80; mergers, 148; national convention, 69–70; 1968 Michigan meeting, 98; *Port Huron Statement of the Students for a Democratic Society*, 21–22; as targets, 76

Student Mobilization Committee to End the War in Vietnam (SMC), 34, 65, 71–72, 140, 162, 183

Student Nonviolent Coordinating Committee, 8, 25, 27, 51, 65

Subversive Activities Control Board, 9

Sullivan, William C., 45, 66–67, 79

Swarthmore Ministers Association, 9

Teach-ins, 29, 199

Union for National Draft, 13

United Campus Christian Fellowship (UCCF), 68

Universities Committee on Problems of War and Peace, 29

University of Missouri's Freedom of Information Art Center, 15

Venceremos Brigade, 190

Vietnam Day Committee, 31

Vietnam Moratorium Committee (VMC), 132, 138, 154, 161–62, 209

Vietnam Veterans Against the War, 210

War Resisters League, 27, 189

Weathermen, 148, 156, 162–63, 165, 168–69, 209; dissention between New Left groups, 189; wiretaps, 209

Weather Underground, 170, 208; "Days of Rage," 132

Webster, William, 213

Women Against the War, 140

Women Strike for Peace, 31

Women's International League for Peace and Freedom, 24

Young Socialists Alliance (YSA), 71, 176–77, 183, 186, 214

Youth Against War and Fascism (YAWF), 164

"Youth in Rebellion," 130

Youth International Party (Yippies), 71, 79–80

About the Author

JAMES KIRKPATRICK DAVIS is President of Davis Advertising Agency, Inc. in Kansas City. A student of American history for over thirty years, Mr. Davis is the author of *Spying on America: The FBI's Domestic Counterintelligence Program* (Praeger, 1992). He also worked directly with Clarence Kelley, former Director of the FBI, as coauthor of the book *Kelley: The Story of an FBI Director*.